THE PHILOSOPHERS

THE PHILOSOPHERS

INTRODUCING GREAT WESTERN THINKERS

Edited by
TED HONDERICH

OXFORD
UNIVERSITY PRESS

OXFORD
UNIVERSITY PRESS

Great Clarendon Street, Oxford OX2 6DP

Oxford University Press is a department of the University of Oxford.
It furthers the University's objective of excellence in research, scholarship,
and education by publishing worldwide in

Oxford New York

Athens Auckland Bangkok Bogotá Buenos Aires Calcutta
Cape Town Chennai Dar es Salaam Delhi Florence Hong Kong Istanbul
Karachi Kuala Lumpur Madrid Melbourne Mexico City Mumbai
Nairobi Paris São Paulo Singapore Taipei Tokyo Toronto Warsaw

with associated companies in Berlin Ibadan

Oxford is a registered trade mark of Oxford University Press
in the UK and in certain other countries

Published in the United States
by Oxford University Press Inc., New York

British Library Cataloguing in Publication Data

Data available

Library of Congress Cataloging in Publication Data
The philosophers : introducing great western thinkers / edited by Ted Honderich.
Includes bibliographical references and index.
1. Philosophy—History. 2. Philosophers—History. I. Honderich,
Ted. II. Oxford companion to philosophy.
B72.P44 1999 190—dc21 98–54768

ISBN 0-19-823861-4

1 3 5 7 9 10 8 6 4 2

Typeset in Dante
by Jayvee, Trivandrum, India
Printed in Great Britain
on acid-free paper by
Bookcraft Ltd.,
Midsomer Norton, Somerset

CONTENTS

LIST OF CONTRIBUTORS

Henry E. Allison, Boston University
Thomas Baldwin, University of York
David Bostock, University of Oxford
Justin Broackes, Brown University
Alexander Broadie, University of Glasgow
David Charles, University of Oxford
John Cottingham, University of Reading
Bernard Gert, Dartmouth College, New Hampshire
Peter Hacker, University of Oxford
Alastair Hannay, University of Oslo
Ross Harrison, University of Cambridge
Ted Honderich, University College London
C. J. Hookway, University of Sheffield
M. J. Inwood, University of Oxford
Anthony Kenny, University of Oxford
Christopher Kirwan, University of Oxford
A. R. Lacey, King's College London.
Mark Sainsbury, King's College London
Richard Schacht, University of Illinois, Urbana-Champaign
Peter Singer, Monash University
John Skorupski, University of St Andrews
R. C. Sleigh, Jr., University of Massachusetts, Amherst
T. L. S. Sprigge, University of Edinburgh
C. C. W. Taylor, University of Oxford
Geoffrey Warnock, late of the University of Oxford
Allen Wood, Yale University
Roger Woolhouse, University of York

INTRODUCTION

TED HONDERICH

I N the first philosophy of which we have more than fragments, there was the arguer who did not give up, Socrates. Of him it is possible to think that he stubbornly chose to die in order to bring home to his accusers the error of their ways, to show them they were wrong about him. His taking the hemlock in 399 BC made him as immortal as any of us are. As for his thoughts, they cannot be separated with confidence from those of his pupil Plato, both having been written into the latter's dialogues. But whatever the origins of Plato's thoughts, those of his middle period had to do with the ordinary world in which we live and also with something else, true reality.

Our ordinary world, he suggested, is like a parade of indistinct shadows looked at by captives in a cave. True reality is what by contrast is not approximate or transient. True reality consists in perfect and eternal types of things, not imperfect and passing instances or examples of them. True reality is the Forms or Ideas, above all the Form of the Good, but also the Forms of Horse and Chair and the like. These must exist to give our words their meanings. They are not in the cave but in the sunlight outside, existing there whether or not there are shadows in the cave that weakly resemble them. Only a few of us, the philosophers, ever get out into the light. Through all of this doctrine, somehow, Plato attempts answers to the large questions of how all things are, and how things should be, and who should rule, and how we know what we do of these various matters.

According to Jean-Paul Sartre in 1945, each of us freely chooses the person we are. We may pretend otherwise, like the waiter hiding in his aproned role, or the girl leaving a man's hand on her knee. But in fact we wholly creatively make our existence what it is. We are absolutely responsible for all of it. We make our essences. This piece of bravery in philosophy, though Sartre later had the sense to think better of it, brought Existentialism to the front of the subject.

The proposition of our absolute freedom is part of a story of the ordinary world absolutely unrelated to Plato's. It is not a matter of shadows in a cave or of light outside. All that is fiction, or anyway to be shrugged off on one's way up the *rue de la Sorbonne*. Sartre gives answers to different questions, which we are to see are the right questions, the questions that can yield truth or important truth. His announcement of the falsehood of determinism is by no means all of his thinking, or its conclusion, but an exemplar of it. It helped, as did his Left-Wing politics, to bring 50,000 of the French to his funeral.

The distance between the philosophy of Socrates and Plato and the philosophy of Sartre is not only a result of the 24 centuries between them. Consider Heidegger, nearly contemporary with Sartre. The philosophy of this German, despite including items that can bring to mind the philosophies of both Plato and Sartre, is a long way away from both of them. One part of the concern of his large work *Being and Time* is all of being or is-ness, *Sein*. It is to be approached by way of a consideration of one part or type of being. This is being-there or perhaps beings or man—*Dasein*.

As you might expect, *Dasein* in itself is a subject that requires a good deal of attention. What is the nature of its consciousness or awareness or, as is said, its original discourse? What is the nature, if this is not to speak too plainly, of the consciousness of *us*? It is not a matter of descriptive truths, of correspondence to fact. It is not a matter of such items as 'This hammer is heavy', but of such exclamations and instructions as 'Too heavy! Give me a lighter one'—which philosophical thought certainly predated a similar one at the beginning of Wittgenstein's *Philosophical Investigations*. Heidegger, whose relation to Nazism is taken by some to be a little obscure, and who said for several reasons that 'science does not think', is put above Sartre by many of those who rank great philosophers. But my concern is only to give some indication of the gulf between them.

There is another gulf between each of Sartre and Heidegger and another of their near-contemporaries, Bertrand Russell. An exemplar of his philosophy, indeed the exemplar, is at bottom a piece of philosophy of language. It is one that does indeed presuppose that what is somehow fundamental in our relationship to the world is fact-stating discourse. Giving instructions and the like is dependent on something else—seeing what is there to give instructions about. Russell's Theory of Descriptions proceeds from the truth (sadly overstated by him in the first instance) that the meanings of terms are bound up with the things for which they stand.

But then what of such a term as the definite description 'the King of France'? There has not been anything answering to the description for some time. Yet we know what it means.

Russell's idea, when saved from being bundled up in formal logic and its locutions, as it sometimes was by him, is that our use of the descriptive term amounts to claiming the existence of some one thing or other that rules over France—which claim is such that each term in it *is* satisfactorily bound up with a thing for which it stands—say the large object France. The idea is wonderfully pleasing to the clear-headed inquirer, say the English inquirer, but issues in less feelingful self-reflection than the doctrines about creating oneself in the *rue de la Sorbonne* and about *Dasein*. Was it for this reason that even Russell of the Committee of 100 against The Bomb, and a Lord as well, shared the fate of all British philosophers, which is to make their departures from the world relatively quietly? All of them, save for a few infected by Hegel, have in their thinking been clear instead of emotional.

The gulfs between the great philosophers, despite affinities between some of them and despite some inheritances, are about as easily illustrated by the rest of them. Augustine in the fourth and fifth centuries has a concern with God unlike Aquinas's in the thirteenth. Aquinas, if certainly not a modern, felt more need of proofs of His existence, and provided five. In another way, incidentally, Augustine was ahead of his time, indeed ahead of Aquinas. This was in connection with the philosophical scepticism about the existence of the world, which is to say the irritating question of whether we are just wrong and it is all a dream. The reassuring thought in this situation—'if I am wrong, I exist'—was had not by Descartes in the seventeenth century but by Augustine in his. Still, it does not make him at all like Descartes. Augustine did not have science on hand to inform or distract him, of course—his situation was different. But he also had his own relation to reality, an intellectual character that would have made a large difference between him and Descartes if they had been together in time.

It separates him too from the sturdiness of Thomas Hobbes in the seventeenth century, who escaped much superstition, but, as I am tempted to report, also gave rise to some. The new kind was destined to be tenacious in some of science and in scientized philosophy, and to flourish in America in the later twentieth century. It is to the effect, you might say, that materialism or physicalism is so true that nothing false can possibly be meant by saying that there is a wholly materialist or physicalist explanation of our human behaviour. But something false *is* meant, or so it seems to me, if the physicalist explanation leaves true subjectivity out of an account of our mental lives, the insideness of them.

But to get back to my main theme, consider for a moment the common rationalism of the philosophers called the Rationalists. It cannot obscure their wonderful individuality. To mention only the most salient point of difference, for Spinoza there is proof that there is but one thing, God or Nature, and for Leibniz there is proof that there are quite a lot of things, these being the windowless monads. So with the common empiricism of the philosophers called the Empiricists. Locke is better than his reputation, despite his loose talk of 'ideas', and no mere precursor of the brazen Berkeley and then the mighty and blessed Hume— Hume standing beside Kant in the pantheon, a little higher than all the rest. Each of the Empiricists, and Kant, speaks very differently of what there is, and should be, and how we know. Kant has his place partly for allowing that there is more to the world than what we are aware of. A pity that Hume didn't. As for the many determinists among the philosophical great—ten, by one way of considering the matter—they do not agree on much more than the causal story, having Spinoza and Hume and in his way Russell among them.

But there is no need to to say more of the diversity of the great philosophers. If you happen to have a little awareness of them already, reader, all that is needed is a reminder of the rest of the roll-call—Aristotle and the Golden Mean, Schopenhauer and the nature of true reality being blind, striving Will, Hegel's World Spirit culminating in Hegel's philosophy, Bentham and the Greatest Happiness Principle, Kierkegaard's religiousness A and B, Marx's historicized and economized but high morality, Mill's liberty and logic, Nietzsche's insolent want of concern, Peirce's signs, James's stream of consciousness, Frege's new logic, Husserl's phenomenology, and—I do not say last and least—Wittgenstein.

These philosophies, you may well say, cannot all be true. Many of them, in particular the great pieces of metaphysics, do seem to collide more or less head-on in their accounts of fundamental reality. It cannot be both Forms and blind, striving Will. And, you may say, there is another way in which each of these twenty-eight philosophies is inconsistent with every other one. Each, if in a few cases tacitly, purports to lay out *what should be of greatest importance to us*. In this way a piece of metaphysics can be inconsistent with something other than a piece of metaphysics. It can conflict with a philosophy of life, which is something

Sartre provides, or a philosophy of language and what goes with it, as in the case of Russell, or a perdurable moral philosophy that judges actions by the fairness of their consequences, which may be in Marx and Mill.

Of course, to take it that only one of these philosophies can be true, or, to be less exacting, only a few of them, does not enable us to discard any. We would need to know something else. *Which one* is true, or *which ones*? In fact that question may not really arise, despite what we are inclined to say. There is a still earlier matter that may get in the way. It is that we should at least be cautious about supposing that in fact, although as yet unknown to us, all but one or a few of these philosophies are false and are failures, their makers defeated.

Might it be that the works of the great philosophers, despite their large pretensions, should be taken differently? That they should not really be taken as attempts to convey all of truth, but as aiming at and giving to us what are admittedly large things but still only *sides of truth*? In each case a side of truth discerned through the achievement of a great individual point of view and, at least as necessary, through wonderful persistence in it? To go further, might that be the very nature of truth itself—that it consists in no more than what we are calling sides?

Leibniz saved the good God from the doubts of atheists armed with the Problem of Evil, notably facts of pointless suffering, by establishing to his satisfaction that this world with its shortcomings is the best of all *possible* worlds. Might we do as well by the great philosophers, save their reputations, do more justice to them, reach a better view of them, by reducing truth itself? By seeing that the best that can be achieved and all that can really be aimed at is sides of it?

The thought would be discomfiting to Hegel, say, who would not wish to be joined as successful expositor of the World Spirit by his denigrator Kierkegaard, or his more formidable scoffer Marx. Evidently the thought will be discomfiting to a contributor or two to this book who put their chosen philosopher on a really unique pedestal. But of course the thought goes a good way to explaining what can become more persuasive on reflection—that a great philosophy, by its nature, *cannot* be just a failure and defeat.

I have only a little confidence in this speculation about truth, and you will rightly say that it has not been made crystal-clear. The nature of philosophy, it can seem, it still among philosophy's problems. Also, truth to tell, something else turns up in the course of my thinking about the history of philosophy. Along with some noticeable philosophical passions,

I have a residual inclination to the temporal philistinism of thinking that our philosophy should consider shuffling off its past, like science, even historiography. Should philosophy now begin, at the earliest, with Hobbes? It is a terrible question. Few of my fellow-workers in the subject ask it openly.

I do not press it on you, and do commend all of the introductions in this book to you, Socrates through Wittgenstein, with full confidence. All but the most recent of these thinkers' thinkers, the late-comers, have both taken places in and formed the lives of endless men and women, including men and women unaware of them. The late-comers may well join their predecessors as leaders of the great subject, the greatest of subjects, and thus of so much more. Whatever he thought of the world and felt about it, Hobbes's predecessor Aquinas also made a world. So did Hume and Kant. So too did all the rest.

SOCRATES (470–399 BC)

C. C. W. TAYLOR

ATHENIAN philosopher, teacher of Plato. Socrates is one of the most significant yet most enigmatic figures in the history of philosophy: significant because his relation to Plato was crucial in the development of the latter, and thus indirectly in the development of much later philosophy; enigmatic because he wrote nothing himself, and therefore presents the challenge of reconstructing him from the evidence of others. It is therefore necessary to start with a brief account of that evidence.

Sources

Assuming the truth of the generally (though not universally) accepted view that all Plato's dialogues were written after Socrates' death, the only evidence from Socrates' own lifetime is Aristophanes' *Clouds*, first produced in 423, in which Socrates is a central character. Though the portrayal of this character does preserve some traits of the actual Socrates as recorded elsewhere, e.g. his peculiar gait, it is recognized that the Socrates of the play is not a realistic portrait but a caricature of a representative 'Sophist' combining features of various individuals (e.g. the theory of the divinity of the air of Diogenes of Apollonia) and of stock comic types, such as the half-starved Pythagorean ascetic. The fact that Aristophanes chose Socrates as the peg on which to hang this caricature shows that he was by then a comparatively well-known figure, and the dramatic circumstances of his condemnation and death gave rise to a considerable Socratic literature, comprising both imaginative reproductions of his conversations and controversial works (some hostile, some favourable) focusing on his trial. Apart from fragmentary remains of some other authors (e.g. Aeschines), the only substantial survivors of this literature are the dialogues of Plato and the Socratic writings of Xenophon, which include a version of his speech at his trial and purported 'memoirs' of various conversations. While these are in broad agreement with Plato in attributing to Socrates certain modes of argument (e.g. inductive arguments) and certain specific doctrines (e.g. that virtue is knowledge), their tone is much less speculative and their picture of Socrates much more conventional and practical than Plato's, reflecting the different characters and interests of the respective authors. While Plato's dialogues present a consistent and compelling portrait of the highly individual personality of Socrates, his primary purpose in writing them was not that of a biographer (at least on the modern conception of a chronicler one of whose primary aims is historical accuracy). Rather, he writes as a philosophical apologist, who seeks to present Socrates as the ideal embodiment of philosophy, unjustly traduced by confusion with bogus practitioners and unjustly condemned for his dedication to the philosophic life. It is therefore, given that aim, quite natural that he should in some places put into the mouth of Socrates doctrines of his own which the historical Socrates did not hold. Aristotle, who was born in 384 and came to Athens to study in the Academy in 367, must have derived his knowledge of Socrates primarily (though doubtless not exclusively) from Platonic sources. That is not, of course, to say that his only information was Plato's dialogues; though some of his references to Socrates may be to passages in the dialogues, there is ground for thinking that some are independent (see below).

Life

Socrates spent all his life in Athens, apart from military service abroad. Though the sources represent him as spending his time in philosophical discussion, he was reputedly a stonemason, and may have earned his own living, at least from time to time; Plato is emphatic that he never took money for philosophizing, and makes that a central point of differentiation between him and the (professional) Sophists. The 'intellectual autobiography' which Plato puts into his mouth in the *Phaedo* represents him as having been at one time keenly interested in natural philosophy, but as having become disillusioned with its neglect of teleological explanation. His interests seem to have shifted to questions of conduct and their foundation, while the magnetism of his personality attracted to him a circle of mainly younger men, some of whom, including Plato and some of his relatives, were opposed to the Athenian democratic system. It is impossible to determine how far Socrates himself shared such views; however critical he may have been of democracy in theory, he was in practice a loyal citizen, serving with distinction on the battlefield and adhering strictly to his ideals of legality and justice under severe pressure, once under the democracy, when he was alone in opposing an unconstitutional proposal, and once under the tyrannical regime which briefly ousted the democracy at the end of the Peloponnesian War, when he refused an order to participate in the arrest (and subsequent death) of an innocent man. None the less, his association with notorious anti-democrats, especially Alcibiades and Plato's relatives Critias and Charmides, led to his accusation after the restoration of the democracy on vague charges of impiety and corruption of the young, and to his condemnation to death. The events of his trial and its aftermath are immortalized in three of Plato's works, the *Apology*, an idealized version of his defence at his trial, *Crito*, which gives his reasons for refusing to take the opportunity (which was apparently available) of escape from prison and subsequent exile, and *Phaedo*, a moving re-creation of his final hours, containing first a Platonic treatise on the philosophy of life, death, and immortality and then a depiction of the ideal philosophic death.

Philosophy

It cannot be doubted that Socrates was a major, probably the most significant, influence on Plato's philosophical development, but the nature of this influence is not altogether easy to determine. Because our main access to Socrates is via the works of Plato, we have the problem of determining what, if any, doctrines Socrates himself held (see above). One extreme position is that we can know nothing whatever about the views of the historical Socrates, another that whatever views Plato ascribes to Socrates in any dialogue were actually held by him. Neither seems to me tenable. Aristotle distinguishes the views of Plato from those of Socrates (*Metaphysics* 1078^{b}27–32) by attributing to the former the theory of separate Forms, which, he says, Socrates did not hold. Since Socrates is represented as expounding that theory in the *Phaedo* and other dialogues, it is clear that Aristotle does not derive that information from the dialogues, and it is therefore plausible that he learned either from Plato himself or from other sources in the Academy that the theory was Plato's own. So not everything in the dialogues is Socratic. But is anything Socratic? In the same passage Aristotle ascribes to Socrates an interest in general definitions and the practice of inductive arguments, both of which we find attributed to Socrates by Plato and Xenophon. Both the latter also attribute to Socrates the 'Socratic paradoxes' that virtue is wisdom or knowledge and that no one does wrong willingly. It is at least plausible that those methods of argument were employed, and those doctrines held, by the historical Socrates.

Though Socrates is represented as maintaining these doctrines by Plato, he figures in the dialogues, especially the earlier ones, not primarily as a dogmatic philosopher (indeed he was famous for claiming that he did not know anything), but as a critic, eliciting opinions from his interlocutors and subjecting them to critical scrutiny, usually resulting in a refutation by showing the doctrine in question to be inconsistent with other propositions agreed by both parties to be true. This 'method of elenchus' (a Greek word meaning 'examination') has obvious affinities with the argumentative strategies employed and taught by the Sophists, and Plato is concerned to stress that in Socrates' hands it was intended not to produce victory in a debating contest, but to lead to genuine understanding by purging the person subjected to it of false beliefs. Philosophical inquiry conducted by this method is supposed to be not a contest between opponents (eristic), but a co-operative search for truth and understanding (dialectic). Though Plato's conception of the methods of dialectic clearly developed considerably in the course of his life, the ideal of a co-operative critical inquiry, conducted by the spoken word, remained his paradigm of philosophy, and we have every reason to think that it was his memory of the power of Socratic conversations which gave that ideal its perennial attractiveness for him. Nor did the influence of the figure of Socrates cease with Plato. In the Hellenistic period the various schools each sought to appropriate him as a patron saint, the Cynics appealing to his ascetic mode of life, the Sceptics to his profession of ignorance, and the Stoics to his alleged claim that virtue was the only intrinsic good. It is no exaggeration to claim that as long as personal and intellectual integrity remain compelling ideals, the figure of Socrates will be a suitable embodiment of them.

PLATO (c.428–347 BC)

DAVID BOSTOCK

THE best known and most widely studied of all the ancient Greek philosophers. He was an Athenian, born into a noble family, and might have been expected to play a part in the politics of that city. But in fact he came under the influence of Socrates, who fired him with an enthusiasm for philosophy. When Socrates was condemned to death and executed in 399, Plato gave up all thought of a political career, and left Athens in disgust. It is said that he then travelled to various places, including Egypt, but we have no trustworthy information on this part of his life, until we come to his first visit to Italy and Sicily in 387. From that visit he returned to Athens, and soon after founded his Academy, just outside the city. This may be regarded as the first 'university'. Apart from two further visits to Sicily, in 367 and 361, he remained at the Academy until his death in 347.

It is often assumed that his first philosophical work was the *Apology*; this purports to be a record of the speeches that Socrates delivered at his trial. Apart from this one example, all Plato's philosophical works are dialogues. They are standardly divided into three periods: early, middle, and late. On the usual chronology, the early period includes *Crito, Ion, Hippias minor, Euthyphro, Lysis, Laches, Charmides, Hippias major, Meno, Euthydemus, Protagoras, Gorgias*. Many of these dialogues are short. They are listed here in order of length, from the *Crito* at 9 pages, to the *Euthydemus* at 36, the *Protagoras* at 53, and the *Gorgias* at 80. No one is confident of their order of composition. The usual chronology for the middle period includes *Phaedo, Symposium, Republic, Phaedrus*, in that order. The *Republic* is very long, and is divided into ten books. Some count the *Cratylus* as belonging to this period (placed after the *Republic*); some count it as an early dialogue. Finally, on the usual chronology for the late period, it begins with *Parmenides* and *Theaetetus*, and then (after a break) it contains *Sophist, Statesman, Timaeus* (and *Critias*), *Philebus, Laws*. Again there is one work which is very long, namely the *Laws*, which is divided into twelve books. The orthodox view is that this may be counted as Plato's last work, though in fact the evidence for this claim is very insecure. Another important dispute concerns the date of the *Timaeus*, which some would classify as a middle dialogue (after the *Republic*). A great deal of work has been done, and is still being done, towards establishing the order of the dialogues, but one cannot say that a consensus has been reached. (The above list simply omits all works whose authenticity may be considered doubtful.)

I

The early dialogues are our only worthwhile source for the philosophy of Socrates. They illustrate his preoccupation with ethics, and his insistence that it is vitally important to find correct definitions for ethically significant concepts, since otherwise we will not know how to live. No doubt Plato himself shared these views at the time. But he shows a more independent attitude to the Socratic claim that virtue (*aretē*) is knowledge, and to its associated paradoxes, e.g. that all wrongdoing must be due to ignorance (so that no one does wrong on purpose), and that all virtues must somehow be the same (so that one cannot have one but lack another). The dialogues show Plato to be very *interested* in these claims, but he is not clearly *endorsing* them. On the contrary, he seems rather to be exploring them, and recognizing the problems they involve. He can achieve this neutral stance partly because he is writing dialogues, between Socrates and other speakers, and we need not suppose that Plato believes whatever he makes his character Socrates say; and partly because most of the dialogues are anyway inconclusive. They will begin by propounding some problem for discussion, and during the discussion several answers will be proposed, but all will be rejected, so that officially no conclusion is reached. (Often one is tempted to read between the lines, to find an answer that Plato is recommending, despite its official rejection; but even so one should suppose that he is recommending it for further consideration, not for acceptance.) In these early dialogues, then, Plato is mainly concerned with Socrates' philosophy, but he is trying out lines of thought, and objections to them, and he is not confident that he has found answers. In a few cases (notably the *Meno* and the *Gorgias*) one can see that his confidence is growing, and that he has something to say which he very much wants his audience to believe. But that is because the middle period is dawning.

II

In the middle period Plato's interests broaden very considerably, and we find the metaphysical and epistemological doctrines for which he is best known. They now form the background against which he works out his new thoughts on how one ought to live, and on a number of other topics, ranging from the true role of love (*Symposium, Phaedrus*) to the structure of the physical world (*Timaeus*—assuming that to be a middle dialogue). There is space here only for a brief account of some of the better-known doctrines. Although Socrates remains the chief speaker of these dialogues (except for the *Timaeus*), still one can now be quite confident that the views put into his mouth are Plato's own views, and often they owe very little to the historical Socrates.

Knowledge and the Forms. Socrates had insisted that we must be able to answer the question 'What is *X*?' before we can say anything else about *X*. He understood this question as asking for the one thing common to all the many instances or examples of *X*, and he continued to stress its importance for ethical inquiry, even though he never found any answers that satisfied him. One may conjecture that this led Plato to ask *why* the search was yielding no results, and that he came to the conclusion that it was because even the supposed instances and examples of *X* were unreliable. At any rate, he certainly did come to hold that, in interesting cases such as justice and goodness and beauty, every instance of *X* will *also* be an instance of the opposite to *X*. But this provokes a problem, for instances and examples seem to be crucial for language-learning. That is, one could not come to understand the word 'red' if there were no examples of red things, nor if every example of something red were at the same time an example of something non-red. How, then, do we manage to attach any meaning at all to words such as 'just', 'good', and 'beautiful'? This problem led Plato to suppose that there must *be* an unambiguous example of justice, not in this world but in some other, and that we must once have been acquainted with it. This is what he calls the 'Form' of justice. So his theory is that we are born into this world with a dim recollection of this Form, and that is why we do have *some* conception of what justice is, though it is only an imperfect conception, which explains why we cannot now answer the Socratic question 'What is justice?'

This is the theory of *Phaedo* 73–7. It significantly extends a line of thought introduced earlier in the *Meno*, which had noted that there is such a thing as a priori knowledge (since mathematics is an example), and had offered to explain this as really recollection of what we had once known in an earlier existence. The *Meno* had *hoped* that philosophical inquiry could yield similar knowledge of justice and the like, obtained by examination of what was already latent within us, but had offered no ground for such a hope. The *Phaedo* provides a ground, at the same time adding a new conception of what it is that must be known (or recalled), namely a paradigm example of *X*, a reliable and unambiguous guide to what *X* is, which the perceptible things of this world 'imitate', but always 'fall short of'. These are the Forms. Yet at the same time, and inconsistently, the Forms are thought of as themselves *being* the answers to the question 'What is *X*?', i.e. as being the one thing common to all the many instances of *X*, that in which they all 'participate'. In other words, the Forms are *both* perfect paradigms *and* universals. This ambivalent conception is found in all the middle dialogues (including the *Timaeus*). The associated theory of recollection (*anamnēsis*) is not so constantly mentioned; in fact it is restated only once after the *Phaedo*, i.e. at *Phaedrus* 249.

The Soul (psukhē or psyche) and Morality. In the *Apology* Socrates had been portrayed as agnostic on the immortality of the soul. In the *Phaedo* he is convinced of it, and the dialogue is as a whole a sustained argument for that claim. We find further arguments for the immortality of the soul in *Republic* x and in the *Phaedrus*, but in those dialogues there is also a more complex view of what the soul is. Whereas the *Phaedo*, like the early dialogues, had been content with a simple opposition between soul and body, in *Republic* iv the soul itself is divided into three 'parts', which roughly correspond to reason, emotion, and desire. (But in *Republic* viii–ix the 'reasoning' part is associated with the desire for knowledge, the so-called 'spirited' part with the desire for honour and prestige, and the 'desiring' part—itself recognized to be 'many-headed'—is clearly confined to bodily desires.) An explicit motive for this division is to allow for conflict within the soul, and one consequence of this is that Plato is no longer tempted by the Socratic claim that all virtue is knowledge, and its associated paradoxes. He does retain the early view that virtue is a condition of the soul, but wisdom is now viewed as a virtue of the reasoning part, whereas courage is a virtue of the spirited part, and justice is explained as a suitable 'harmony' between all three parts. Another consequence of the threefold division of the soul is that Plato seems to have become uncertain how much of the soul is immortal. (*Republic* x. 611–12 is deliberately evasive; *Phaedrus* 245–9 clearly claims that the team of all three parts is immortal; *Timaeus* 69–72 is equally clear in its claim that only the reasoning part is immortal.) Plato thinks of the immortal soul as subject to reincarnation from one life to another. Those who live virtuous lives will be somehow rewarded, but the detail differs from one treatment to another.

Political Theory. In the *Republic* Plato sets out his 'ideal state'. It is very decidedly authoritarian. He begins from the premiss that only those who know what the good is are fit to rule, and he prescribes a long and rigorous period of intellectual training, which he thinks will yield this knowledge. In a famous analogy, it will loose the bonds that keep most men confined in a cave underground, and allow us to ascend to the 'real' world outside, which is a world of Forms, available to the intellect but not to the senses. This is to be accomplished by a full study of mathematics, which will turn one's attention towards the Forms, since it is an a priori study and does not concern itself with what is perceptible; and after that a study in 'dialectic', i.e. in philosophical debate. Those who complete this training successfully, and so know what the good is, will form the ruling élite. From time to time they will be required to give up their intellectual delights and go back into the cave to govern it. They will govern with a view to maximizing the happiness of the state as a whole, but Plato thinks that the way to achieve this is to impose a strict censorship to prevent wrong ideas being expressed, to ensure that each person sticks to his own allotted job, so that he does not meddle with affairs that are not his concern, and so on. Plato was firmly against democracy, and seems to have seen no connection between happiness and individual liberty.

III

The late dialogues open with two criticisms of the theories of the middle period, in the *Parmenides* and the *Theaetetus*. The *Parmenides* is concerned with metaphysics, and its first part raises a series of objections to the middle period's theory of Forms. The most famous of these is the so-called third man argument, which evidently exploits the fact that Forms are supposed to be *both* universals *and* perfect paradigms. Scholars differ in their view of how Plato himself reacted to these objections. Provided that the *Timaeus* is regarded as a middle dialogue, one can hold that Plato saw that the objections depend upon Forms being both universals and paradigms, and thereupon ceased to think of them as paradigms. But if the *Timaeus* is later than the *Parmenides*, as stylometric studies appear to indicate, then one is forced to conclude that Plato made no such modification to his theory. The second part of the *Parmenides* is a riddle. It draws a bewildering array of contradictory conclusions, first from the hypothesis 'The One is' and then from its negation 'The One is not', and then it just ends without further comment. There have been many attempts to extract a serious moral that Plato may have intended, but none have won general approval.

As the *Parmenides* attacks the metaphysics of the middle dialogues, so the *Theaetetus* attacks their epistemology, but again the attack has its puzzling features. The middle dialogues (and in particular the *Timaeus*) claim that perceptible things are not stable, and for that reason there can be no knowledge of them; rather, only Forms can be known. The first part of the *Theaetetus*, however, argues that it is self-refuting to ascribe such radical instability to perceptible things, and it proceeds to assume that we do know about them. But it nevertheless insists upon distinguishing this knowledge from perception, on the ground that knowledge requires belief (or judgement) while mere perception does not. The second part of the dialogue then professes to be exploring the claims that knowledge is to be identified with true belief, or with true belief plus an 'account'. But what is puzzling about this discussion is that it appears to focus not upon knowledge of facts (*savoir*) but upon knowledge of objects (*connaître*), and on the face of it the latter does not involve belief or judgement at all. Again, the solution to this puzzle is a matter of controversy.

Although the late dialogues begin with two enigmatic and self-critical pieces, in which Plato's own position is once more unclear, in subsequent writings he has evidently recovered the confidence of his middle period. In the *Sophist* he gives us a new metaphysics and a more sophisticated investigation of language, in the course of a long investigation of 'not being'. This includes the important point that even in the simplest sentences one may distinguish two expressions, subject and predicate, that have different roles to play. In the *Statesman* he reaffirms his view that ruling is a task for experts, and argues that the expert should not be bound either by law or by the wishes of the people. But it is admitted that law is a second best, where no expert is available. Of constitutions bound by law he considers that monarchy is best, oligarchy in the middle, and democracy worst. But in the absence of law this order is reversed. In the *Philebus* he once more weighs the claims of knowledge and of pleasure to be the good, and at the same time undertakes a full examination of what pleasure is. He does not award victory to either contestant, arguing instead for the mixed life, but knowledge is ranked higher.

In all three of these dialogues Plato pays much attention to what he calls the method of 'collection and division'. At an earlier stage he had recommended the different method of 'hypothesis'. This is introduced in the *Meno*, apparently as a device which allows us to make progress with philosophical problems without first having to answer the awkward question 'What is *X*?' Then in the *Phaedo* and the *Republic* it receives a much fuller exposition, and becomes Plato's account of how a priori knowledge is possible. This method makes its final appearance in the *Parmenides*, and one way of reading the second part of that dialogue is as a prolonged demonstration of its inadequacy. Meanwhile, the new method of 'collection and division' has been introduced in the *Phaedrus*, and it is then both preached and practised at some length in the *Sophist* and the *Statesman*. It is presented as a method of finding definitions, though it is clear from what those dialogues say about it that it must be handled very carefully if it is not to lead us astray. The version in the *Philebus* introduces some new, and very puzzling, considerations concerning 'the indefinite'. This appears to connect with what Aristotle tells us about Plato's so-called 'unwritten doctrines', but that topic is too obscure to be pursued here.

Finally, in the *Laws* we find Plato again building an ideal state, but now in a very different mood from that of the *Republic* and the *Statesman*. He is now much more ready to compromise with principle in order to find something that will work in practice, and he puts a very high value on the law. In fact the work is remarkable for proposing a great deal of extremely detailed legislation. But Plato's general attitude remains very authoritarian, and he still pays no attention to individual liberty. It is justly said that the 'Nocturnal Council', which turns out to be the supreme authority in this state, would certainly not have tolerated the subversive ideas of Socrates, from which Plato began.

ARISTOTLE (384–322 BC)

DAVID CHARLES

ARISTOTLE was born at Stagira in Chalcidice in northern Greece. His father was a doctor whose patients included Amyntas, King of Macedonia. At the age of 17, Aristotle went to Athens to study under Plato, and remained at the Academy for nearly twenty years until Plato's death in 348/7. When Speusippus succeeded Plato as its head, Aristotle left Athens, lived for a while in Assos and Mytilene, and then was invited to return to Macedonia by Philip to tutor Alexander. Aristotle returned to Athens in 335 at the age of 49, and founded his own philosophical school. He worked there for twelve years until Alexander's death in 323, when the Athenians in strongly anti-Macedonian mood brought a formal charge of impiety against him. Aristotle escaped with his life to Chalcis, but died there in the following year at the age of 62. He married twice, and had a son, Nicomachus, by his second wife.

Aristotle's philosophical interests covered an extremely wide area. He composed major studies of logic, ethics, and metaphysics, but also wrote on epistemology, physics, biology, meteorology, dynamics, mathematics, psychology, rhetoric, dialectic, aesthetics, and politics. Many of his treatises constitute an attempt to see the topics studied through the perspective of one set of fundamental concepts and ideas. All reflect similar virtues: a careful weighing of arguments and considerations, acute insight, a sense of what is philosophically plausible, and a desire to separate and classify distinct issues and phenomena. They also exhibit considerable reflection on the nature of philosophical activity and the goals of philosophy itself.

Aristotle's philosophical development is difficult to determine chronologically. He probably worked on a range of concerns simultaneously, and did not always see clearly how far his thinking on logic or philosophy of science fitted with his current work on (for example) metaphysics or biology. He may have returned more than once to similar topics, and added to existing drafts in a piecemeal fashion at different times. It is, in general, more fruitful to inquire how far different elements in his thinking cohere rather than what preceded what. Further, many of his extant works read more like notebooks of work in progress or notes for discussion than books finished and ready for publication. His writings (like Wittgenstein's) reflect the activity of thinking itself, uncluttered by rhetoric or stylistic affectation. Their consequent freshness of tone should make one cautious of accepting over-regimented accounts of his overall project: for it may well have been developing as he proceeded.

In what follows, I shall aim to introduce a few of Aristotle's leading ideas in three areas only: logic and philosophy of science, ethics, and metaphysics. While these subjects differ widely, there is considerable overlap of concerns and interests between them.

Logic and Philosophy of Science

Aristotle was the first to develop the study of deductive inference. He defined the syllogism as a 'discourse in which certain things having been stated, something else follows of necessity from their being so'. Syllogisms are deductively valid arguments, and include both arguments of the form:

> All as are b,
> All bs are c,
> All as are c,

and

> as are red,
> as are coloured.

Both these arguments are *perfect* syllogisms since nothing needs to be added to make clear what necessarily follows. By contrast, arguments form *imperfect* syllogisms when more needs to be added beyond the premisses to make clear that the conclusion follows of necessity. It is a distinctive feature of Aristotle's account that it takes as its starting-point the notion of 'following of necessity', which is not itself defined in formal or axiomatic terms. If this notion has a further basis, it lies in Aristotle's semantical account of the predicate as what affirms that a given property belongs to a substance (and so rests on his metaphysics of substance and property).

Aristotle focused on perfect syllogisms which share a certain form involving three terms: two premisses and a conclusion. Examples of such syllogisms are:

All *a*s are *b*,	All *a*s are *b*,	Some *a*s are *b*,	Some *a*s are *b*,
All *b*s are *c*,	No *b*s are *c*,	All *b*s are *c*,	No *b*s are *c*,
All *a*s are *c*.	No *a* is *c*.	Some *a*s are *c*.	Not all *a*s are *c*.

He claimed that other syllogisms with a similar form and the same crucial terms ('all', 'some', 'none', 'not all') could be expressed using one of these perfect cases if one adds three conversion rules:

From No *b*s are *a*	*infer*	No *a*s are *b*.
From All *b*s are *a*	*infer*	Some *a*s are *b*.
From Some *b*s are *a*	*infer*	Some *a*s are *b*.

Finally, he proposed that any deductively valid argument can be expressed in one of the four obvious perfect syllogisms specified above or reduced to these by means of the conversion rules. If so, any such argument can be reformulated as one of the basic cases of perfect syllogisms in which the conclusion obviously follows of necessity.

Aristotle was interested in this logical system in part because he was interested in explanation (or demonstration). Every demonstration is a syllogism, but not every syllogism is a demonstration. In a demonstration, the aim is to explain why the conclusion is true. Thus, if the conclusion states that (for example) trees of a given type are deciduous, the premiss of the relevant demonstration will state this is so because their sap solidifies. If no further explanation can be given of why their leaves fall, this premiss states the basic nature of their shedding leaves. Premisses in demonstrations are absolutely prior, when no further explanation can be offered of why they are true. These constitute the starting-points for explanation in a given area.

Aristotle's ideas about the nature of valid inference and explanation form the basis of his account of the form a successful science should take. In terms of these, he outlined an account of what each thing's essence is (the feature which provides the fundamental account of its other genuine properties), of how things should be defined (in terms of their basic explanatory features), and of the ideal of a complete science in which a set of truths is represented as a sequence of consequences drawn from a few basic postulates or common principles. These ideas, which underlie his *Analytics*, determined the course of logic and philosophy of science, and to some extent that of science itself, for two millennia.

Aristotle's system has its own shortcomings and idiosyncrasies. His treatment of the syllogistic does not exhaust all of logic, and not all arguments of a developed science can be formulated into the favoured Aristotelian form. His system was a pioneering one which required supplementation. It was unfortunate, not least for his own subsequent reputation, that it came to be regarded as the complete solution to all the problems it raised.

It is important to note that Aristotle's logical project was directly connected with his metaphysical goals. His aim was to develop a logical theory for a natural language capable of describing the fundamental types of object required for a full understanding of reality (individual substances, species, processes, states, etc.). He had no interest in artificial languages, which speak of entities beyond his favoured metaphysical and epistemological theory. His goal was rather to develop a logical theory 'of a piece' with his philosophical conception of what exists in the world and how it can be understood. In this respect, his goals differ markedly from those of metalogicians since Frege, who speak of artificial as well as natural languages, and domains of objects unconstrained by any privileged metaphysics.

Ethics and Politics

Aristotle's *Ethics* contains several major strands.

1. It aims to give a reflective understanding of well-being or the good life for humans.

2. It suggests that well-being consists in excellent activity such as intellectual contemplation and virtuous actions stemming from a virtuous character. Virtuous action is what the person with practical wisdom would choose; and the practically wise are those who can deliberate successfully towards well-being. This might be termed the *Aristotelian circle*, as the key terms (well-being, virtue, and practical wisdom) appear to be interdefined.

3. It develops a theory of virtue (*aretē*) which aims to explain the fact that what is good seems so to the virtuous. Aristotle examines the characteristic roles of desire, goals, imagination, emotion, and intuition in the choices and intentional actions of the virtuous, and explains in these terms how virtue differs from self-control, incontinence (*akrasia*), and self-indulgence. This is a study in moral psychology and epistemology, involving detailed discussion of particular virtues involved in the good life.

Each of these is important but controversial, and Aristotle's own viewpoint is far from clear. Sometimes it appears that the self-sufficient contemplation (of truth) by the individual sage constitutes the ideal good life, but elsewhere man is represented as a 'political animal' who needs friendship and other-directed virtues (such as courage, generosity, and justice) if he is to achieve human well-being. On occasion, Aristotle seems to found his account of the good life on background assumptions about human nature, but elsewhere bases his account of human nature on what it is good for humans to achieve. He remarks that the virtuous see what is good, but elsewhere writes that what is good is so because it appears good to the virtuous.

One way (there are many) to fit these strands together runs as follows. The paradigm case of activity which manifests well-being is intellectual contemplation, and everything else that is an element in the good life is in some relevant way like intellectual contemplation. Practical wisdom is akin to theoretical activity: both are excellences of the rational intellect, both involve a proper grasp of first principles and the integration of relevant psychological states, and both require a grasp of truth in their respective areas. Intellectual contemplation is the activity which best exemplifies what is good for humans; anything else which is good for us in some way resembles it.

But what counts as truth in practical matters? Is this is to be understood merely as what seems to be the case to the virtuous agent? Alternatively, practical truth might be taken as a basic notion. Or perhaps the virtuous agent is the proper judge because the virtue she possesses, when allied with practical wisdom, constitutes part of well-being. On this view, the interconnections between virtue and well-being would explain why her practical reasoning is as it is (in a way consistent with reputable and well-established opinion). This preserves the analogy with truth in theoretical matters, where interconnections between kinds, essences, and causal powers explain why our theoretical reasoning is as it is (in a way consistent with reputable opinion). While the third of these interpretations captures substantial parts of Aristotle's discussion, he proceeds with characteristic caution and appears reluctant to commit himself finally on this issue.

Aristotle wrote his *Ethics* as a prolegomenon to his study of *Politics*. This too reflects his interest in virtue and well-being, but also contains several other major themes. Thus Aristotle holds the following theses.

1. A city-state has as its goal well-being, and the ideal constitution is one in which every citizen achieves well-being.

2. In practice, democracy is preferable to oligarchy because it is more stable and its judgements are likely to be wiser since individuals when grouped together have more wisdom than a few.

3. The practice of slavery, with regard to both 'natural' and 'non-natural' slaves required to till the soil and maintain the state (1330ᵃ32–3), is justifiable.

4. Plato's 'communist' society of guardians in the *Republic* is to be condemned because it leads to social disturbances, undermines private property and friendship, 'which is the greatest safeguard against revolution', and is unobtainable.

What holds these diverse views together? Sometimes, Aristotle writes as if his aim is for each citizen to achieve the perfectionist goals set out in the *Ethics*. However, his commitment to this ideal is mitigated by other factors including the need for stability and social harmony. When these conflict (as in his discussion of non-natural slaves), he does not give authority to perfectionist values in a direct or systematic way. It may be that Aristotle thought that there would be more excellent activity in the long run if considerations of harmony and stability were taken seriously. But he fails to spell this out or to specify in detail the distributional policies which are to be implemented by the wise rulers who hold power in his preferred constitution. While the *Politics* contains many influential remarks, such as those condemning the practice of lending money for profit and analysing the nature of revolutions, it is incomplete as a work of political theory. It also exhibits some of the less attractive aspects of perfectionist theory: if people lack the abilities required for a life of excellence, they are natural slaves rightfully deprived of the basic freedoms enjoyed by those with higher-grade capacities. Similarly, if children are born with serious physical handicaps, they are to be left to die. Aristotle does not seriously address the intuitions of liberty or equality of treatment which run contrary to the demands of perfectionist theory in these cases.

Metaphysics and Biology

Aristotle's metaphysical proposals have a number of different sources. Three of them can be summarized as follows.

1. Aristotle's logical system (as set out above) required a metaphysical underpinning—an account of species, substances, and essences—to underwrite his treatment of logical necessity and demonstration. The same was true of his semantical discussion of the signification of names and the principle of non-contradiction. Names signify (in his view) substances with essences. 'Man' has the significance it does because it signifies the same species on all occasions when it is used. But what makes this the

same species is that it possesses a distinctive essence which it cannot lack. The kind occupies its own slot in the intelligible structure of the world in virtue of its possession of this essence. The essence is the fundamental feature which makes the substance what it is, and explains the other properties of the substance. Aristotle was faced with two problems: he required a metaphysical account of substances, species, and essence to sustain this view, and a psychological account of how we grasp these substances and kinds. (The latter issue is addressed in *De anima*, where Aristotle proposed that our thoughts and perceptions are of objects and kinds when we are in appropriate causal contact with them, and are thus 'likened' to them.)

2. Aristotle was convinced that teleological explanation was the key to the proper study of natural organisms. What determined a thing's nature was what counted as its successful operation: its achieving what it is good for it to achieve (as is implicit in his ethical writings). These goals, and being organized so as to achieve them, are what makes the species the one it is. Some goals are extrinsic; the goal of an axe is to cut wood, and this explains the arrangement of the metal in the axe. But the teleological goal of man is to live a life of a given kind (e.g. of rational activity), and the rest of his nature is designed so as to achieve this intrinsic goal. The distinctive goal of each biological kind is what determines its respective essence.

3. Aristotle's critical study of Plato's theory of universals had convinced him that universals could not exist by themselves, but only in particular things. Since substances must be capable of independent existence, it appears that they cannot be universals but must be particulars. However, this generated a dilemma since Aristotle also believed that only universals were definable and the objects of scientific knowledge (in the *Analytics* model). Thus if substances are knowable, they cannot be particulars. But now it looks as if substances cannot exist at all since they cannot be either universals or particulars. Aristotle's dilemma arises because he was tempted to regard particular substances as ontologically primary, while (at the same time) insisting that understanding and definition are of universals. The latter thought he shared with Plato; but the former is very much his own, and one which led to a fundamentally different account of numbers and universals than the one Plato offered.

In addressing the first two issues, Aristotle needed to represent the essences of substances in a way which respected two ideas: (*a*) that each substance has one fundamental feature which causes its other features to be as they are, (*b*) this feature is teleologically basic. *Form* is the candidate proposed as the relevant essence of substances, composed of form and matter. But is the form particular or universal? How is it related to matter? Is it itself *one* unitary thing? These questions dominate Aristotle's reflections in the *Metaphysics*, and parts of his account of the soul in *De anima* and natural kinds in the biological writings.

Aristotle's discussion of these issues has generated several major scholarly controversies. First, did he take the notion of one unified substance as basic, and regard its matter and form as abstractions from this basic notion? Or did he regard form and matter as independent starting-points which, when related in a given way, yield a unified substance? Second, if each individual substance's form is unique, how is the form itself individuated? Is its identity fixed independently of the matter (or the composite) it informs? Or is it rather a distinct form precisely because it is the result of a general form informing certain quantities of matter? Third, did Aristotle regard general forms as abstractions from the forms of particular substances, which served as his basic case? Or is the order of explanation reversed, general forms taken as explanatorily prior and forms of particular substances derived from general forms enmattered in particular quantities of matter?

One approach (there are again many) takes general forms as explanatorily basic, and construes particular forms as the result of their instantiation in different quantities of matter. On this view, Aristotle regards form and matter as prior to the composite substance, while maintaining as a separate thesis that universals cannot exist uninstantiated. Composites such as humans are to be understood as the result of the operation of form on matter. They are composed from arms and legs, composed in turn from flesh and blood, themselves composed from basic elements. At each level above the lowest, the relevant entities are defined by representing the matter as serving certain teleological goals. While matter is described as potentiality, this means no more than that it can be informed in favourable conditions. This perspective is at work in *The Parts of Animals* and *De anima*, yielding a distinctive picture of the soul and of animal. The teleological operations which introduce such phenomena as desire or perception are not definable in terms of efficient causation, but refer essentially to the creature's own goals, such as well-being or survival. Nor can they be defined as 'whatever plays a given role in a system of explanation', as they are genuine entities in their own right with their own causal powers and essential features. On this view, Aristotle is neither offering a reductive account of psychological states, nor regarding them as inexplicable or mysterious (as in Platonic dualism).

These scholarly issues remain highly controversial, and are at the centre of current debate. Other more general problems are raised by Aristotle's discussion. First, is it possible to explain the unity or identity of a particular substance at all? Second, what is the nature of a metaphysical explanation which Aristotle is seeking? He appears to offer a constructive account of higher-order states, in some way intermediate between reductionism and dualism. But is this a genuine alternative, and how is the relevant construction itself constrained? Third, is there always one teleologically basic feature which explains the presence and nature of the other genuine properties of substances?

As already indicated, Aristotle made substantial progress with each of these questions in his treatises on psychology and biology. Indeed, much of their philosophical interest lies in tracing how far he succeeded in explaining the nature of the relevant phenomena in terms of his central concepts and favoured methodology. The results, particularly in his psychological writings, are often exciting and compelling but sometimes inconclusive. Aristotle encountered serious difficulties in his study of biological natural kinds. He did not succeed in finding one basic feature to explain the remainder of their genuine properties (as required by the *Analytics* model). Thus, he saw that fish are so constituted as to fulfil a range of diverse functions—swimming, feeding, reproducing, living in water—which cannot all easily be unified in a unitary essence of the type proposed in the *Analytics*. The model he had developed to analyse physical phenomena (such as thunder) could not be applied without major changes to central aspects of the biological world. Aristotle's commitment to teleological explanation generated results apparently contrary to the guiding idea of non-complex unifying forms proposed in the *Metaphysics*. It is not clear whether he believed that these problems could be overcome, or concluded that the model of explanation which applied elsewhere could not successfully analyse biological kinds. He did not succeed in integrating all his beliefs into a complete and unified theory.

Aristotle's writings in metaphysics, morals, biology, and psychology are unified by common interests in natural kinds, teleology, and essence, but they are not parts of the seamless web of a perfectly unified and finished theory. Aristotle was too cautious and scrupulous a thinker to carry through a 'research programme' without constant refinement and attention to recalcitrant detail. In this respect his writings seem to reflect the nature of intellectual contemplation itself.

AUGUSTINE (354–430)

CHRISTOPHER KIRWAN

S AINT, Bishop of Hippo Regius (now Annaba, Algeria), Doctor of the
Western Church. His enormous influence on the doctrines of Western Christianity owes much to his skill and perseverance as a philosopher. In the history of philosophy itself he is a secondary figure, partly
because he didn't have the taste or leisure to acquire more than a scrappy
knowledge of the 800-year tradition preceding him.

As a young student at Carthage he formed the ambition, according to
his *Confessions* (397–400), to lead a philosophical life pursuing truth. The
opportunity to fulfil this ambition came when, aged 31, he resumed his
childhood Christianity at Milan (386) and gave up his career as a school-
master. With some friends he spent a winter at Cassiciacum by the north
Italian lakes, discussing philosophy and composing dialogues on scepticism, the happy life, and the soul's immortality. Returning from there
(388) to his birthplace Thagaste in Numidia (Souk-Ahras, Algeria), he set
up a community of young disciples and wrote on the problem of evil,
order, prosody, and language and learning. But that life soon ended,
when the Catholic congregation at Hippo on the Numidian coast pre-
vailed on him in 391 to become their presbyter and later bishop. From
then on he was never free of pastoral business. He by no means stopped
writing (his written output, nearly all of which survives, is bulkier than
from any other ancient author), but the subject-matter became mainly
polemical, against schismatics and heretics. Even his masterpieces, the
Confessions and *City of God* (413–26), have a pastoral purpose, the one
being a public meditation on his own slow road to Catholic Christianity,
and the other an attack (which was to have important historical effect) on
the pretensions of pagans to possess a valuable independent culture. At
the end of his life he catalogued and reviewed ninety-three of his works,
excluding the numerous sermons and letters, in his *Retractationes* (426–7).

In spite of his hostility to the pagan past, Augustine was formed by clas-
sicism (all through Latin—he hardly read Greek), and he commended its

contributions to knowledge and helped to transmit some of its flavour to the Western Middle Ages. In philosophy the chief influence on him was Platonist.

The Platonism came from Plotinus. For Augustine, as for the circle from whom he imbibed it during the Milan years (384–7), it was a route to Christianity, rescuing him from Cicero's scepticism and from the materialism and good–evil dualism of the Manichees, whose sect he had joined at Carthage. Now he could agree with 'the Platonic philosophers, who said that the true God is at once the author of things, the illuminator of truth, and the giver of happiness' (*City of God*, 8. 5). He could believe that there are three 'natures' or kinds of substance: bodies, mutable in time and place; souls, incorporeal but mutable in time; and God, incorporeal and immutable (*De Genesi ad Litteram (c.*410), 8. 20. 39). God makes everything, and all that he makes is good. Badness arises from the tendency of things to decay: 'for a thing to be bad is for it to fall away from being (*deficere ab essentia*) and tend to a state in which it is not' (*De Moribus Manichaeorum* (388), 2. 2). The 'ordinary course of nature' is the regular and planned unfolding of causal or 'seminal' reasons, which date from the creation when God 'completed' his work (*De Genesi ad Litteram*, 9. 17. 32, 6. 11. 18–19).

Like Plato's Form of the Good, Augustine's God is not only the cause of things' being but the cause of our knowing them. God illuminates truths as the sun illuminates visible things. The senses do not supply knowledge, because their objects are mutable (*Soliloquia* (386–7), 1. 3. 8). But understanding (which is the actualization of knowledge) can be *compared* to vision as the successful exercise, like successful looking, of the faculty of reason, which is like sight, in the presence of God or wisdom, which is like light (*Soliloquia*, 1. 6. 12–15). This analogy with one of the five senses was enough to convince Augustine that knowledge is enlightenment by God, the only teacher who can do more than provide an occasion for learning (*De Magistro*, 389).

Platonism also helped to shape Augustine's views about the relation of men and other animals to their souls (*animae*), at least to the extent of persuading him that souls are incorporeal, against the Stoic influence that had been felt by some earlier Christians. Soul, he thought, is a nature, or substance (*De Trinitate* (400–20), 2. 8. 14), and he was content to believe that until the general resurrection the souls of the dead will 'live' without bodies (*City of God*, 13. 19). But confronting the question whether a man not yet dead 'is both [a body and a soul], or only a body, or only a soul'

(*De Moribus Catholicae Ecclesiae* (388), 4. 6) he chose the first answer, while also confessing that 'the *way* in which spirits adhere to bodies and become animals is altogether mysterious' (*City of God*, 21. 10. 1). The adherence may be like mixture of light with air, but perhaps should not be called mixture at all (*Epistulae*, 137. 7. 11).

In brooding on scepticism Augustine gradually came to think that even the tough 'criterion' of knowledge that had been agreed, seven centuries before, between Stoics and their adversaries the Academic Sceptics could be satisfied by assent to 'I exist' and 'I am alive'. In scattered passages of his works we can see developing an argument that finds final, Descartes-anticipating form at *City of God*, 11. 26: 'if I am wrong, I exist (*si fallor, sum*)'—hence one's own existence is something one cannot believe in erroneously.

Augustine made some casual remarks about language-learning in the *Confessions*, but also discussed language quite thoroughly elsewhere. He accepted the standard view that speech 'signifies', not only in the sense of *indicating* thoughts (and perhaps things) but also, apparently, in the sense of *representing* the structure of thoughts in its own verbal structure, each unit of thought being itself a word 'that we say in the heart' (*De Trinitate*, 15. 10. 19), not in any language. The theme of such inner words seemed to him important enough to be gently and lucidly expounded in more than one sermon.

Among the Christian controversies which he entered into with great zest and skill were some that involved the major philosophical themes of time and free will. Both Manichees and pagans had mocked the Genesis story of Creation. In *Confessions*, and *City of God*, 11–12, Augustine met the pagan challenge 'Why did God create *then*?' with a response inherited from Philo Judaeus that God made time too. It then follows—or at any rate Augustine asserted—that God himself, being beginningless, must be outside time: his years do not pass but 'stand simultaneously' (*Confessions*, 11. 13. 16). Augustine proceeded to treat Aristotle's puzzle how times can exist, seeing that all of them are past or future or durationless. Starting from the insight that we measure times by memorizing their length (as when, in reciting the long syllables of the hymn 'Deūs creātor ōmniūm', we remember the duration of the short syllables and double it), he speculates whether times are affections of the mind (*Confessions*, 11. 27. 36).

Augustine saw human free will—more exactly free decision, or perhaps free control, of the will, *liberum voluntatis arbitrium*—as essential to

Catholic theology because otherwise an almighty God, exempt from the limitations of Manichaean dualism, could not be justified in tolerating ill deeds and punishing ill-doers. The latter requires original guilt, *originalis reatus*, so that the sin we inherit from Adam must be 'penal' (*De Peccatorum Meritis* (411), 1. 37. 68); and both require the two-way power of acting and not acting, a 'movement of the mind free both for doing and for not doing' (*De Duabus Animabus* (392–3), 12. 17). In *De Libero Arbitrio* (391–5) and *City of God*, 5, Augustine made useful moves towards reconciling such freedom of decision with divine foreknowledge.

By the 390s he also believed, and later against Pelagius felt obliged to proclaim, that men are not able to 'fulfil the divine commands' without God's aid (*De Gratia et Libero Arbitrio* (426), 15. 31), nor even to 'will and believe' aright without God's 'acting' (*De Spiritu et Littera* (412), 34. 60). To those who receive them these benefits come as grace, unmerited, and God's will in bringing them 'cannot be resisted' (*De Corruptione et Gratia* (426), 14. 45). Yet it seems that what cannot be resisted is not received freely and—in one mood—Augustine at last confessed that though 'I tried hard to maintain the free decision of the human will, the grace of God was victorious' (*Retractationes*, 2. 1).

In one of his two works about lying Augustine criticized consequentialism as a decision procedure on the ground of its neutrality between doing ill oneself and acquiescing in the ill deeds of others. He advised that a Christian in penal times threatened with sexual abuse unless he sacrificed to pagan gods 'more ought' to avoid 'his own sin than somebody else's, and a lesser sin of his own than a graver sin of somebody else's' (*De Mendacio* (396), 9. 14). Although this is not a licence to 'wash your hands', it does mean that sins cannot be exculpated by their good consequences. Augustine doggedly inferred that lies, being sinful, are never justified. But like St Paul disavowing 'Let us do ill that good may come' (Romans 3: 8), he did not pause to ask how sins or ill deeds are to be recognized: homicide, for example, he thought only sometimes sinful, because it is permitted to properly authorized soldiers (*Contra Faustum* (400), 22. 70) and executioners (*City of God*, 1. 21).

Augustine shared the asceticism common among Christian and pagan intellectuals of his time. In particular sexual activity, and therefore marriage, would not fit well with philosophy. In his twenties he lived with a woman (he never names her), the mother of his son; and he says in the *Confessions* that what chiefly held him back from the plunge into Christianity was desire for a woman's arms (6. 11. 20). As a bishop he commended to others the partnership of marriage, but even more highly he commended marital continence and virginity. There was something inescapably *low* about sex.

Beginning as a champion of religious toleration, Augustine was gradually drawn into a campaign by the Catholics of north Africa to encourage state coercion of the schismatic Donatist Church, a popular and turbulent movement in the area. His chief motive may have been the same as later persuaded English liberals like Locke to stop short of advocating toleration of Roman Catholics: civil peace. His attitude to the Roman imperial power, Christian since forty years before his birth, was compliant. No one should despise the services it continued to render in increasingly 'barbarian times', while release from its evils must await the end of life's pilgrimage in this 'earthly city' and the home-coming of the saved to heaven.

ST THOMAS AQUINAS (1224/5–1274)

ALEXANDER BROADIE

THE greatest of the medieval philosopher-theologians. After centuries of neglect by thinkers outside the Catholic Church, his writings are increasingly studied by members of the wider philosophical community and his insights put to work in present-day philosophical debates in the fields of philosophical logic, metaphysics, epistemology, philosophy of mind, moral philosophy, and the philosophy of religion.

He was born in Roccasecca in the Kingdom of Naples and sent at the age of 5 to the Abbey of Monte Cassino, from where in his mid-teens he progressed to the University of Naples. In 1242 or the following year he entered the Order of Preachers (the Dominican Order), and spent the rest of his life exemplifying the Order's commitment to study and preaching. In 1256 he received from the University of Paris his licence to teach, and subsequently taught also at Orvieto, Rome, and Naples, all the while developing and refining a vast intellectual system which has come to acquire in the Church an authority unrivalled by the system of any other theologian. That authority was not, however, immediately forthcoming. His canonization in 1323 puts in perspective the fact that a number of propositions he defended were condemned by Church leaders in Paris and Oxford in 1277 shortly after his death.

His written output is vast, 8 million words at a conservative estimate, the more remarkable as he died aged no more than 50. Many of his works are in the form of commentaries, especially upon the Gospels, upon Aristotelian treatises, several of which had only recently reached the Christian West, and upon the *Sentences* of Peter Lombard, the main vehicle in the Middle Ages for the teaching of theology. He also conducted a number of disputations, dealing with questions on truth, on the power of God, on the soul, and on evil, and these disputations were duly committed to paper. Finally, and most famously, he wrote two *Summae* (Summations) of theology, the first, *On the Truth of the Catholic Faith against the Gentiles*, known as the *Summa contra Gentiles*, may have been written as a handbook for those seeking to convert others, in particular Muslims, to the Catholic faith. The second, his chief masterpiece, is the *Summa Theologiae* (Summation of Theology), left unfinished at his death. On 6 December 1273 he underwent an experience during Mass, and thereafter wrote nothing. His reported explanation for the cessation was: 'All that I have written seems to me like straw compared to what has now been revealed to me.' He died four months after the revelation.

That Aquinas wrote commentaries on several of Aristotle's books is indicative of the fact that Aquinas recognized the necessity of showing that Aristotle's system could be squared, more or less, with Christianity. Aristotle had constructed a system of immense range and persuasive power; persuasive not because of the rhetorical skill of the author but by virtue of his remorseless application of logic to propositions that all people of sound mind would accept. Aquinas was not the first to recognize the need to determine the extent to which Aristotle's system was compatible with Christian teaching, and to wonder how the latter teaching was to be defended in those cases where Aristotle clashed with it. But Aquinas more than anyone else rose to the challenge, and produced what must be as nearly the definitive resolution as any that we shall ever have. The resolution is the system of Christian Aristotelian philosophy which was most fully expounded in the *Summa Theologiae*. There we find Aristotelian metaphysics, philosophy of mind, and moral philosophy forming a large part of an unmistakably Christian vision of the created world and of God.

Aquinas draws a sharp distinction between two routes to knowledge of God. One is revelation and the other is human reason. There are many things it is better for us to know than not to know, for example that God exists and that he is one and incorporeal, and in general our reason is a less sure guide than is revelation to the acquisition of this valuable knowledge. Nevertheless, Aquinas believes that it is possible for us to reach these truths without the aid of revelation, by arguing, in particular on the basis of the facts of common experience, such as the existence of motion in the world. To argue to the foregoing propositions about God on such a basis and by rigorous logic is to do philosophy; it is not to do theology, and even less is it simply to rely on revelation. Such exercises of logic are to be found scattered throughout Aquinas's writings, and for this reason he is to be considered a philosopher even in those contexts where he is dealing with overtly religious matters such as the existence and nature of God.

Aquinas is compelled to seek a demonstration of God's existence because he recognizes that the proposition 'God exists' is not self-evident to us, though it is self-evidence in itself. A demonstration can proceed in either of two directions: from consideration of a cause we can infer its effect, and from an effect we can infer its cause. Aquinas presents five proofs of God's existence, the *quinque viae* (five ways), each of which starts with an effect of a divine act and argues back to its cause. In Aquinas's view no demonstration can start from God and work to his effects, for such a procedure would require us to have insight into God's nature, and in fact we cannot naturally have such a thing—we know of God *that* he is but not *what*.

Aquinas argues first from the fact that things move in this world to the conclusion that there must be a first mover which is not moved by anything, 'and everyone thinks of this as God'. The second way starts from the fact that we find in the world an order of efficient causes, and the conclusion drawn is that there must be some efficient cause, which everyone calls 'God', which is first in the chain of such causes. Thirdly, Aquinas begins with the fact that we find things that have the possibility of both being and not being, for they are things that are generated and will be destroyed. And, arguing that not everything can be like that, he concludes that there must exist something, called 'God' by everyone, which is necessary of itself and does not have a cause of its necessity outside itself. The fourth way starts from the fact that we find gradations in things, for some things are more good, some less, some more true, some less, and so on; and concludes that there must be something, which we call 'God', which is the cause of being, and goodness, and every perfection in things. And finally Aquinas notes that things in nature act for the sake of an end even though they lack awareness, and concludes that there must be an intelligent being, whom we call 'God', by whom all natural things are directed to an end. It has been argued that several of these arguments are fatally flawed by their reliance upon an antiquated physics, though other modern commentators have raised doubts about this line of criticism.

Aquinas's belief that we do not have an insight into God's nature forced him to deal with the problem of how we are to understand the terms used in the Bible to describe God. What do terms such as 'good', 'wise', and 'just' mean when predicated of God? Their meaning is otherwise than when predicated of human beings, for if not we would indeed have insight into God's nature. Should the terms therefore be understood merely negatively, as meaning 'not wicked', 'not foolish', and so on? This solution, especially associated with Maimonides (1135–1204), was rejected by Aquinas because this is not what people intend when they use such words. Aquinas's own answer is that the terms are used analogically of God. Since we cannot have an adequate conception of God, that is, since our idea of him falls short of reality, we have to recognize that the qualities that the terms for the perfections normally signify exist (or 'pre-exist') in God in a higher way than in us. It is not that God is not really, or in the fullest sense, good, wise, just, and so on. On the contrary, he has these perfections in the fullest way possible, and it is we creatures who fall short in respect of these perfections.

Among the divine perfections to which Aquinas attends is that of knowledge. God knows everything knowable. As regards his knowledge of the created world he does not know it as a spectator knows an object he happens upon. God, as absolute first cause, is not dependent upon anything for anything. His knowledge of things is therefore not dependent upon the prior existence of the things he knows. On the contrary, it is the act of knowing that brings the things into existence. We can, thinks Aquinas, get a small glimpse into the nature of such knowledge by thinking of it as the kind of knowledge an architect has of a house before he has built it, as compared with the knowledge that a passer-by has of it. It is because of the conception of the house in the architect's mind that the house comes into existence, whereas it is because the house already exists that the passer-by comes to form a conception of it.

Since God knows everything knowable, he must know every act that any human being will ever perform, which raises the notorious problem of whether human beings are free if God is indeed omniscient. In tackling this problem Aquinas offers us a metaphor. A man standing on top of a hill sees simultaneously all the travellers walking along the path that goes round the hillside even though the travellers on the path cannot see each other. Likewise the eternal God sees simultaneously everything past, present, and future, for 'eternity includes all time'. And just as my present certain knowledge of the action you are performing before my eyes does not imply that your action is unfree, so also God's timelessly present knowledge of our acts, past, present, and future, does not imply that our acts are unfree. One prominent problem associated with this solution concerns the fact, mentioned earlier, that Aquinas does not believe God's knowledge of the world to be like that of a spectator but instead to be more like the knowledge an agent has of what he makes. If the history of the world is to be seen as the gradual unfolding of a divinely ordained plan then it is indeed difficult to see in what sense, relevant at least to morality, human acts can be free. Aquinas's solution is still the subject of intense debate.

Given the close relation at many levels between knowledge and truth, Aquinas recognizes that his exposition of the nature of knowledge would be incomplete without a discussion of truth—a concept in which he is in any case bound to be interested given the biblical assertion 'I am the truth'. Truth is to be sought either in the knowing mind or in the things which are known, and Aquinas sees point to accepting both alternatives, so long as distinctions are made. He builds on a comparison with good-ness. We use the term 'good' to refer to that to which our desire tends and use 'true' to refer to that to which our intellect tends. But whereas our desire directs us outward to the thing desired, our intellect directs us inward to the truth which is in our mind. In that sense desire and intellect point in opposite directions, and they do so in a further sense also, for in the case of desire we say that the thing desired is good, but then the desire itself is said to be good in so far as what is desired is good. And likewise, though the knowledge in our mind is primarily true, the outer object is said to be true in virtue of its relation to the truth in the mind.

As regards the relation between the inner truth and the outer, a dis-tinction has to be made because something can have either an essential or an accidental relation to the knowing mind. If the thing known depends for its existence upon the knowing mind then the relation between it and the mind is essential. Thus the relation that something planned has to the plan is an essential relation. The house would not have had the features it has if the architect had not planned it that way, and those features are therefore related essentially to the idea in the architect's mind. Likewise as regards natural things, they are essentially related to the mind of God, who created them, since they depend for their existence upon the idea which he had of them. This contrasts with the relation between an object and a passer-by. The relation in which the house stands to the mind of the passer-by is accidental, for the house does not depend upon the passer-by. In making this distinction Aquinas is developing the concept now known as 'direction of fit'. It is primarily the idea in the mind of the architect that is true and the house built according to his plan is said to be true only derivatively. If the house constructed by the builder does not correspond to the architect's plan then the builder has made a mistake—the house is not true to the architect's plan. It is not that the plan does not fit the house but that the house does not fit the plan. On the other hand if the passer-by does not form an accurate idea of the house then it is his idea that does not fit the house—it is not true to the house.

This distinction enables Aquinas to say that truth is, though in different ways, in both the mind and in that to which the mind is directed. Or if the thing is essentially related to the knowing mind then truth is primarily in the mind and secondarily in the thing, whereas if the thing is accidentally related to the knowing mind then truth is primarily in the thing and secondarily in the mind that knows it. In each case what is said is determined by the order of dependency. Truth is secondarily in that which is dependent.

The truth of the house lies in its conformity to the plan, and the truth of the passer-by's idea of the house lies in its conformity to the house. In each case there is truth where there is a form shared by an intellect and a thing. In view of this Aquinas affirms that truth is defined as conformity of intellect and thing. But for there to be such a conformity does not imply that the knowing mind knows also that the conformity exists. That knowledge involves a further stage in which the intellect judges that the thing has a given form or that it does not have a given form. Here we are dealing not merely with a concept corresponding to an outer thing, we are dealing instead with a judgement in which two concepts are related affirmatively or negatively. And it is such truth, the truth as known, that Aquinas identifies as the perfection of the intellect.

Aquinas is impelled thereafter to describe ways in which something can be false, for otherwise he might be thought to hold that falsity cannot exist. A central doctrine in the *Summa Theologiae* is that truth is a transcendental term, that is, it is truly predicable of all things. In short, whatever exists is true. It is clear why Aquinas maintains this, for truth lies in the conformity between a thing and an intellect, and everything conforms with some intellect, whether human or divine. But if everything is true there is no room for falsity. Aquinas's conclusions concerning truth dictate his principal doctrines concerning falsity. Since truth and falsity are opposites, falsity is to be found where it is natural for truth to be. It occupies the space reserved for truth. That space is primarily in the intellect, and secondarily in things related to an intellect. A natural thing, as produced by an act of the divine will, will not be false to God's idea of it, but a human artefact is false in so far as it does not conform to the artificer's plan. But both divinely and humanly made things may be called false in a qualified way, in so far as they have a natural tendency to produce in us false opinions about them. Thus tin is called 'false silver' because of its deceptive appearance, and a confidence-trickster is a false person because of the plausibility of his self-presentation. In a sense there must on Aquinas's account be more, infinitely more, truth in the world than falsity, for the truths about the created order known by God are infinite, unlike the false opinions which we creatures have, which though numerous are nothing as compared with the truth which God has.

Aquinas had a great deal to say about the human soul. He had inherited from Aristotle the doctrine that every living thing, whether plant, dumb animal, or human being, has a soul. In the first case the soul is nutritive, in the second nutritive and sensitive, and in the third nutritive and sensitive and rational. Since in each case there is a body which has the soul, a question arises concerning how the soul relates to the body. Is it perhaps a corporeal part of the body it vivifies? Aquinas's answer is this. The soul is the 'first principle of life in things which live amongst us'. No body is alive merely in virtue of being corporeal, for otherwise every body would be alive. A body is alive in virtue of being a body of such-and-such a kind. Aquinas uses the term 'substantial form' to signify that by which something is the kind of thing it is, and hence the soul of a particular body is the substantial form of that body. And it is plain that a substantial form of a body cannot itself be corporeal, any more than the circularity of a rose window, which is the window's geometrical form, can be corporeal. The window is corporeal, but its circularity is not.

Turnips and tortoises, though having souls, are not spiritual beings. Humans are spiritual in virtue of having specifically rational souls. Unlike vegetables and dumb animals we have intellect. Aquinas held, following Aristotle, that human knowledge involves the non-material assimilation of the knower's mind to the thing known, thus becoming in a sense identical with that thing. Our intellect has two functions, one active and one passive. The intellect *qua* active abstracts from 'phantasms', that is, from our sense-experience. What is abstracted is stored in the intellect *qua* passive, and is available so that even when corporeal objects are not present to our senses we can none the less think about them.

The bodies we experience with our senses are compounds of matter and form. 'Abstraction' is the metaphor Aquinas uses to signify that the form of the body sensorily experienced becomes also the form of the knower's intellect. The form in the intellect does not, however, have the same mode of existence as the form in the body known. In the latter case the form is said to have 'natural existence' and in the former 'intentional existence'. The knowledge of the object gained by this abstractive act is universal in the sense that it is not the object itself in its individuality that is being thought about, but rather the nature of the object. Such universal knowledge is available only to creatures with intellect, and not to creatures whose highest faculty is that of sense.

The rational soul of a human being has two parts. It is intellect plus will. As is to be expected, the concept of will plays a large role in Aquinas's extensive examination, in the *Summa Theologiae*, of morality. That examination is systematically related to the long discussion which precedes it concerning God, his knowledge and powers, and the world considered precisely as a created thing. For human beings have, according to Aquinas, a twin status as coming from God, in the sense that we owe to him our existence, and also as turned towards him as the end to which we are by nature directed. Indeed the concepts of *exitus* and *reditus*, departure from and return to God, not only define our status but also give the fundamental structuring principle of the *Summa Theologiae*. Building upon Aristotle's teaching, particularly the *Nicomachean Ethics* III and VI, Aquinas gives a detailed analysis of human acts, focusing upon voluntariness, intention, choice, and deliberation, and argues that these features have to be present if an act is to be human, and not merely, like sneezing or twitching, an act which might as truly be said to happen to us as to be something we do, and which could equally happen to a non-human animal. Human acts are those that we see ourselves as having a reason for performing, our reason being the value that we attach to something which is therefore the end in relation to our act. Aquinas argues that beyond all the subsidiary ends at which we might aim, there is an ultimate end, happiness, which we cannot reject, though through ignorance or incompetence we may in fact act in such a way as to put obstacles in the way of our achieving it. However, the fundamental practical principle 'Eschew evil and do good' is built into all of us in such a way that no person can be ignorant of it. This practical principle and others following from it form, in the *Summa Theologiae*, a full and detailed system of natural law which has had a major impact on modern discussions in the philosophy of law.

In this area as in others the discussions that Aquinas's writings have provoked in modern times are as much between, and with, secular-minded philosophers as between Christian theologians, and in that sense the title *doctor communis*, by which he used to be known, applies now as never before.

THOMAS HOBBES (1588–1679)

BERNARD GERT

ENGLISH philosopher, generally regarded as the founder of English moral and political philosophy. His most famous work is *Leviathan* (English edition 1651; Latin edition 1668), but he published translations of Thucydides (1628) and Homer (1674–6) as well as a philosophical trilogy in Latin—*De Corpore* (1655), *De Cive* (1642; English translation, 1651), and *De Homine* (1658)—covering logic, language, optics, human nature, law, and religion, as well as moral and political theory. He also wrote on aesthetics, free will, and determinism, and authored a somewhat biased history of the period of the Civil War. He even entered into some unfortunate mathematical controversies by claiming that he had squared the circle. He was a secretary to Francis Bacon, visited Galileo, and engaged in disputes with Descartes.

Hobbes seems to have been proud of being fearful, proclaiming that he was the first of all who fled the Civil War; and he did leave England for France in 1640 and remained in Paris for eleven years. He explains his fearfulness by claiming that he was born prematurely (5 April 1588) because of his mother's fright over the coming of the Spanish Armada. However, his writings are very bold. He published views that he knew would be strongly disliked by both parties to the English Civil War. He supported the king over Parliament, which earned him the enmity of those supporting Parliament, but he also denied the divine right of the king, which earned him the enmity of many royalists, though not of the king. He also put forward views concerning God and religion that he knew would make him extremely unpopular. The Roman Catholic Church put his books on the Index and Oxford University dismissed faculty for being Hobbists. Some people recommended burning not only his books but himself. He died on 4 December 1679 at the age of 91, and though he had gained great fame on the Continent as well as in England, he remained a controversial person throughout his entire professional life.

Hobbes clearly and explicitly holds a materialist view. He tries to show that there is a plausible explanation of all the features of human psychology, e.g. sense, imagination, dreams, appetites, and aversions, in terms of the motions in the body. He does not claim to demonstrate how the motions of sense and imagination actually interact with the vital motion, e.g. breathing and blood flow, in order to explain voluntary motion. All that Hobbes wants to establish is that there is a plausible materialist explanation of human behaviour and feelings. The key concept in Hobbes's attempt to show the compatibility of his philosophy of motion with the explanation of voluntary behaviour is *endeavour*.

After defining the theoretical concept of endeavour as the invisible beginnings of voluntary motion, he uses endeavour to define the more common psychological terms that are part of his analyses of particular passions. 'This endeavour, when it is toward something that causes it, is called APPETITE or DESIRE . . . And when the endeavour is fromward something, it is generally called AVERSION.' Pleasure and pain are intimately related to appetite and aversions. Sometimes Hobbes regards pleasure and pain as epiphenomena, i.e. simply as appearances of the motions of desire and aversion. However, in other places Hobbes puts forward a more sophisticated materialist account of pleasure and pain—pleasure simply is a desire for what one already has. On this account to take pleasure in something is to desire for it to continue.

Once Hobbes has the concepts of appetite and aversion, pleasure and pain, his account of the individual passions completely ignores the relation between human psychology and his materialist philosophy. He simply proceeds by way of introspection and experience, along with liberal borrowings from Aristotle's account of the passions. Hobbes explicitly maintains that introspection and experience, not a materialist philosophy, provide the key to understanding human psychology. In the Introduction to *Leviathan* he says, 'whosoever looketh into himself, and considereth what he doth, when he does *think, opine, reason, hope, fear,* &c. and upon what grounds, he shall thereby read and know, what are the thoughts and passions of all other men upon the like occasions'. He closes his Introduction with the claim that he has provided an account of mankind, and that all that anyone else has to do is 'to consider, if he also find not the same in himself. For this kind of doctrine admitteth no other demonstration.'

Just as Hobbes finds no incompatibility between his materialist metaphysics and an ordinary account of human psychology, so he finds no incompatibility between holding determinism and accepting an ordinary account of human freedom. Hobbes claims that there is no incompatibility between human freedom and either materialistic determinism or God's omniscience and omnipotence. On his view, all that is required for one to be free is that one's action proceeds from one's will. Since Hobbes defines the 'will' as 'The last appetite (either of doing or omitting), the one that leads immediately to action or omission', all that is necessary for one to be free is that one acts as one wants. It should be clear that this kind of freedom is compatible with both materialistic determinism and God's omnipotence and omniscience. However, at least since Freud, doing what one wants has not been taken by many philosophers as sufficient for free will. Unlike Hobbes, they do not take free will to mean 'the liberty of the man [to do] what he has the will, desire, or inclination to do'. Rather they take free will to refer to some power within the person with regard to his desires, e.g. the ability to change one's desires in response to changes in the circumstances. For Hobbes, that power is reason, and though he does not explicitly relate reason to free will, he may be regarded as the forerunner of contemporary compatibilist views that do so.

Hobbes has a rather ordinary, though somewhat pessimistic, view of human nature. He thinks that children are born concerned only with themselves, but that with appropriate education and training they may come to be concerned with others and with acting in a morally acceptable way. He thinks that, unfortunately, most children are not provided with such training. Thus he holds that most people care primarily for themselves and their families, and that very few are strongly motivated by a more general concern for other people. He does not deny that some people are concerned with others, and, in *Leviathan*, he includes in his list of the passions the following definitions: '*Desire* of good to another, BENEVOLENCE, GOOD WILL, CHARITY. If to man generally, GOOD NATURE' and '*Love* of persons for society, KINDNESS'. But he does not think that such passions are widespread enough to count on them when constructing a civil society.

Given Hobbes's definition of the will as the appetite that leads to action, it follows that we always act on our desires. Since Hobbes further holds that 'The common name for all things that are desired, in so far as they are desired, is good', it follows that every man seeks what is good to him. This has led some to claim mistakenly that Hobbes holds that all people always act in their own self-interest (a view called psychological egoism), and that therefore no one ever is benevolent or desires to act justly. We have seen from the definitions quoted in the previous paragraph that Hobbes acknowledges the existence of benevolence and kindness, even though he does not think that they are very widespread. Similarly, he does not deny that a few are strongly motivated by a desire to act justly. This is shown by the definitions that he offers; for example, a just person is one who is 'delighted in just dealings', studies 'how to do righteousness', and endeavours 'in all things to do that which is just'. He also acknowledges that we can be strongly affected by injustice or injury, as is shown by his definition of indignation as 'Anger for great hurt done to another, when we consider the same to be done by injury'.

For several reasons it is important for Hobbes to hold that people are motivated by their moral views. First, he claims that false moral views were one of the main causes of the Civil War, and so thinks his attempt to provide the correct account of morality may have significant practical benefits. Second, Hobbes grounds the citizens' obligation to obey the law on their promise of obedience. He explicitly says that a person 'is obliged by his contracts, that is, that he ought to perform for his promise sake'. Third, Hobbes knew that the danger to the stability of the state did not arise from the self-interest of all its ordinary citizens, but rather from the self-interest of a few powerful persons who would exploit false moral views. He regarded it as one of the most important duties of the sovereign to combat these false views, and to put forward true views about morality, including its relationship to religion.

Hobbes's account of the relationship between reason and the passions is very complex and subtle. Not only is reason not the slave of the passions, as Hume maintains, but the passions do not necessarily oppose reason, as Kant seems to hold. Rather, the reason of all has the same life-long, long-term goals, namely, the avoidance of avoidable death, pain, and disability. However, people have differing passions, some leading people to act in ways that conflict with reason's obtaining its goals while other passions lead people to act in ways that support the goals of reason. Reason also differs from the passions in that, since it is concerned with life-long, long-term goals, it considers not merely immediate consequences but also the long-term consequences of an action. It also is concerned with determining the most effective means of obtaining these goals. By contrast, the passions react to the immediate desirable consequences, without considering the long-term undesirable consequences.

I think Hobbes's account of rationality and the emotions is a fairly accurate account of the ordinary view. We hold that though people have different passions, rationality is the same in all. Many of us also acknowledge, with Hobbes, that in a conflict between reason and passion, people often follow their passions, although they ought to follow reason; for example, many people act on their passions when doing so threatens their life, and this is acting irrationally. That Hobbes's account of reason is so different from the current philosophically dominant, but mistaken, Humean view of reason as purely instrumental may explain why it has been so widely misinterpreted.

Hobbes's views about the universality of reason make it possible for him to formulate general rules of reason, the laws of nature, that apply to all men. Throughout all his works Hobbes is completely consistent on the point that the laws of nature are the dictates of reason and that, as such, they are concerned with self-preservation. But the dictates of reason that Hobbes discusses as the laws of nature are not concerned with the preservation of particular persons but, as Hobbes puts it, with 'the conservation of men in multitudes'. These are the dictates of reason that concern the threats to life and limb that come from war and civil discord. The goal of these dictates is peace. It is these laws of nature that Hobbes holds provide an objective basis for morality. 'Reason declaring peace to be good, it follows by the same reason, that all the necessary means to peace be good also; and therefore that modesty, equity, trust, humanity, mercy (which we have demonstrated to be necessary to peace), are good manners or habits, that is, virtues.' Hobbes, following Aristotle, considers morality as applying primarily to manners or habits.

The account outlined above allows Hobbes to regard courage, prudence, and temperance as personal virtues, because they lead to the preservation of the individual person who has them, and yet to distinguish them from the moral virtues, which, by leading to peace, lead to the preservation of everyone. This account of reason as seeking self-preservation therefore provides a justification of both the personal and the moral virtues. The personal virtues directly aid self-preservation, and the moral virtues are means to peace and a stable society, which are essential for lasting preservation. This simple and elegant attempt to reconcile rational self-interest and morality is as successful as it is because of the limited view Hobbes takes of the goal of reason. It may be implausible to maintain that it is always in one's self-interest, widely conceived, to have all the moral virtues. It is extremely plausible to maintain this, when the goal of reason is limited to self-preservation.

The importance of reason for Hobbes can be seen from the fact that both the laws of nature and the right of nature are based on it. In the state of nature reason dictates to everyone that they seek peace when they can do so safely, which yields the laws of nature; but when they believe themselves to be in danger, even in the distant future, reason allows them to use any means they see fit to best achieve lasting preservation, which yields the right of nature. But if each person retains the right of nature, the result would be what Hobbes calls the state of nature, in which the life of man is 'solitary, poor, nasty, brutish, and short'. In order to gain lasting preservation, the goal of reason, people must create a stable society; and this requires them to give up their right of nature. This only means giving up the right to decide what is best for one's own long-term preservation; it does not mean giving up one's right to respond to what is immediately threatening. It would be irrational for one not to respond to an immediate threat, and so, for Hobbes, if one seems to give up the right to respond to such threats, that indicates that either one does not mean what one seems to mean, or one is irrational and hence one cannot give up any right. That is why Hobbes regards self-defence as an inalienable right— nothing counts as giving it up.

However, Hobbes argues that giving up one's right to decide what is best for one's long-term preservation, and letting that be decided by a designated person or group of persons called a sovereign, is actually the best way to guarantee one's long-term preservation, provided that other people have also given up their right of nature to the sovereign. Since the sovereign makes the laws, this powerful but paradoxical-sounding argument is equivalent to an argument for obeying the law as long as it is generally obeyed; failing to obey the law increases the chances of unrest and civil war, and hence goes against the dictate of reason, which commands one to seek self-preservation through peace. By allowing for the exception of self-defence, Hobbes has a strong case for saying that reason always supports obeying the civil law.

Although Hobbes is called a social contract theorist, he regards the foundation of the state not to be a mutual contract or covenant, but what he calls a free gift. Theoretically, this free gift may be viewed as the result of people contracting among themselves to make a free gift of their right of nature to some sovereign because of their fear of living with each other without a sovereign, i.e. in the state of nature. However, Hobbes thought that states were naturally formed when people, because of their fear of some person or group who had the power to kill them, made a free gift of their right of nature directly to that sovereign. They believed that only by giving up their right of nature to the sovereign could they save their lives. No matter how the state is formed, the subject does not contract with the sovereign, but rather gives him a free gift of obedience in the hope of living in greater security.

By making a free gift of one's right to the sovereign, the subject becomes obliged to obey the sovereign and is unjust if he disobeys, for injustice is doing what one has given up the right to do. Since the sovereign has not conveyed any right to the subjects, he cannot be unjust; however, in accepting the free gift of the subject, he comes under the law of nature prohibiting ingratitude. Thus, he is required to act so 'that the giver shall have no just occasion to repent him of his gift', which is why Hobbes says, 'Now all the duties of the rulers are contained in this one sentence, the safety of the people is the supreme law.'

Hobbes regards injustice as the only kind of immorality that can be legitimately punished and this is why it is important for him to show that the sovereign cannot commit injustice. He never claims that the sovereign cannot be immoral or that there cannot be immoral or bad laws. However, if immoral behaviour by sovereigns is unjust, any immoral act by the sovereign would serve as a pretext for punishing the sovereign, that is, for civil war. To avoid this possibility Hobbes argues that the sovereign can never be unjust and that there cannot be unjust laws. What is moral and immoral is determined by what leads to lasting peace, what is just and unjust is determined by the laws of the state. On this account, it is immoral to hold that the sovereign can act unjustly, for to hold this is contrary to the stability of the state and hence to lasting peace.

Hobbes believed that if one were forced to choose between what God commands and what the sovereign commands, most would follow God. Thus, he spends much effort trying to show that Scripture supports his moral and political views. He also tries hard to discredit those religious views that lead to disobeying the law. I find no reason to doubt that Hobbes, like Aquinas, sincerely thought that reason and the Scriptures must agree, for both came from the same source, God. But, even if Hobbes held genuine religious views, God still does not play an essential role in his moral or political philosophy. He holds that all rational persons, including atheists and deists, are subject to the laws of nature and to the laws of the civil state, but he explicitly denies that atheists and deists are subject to the commands of God. Since, for Hobbes, reason by itself provides a guide to conduct to be followed by all men, God as the source of reason is completely dispensable.

For Hobbes, moral and political philosophy were not merely academic exercises; he believed that they could be of tremendous practical importance. He held that 'questions concerning the rights of dominion, and the obedience due from subjects [were] the true forerunners of an approaching war'. And he explains his writing of *De Cive* prior to the works that should have preceded it as an attempt to forestall that war. Hobbes's moral and political philosophy is informed by a purpose: the attainment of peace and the avoidance of war, especially civil war. When he errs, it is generally in his attempt to state the cause of peace in the strongest possible form. In this day of nuclear weapons, when whole nations can be destroyed almost as easily as a single person in Hobbes's day, we would do well to pay increased attention to the one philosopher for whom the attainment of peace was the primary goal of moral and political philosophy.

RENÉ DESCARTES (1596–1650)

JOHN COTTINGHAM

BEYOND question, Descartes was the chief architect of the seventeenth-century intellectual revolution which destabilized the traditional doctrines of medieval and Renaissance scholasticism, and laid down the philosophical foundations for what we think of as the 'modern' scientific age. As a small boy Descartes was sent to the newly founded college of La Flèche in Anjou, where he received from the Jesuits a firm grounding in the very scholastic philosophy he was subsequently to challenge. 'I observed with regard to philosophy', he later wrote, 'that despite being cultivated for many centuries by the best minds, it contained no point which was not disputed and hence doubtful' (*Discourse on the Method*, pt. I). In his early adulthood Descartes came to see in the methods and reasoning of mathematics the kind of precision and certainty which traditional philosophy lacked: 'those long chains, composed of very simple and easy reasonings, which geometers customarily use to arrive at their most difficult demonstrations, gave me occasion to suppose that all the things which fall within the scope of human knowledge are interconnected in the same way' (*Discourse*, pt. II).

Much of Descartes's early work as a 'philosopher' was what we should now call scientific. His *Le Monde* (The World, or The Universe), composed in the early 1630s, was a treatise on physics and cosmology, which resolutely avoided the old scholastic apparatus of 'substantial forms' and 'real qualities', and instead offered a comprehensive explanatory schema invoking only simple mechanical principles. A corner-stone of Descartes's approach was that the matter throughout the universe was of essentially the same type; hence there was no difference in principle between 'terrestrial' and 'celestial' phenomena, and the earth was merely one part of a homogeneous universe obeying uniform physical laws. In the climate of the mid-seventeenth century such views could still be dangerous, and Descartes cautiously withdrew his *World* from publication in 1633 on hearing of the condemnation of Galileo by the Roman Inquisition for advocating the heliocentric hypothesis (which Descartes too supported). But in 1637 he ventured to release to the public (anonymously) a sample of his work, the *Geometry*, *Optics*, and *Meteorology*. Prefaced to these three 'specimen essays', was what was to become an acknowledged philosophical classic—the *Discourse on the Method of Rightly Conducting Reason and Reaching the Truth in the Sciences*. The *Discourse* is part intellectual biography, part summary of the author's scientific views (including a presentation of some central themes from the earlier suppressed treatise *Le Monde*). But the book's fame rests on the short central section where Descartes discusses the foundations of knowledge, the existence of God, and the distinction between mind and body. The metaphysical arguments contained here, and greatly expanded in Descartes's philosophical masterpiece, the *Meditations on First Philosophy* (published four years later in 1641), constitute the philosophical core of the Cartesian system.

It is often said that Descartes inaugurated modern philosophy by making questions about the validation of knowledge the first questions to be dealt with in the subject. But while he certainly aimed in the *Discourse* and the *Meditations* to establish epistemically reliable foundations for his new system, it is a distortion to see his interests as primarily epistemological in the modern academic sense. The Descartes who is often presented in today's textbooks is a philosopher obsessively preoccupied with questions like 'How do I know I am really awake?', or 'Could the whole of reality be a dream?' But although the sixteenth-century revival of interest in classical problems about scepticism certainly influenced the framework within which Descartes chose to present his arguments, he was not chiefly interested in contributing to these debates. 'The purpose of my arguments', he wrote in the Synopsis to the *Meditations*, 'is not that they prove what they establish—that there really is a world and that human beings have bodies and so on—since no one has ever seriously doubted these things.' Descartes's main aim was to show how the world of physics, the mathematically describable world, could be reliably mapped out independently of the often vague and misleading deliverances of our sensory organs.

Descartes begins his project of 'leading the mind away from the senses' by observing that 'the senses deceive from time to time, and it is prudent never to trust wholly those who have deceived us even once' (First Meditation). No examples are given of such 'deception', but Descartes later cited standard cases like that of the straight stick which looks bent in water: visual appearances may be misleading. But in some situations, Descartes goes on to concede, such doubts would be absurd: no amount of evidence on the supposed unreliability of my sense-organs could lead me to doubt that I am now sitting by the fire holding a piece of paper in my hands. At this stage, Descartes introduces his famous 'dreaming argument': 'there are no certain marks to distinguish being awake from being asleep', and hence my belief that I am sitting by the fire could turn out to be false (I might be asleep in bed). As first presented, the dreaming argument impugns only particular judgements I may make about what I am doing, or what I think is in front of me; but Descartes goes on to raise more radical doubts about the existence of whole classes of external objects. In their most exaggerated or 'hyperbolical' form (to use Descartes's own epithet), these doubts are expressed in the deliberately conjured up supposition of a 'malicious demon of the utmost power and cunning' bent on deceiving me in every possible way. Perhaps 'the sky, the earth, colours, shapes, sounds and all external things' are merely 'the delusions of dreams which he has devised to ensnare my judgement' (end of First Meditation).

The first truth to emerge unscathed from this barrage of doubt is the meditator's certainty of his own existence. 'Let the demon deceive me as much as he may . . . I am, I exist is certain, so long as it is put forward by me or conceived in my mind' (Second Meditation). This is often known as the Cogito argument, from the Latin phrase Cogito ergo sum ('I am thinking, therefore I exist'). The certainty of the Cogito is, for Descartes, a curiously temporary affair: I can be sure of my existence only for as long as I am thinking. But from this fleeting and flickering insight, Descartes attempts to reconstruct a whole system of reliable knowledge. The route outwards from subjective certainty to objective science depends on the meditator's being able to prove the existence of a perfect God who is the source of all truth. In a much criticized causal argument, Descartes reasons that the representative content of the idea of infinite perfection which he finds within himself is so great that he could not have constructed it from the resources of his own mind; the cause of an idea containing so much perfection must itself be perfect, and hence the idea must have been placed in his mind ('like the mark of the craftsman stamped on his work') by an actually existing perfect being—God

(Third Meditation). Later Descartes supplements this proof by a version of what has come to be known as the ontological argument: since God is, by definition, the sum of all perfections, and since existence is itself a perfection, it follows that 'existence can no more be separated from the essence of God than the fact that its angles equal two right angles can be separated from the essence of a triangle' (Fifth Meditation).

The central importance of God in Descartes's system lies in the deity's role as guarantor of the reliability of human cognition. Humans often go astray in their thinking, but this is because they rashly jump in and give their assent to propositions whose truth is not clear. But provided they use their God-given power of reason correctly, assenting only to what they clearly and distinctly perceive, they can be sure of avoiding error (Fourth Meditation). One problem with this argument was seized on by one of Descartes's contemporary critics, Antoine Arnauld: if we need to prove God's existence in order to underwrite the reliability of the human mind, how can we be sure of the reliability of the reasoning needed to establish his existence in the first place?

Descartes's attempts to extricate himself from this 'Cartesian circle' have been the subject of endless discussion; roughly, his starting position seems to be that there are certain basic truths whose content is so simple and self-evident that we can be sure of them even prior to proving God's existence, and hence the circle can be broken. Truths such as the Cogito —that I must exist so long as I am thinking—are of this kind. The idea of self-standing truths guaranteed merely by their extreme simplicity of content has a certain attraction. But the problem remains—raised indeed by Descartes himself—that it seems possible to imagine that our grasp of such truths could be systematically distorted. The First Meditation had raised the nightmarish doubt that an omnipotent creator might make me able to go wrong 'every time I add two and three or count the sides of a square, or in some even simpler matter if that is imaginable'. If the most fundamental intuitions of the intellect are called into question, then the circle seems to remain as an insoluble puzzle: the intellect cannot without circularity be used to validate its own intuitions. In so far as Descartes got to grips with this problem, he apparently maintained that the irresistible psychological certainty of such elementary truths dispels any reasonable doubt that could be raised: 'If a conviction is so firm that it is impossible for us ever to have any reason for doubting what we are convinced of, then there are no further questions for us to ask; we have everything we could reasonably want' (Second Set of Replies to

Objections to the *Meditations*). On one possible interpretation of this much discussed passage, Descartes is in effect retreating from the claim to provide guaranteed and unshakeably validated foundations for knowledge, and moving towards a position which in some respects anticipates that of David Hume a century later: human beings have to rest content with what their nature irresistibly inclines them to believe; there are no 'absolute' guarantees.

Whatever the solution to the vexed problem of the foundations of Descartes's system, and their epistemic status, Descartes himself clearly believed that if he could get as far as establishing the existence of God, 'in whom all the wisdom of the sciences lies hid', he could proceed to establish a systematic physical science, covering 'the whole of that corporeal nature which is the subject matter of pure mathematics' (Fifth Meditation). The resulting system of 'mathematicized' science was developed most fully by Descartes in his mammoth *Principles of Philosophy* (published in Latin in 1644). Matter is defined as that which has extension (length, breadth, and height), and all observed phenomena explained simply in terms of the various modifications (or 'modes') of this extended stuff—namely the size and shape of the various particles into which it is divided (cf. *Principles of Philosophy*, pt. ii. art. 64). While this quantitative approach to physics clearly constituted an extremely fruitful advance (it remains the basis of our modern scientific outlook), Descartes had problems in accounting for all the properties of the universe as simple modes of extended substance. Even the fact that the matter of the universe is in *motion* seems to take us beyond mere extension in three dimensions—something which leads Descartes to invoke the power of the Deity: 'in the beginning God created matter, along with its motion and rest, and now . . . he conserves the same quantity of motion in the universe as he put there in the beginning'. From the uniformity and constancy of God, Descartes proceeds to deduce important general principles such as the law of the conservation of rectilinear motion; he also arrives at seven mathematical rules for calculating the results of impacts between bodies, all of which presuppose that the quantity of motion (measured as size times speed) is conserved. Although Descartes is often described as an apriorist in science, and although the main structural principles of his physics are arrived at independently of experience, Descartes nevertheless insists that at a lower level reason alone cannot determine which of the various hypotheses consistent with these general principles is in fact correct: 'here I know of no other way than to seek various observations whose outcomes vary according to which is the correct explanation' (*Discourse*, pt. VI).

Descartes's general ambitions in philosophy–science were unificatory: the whole of philosophy, he observed, is like a tree of which the roots are metaphysics, the trunk physics, and the branches the specific sciences, reducible to three principal subjects—medicine, mechanics, and morals. But the Cartesian vision of a comprehensive and unified system of knowledge abruptly disintegrates when it comes to the phenomenon of thought. For a variety of reasons—theological, metaphysical, and scientific—Descartes believed that mind, or 'thinking substance' (*res cogitans*), was wholly distinct from the world of matter. Matter was extended, divisible, spatial; mind unextended, indivisible, and non-spatial. The result is the theory known as Cartesian dualism—the view that the mind or soul (Descartes makes no distinction between these two terms) is 'entirely distinct from the body, and would not fail to be what it is even if the body did not exist' (*Discourse*, pt. IV). Some of Descartes's arguments for the incorporeality of the mind are decidedly weak: in the *Discourse* he baldly concludes, from his (alleged) ability to think of himself existing without a body, that the body is not necessary to his essence as a thinking thing. Other arguments are more interesting: in part V of the *Discourse* he notes that the ability to reason, and to use language, involves the capacity to respond in indefinitely complex ways to 'all the contingencies of life', and that this power goes beyond anything that could be generated by a mere stimulus–response device. The utterances of animals are not genuine language, but simply automatic responses to external and internal stimuli, and hence 'the beasts' are wholly lacking in mind—mere mechanical automata.

One reason this last conclusion seems counter-intuitive is that even if we agree that animals lack genuine thought and reason, this does not seem to rule out their having at least some 'mental' attributes—sensory awareness, for example. Sensation turns out to be a problem for Descartes even in the case of human beings. If the essential self is a pure incorporeal mind, wholly distinct from the body, then it is hard to account for the character of our ordinary feelings and sensations, which seem intimately bound up with our bodily nature as creatures of flesh and blood. A pure spirit, like an angel, could hardly have a tummy-ache. Descartes himself admits that 'nature teaches me by these sensations of hunger, thirst, pleasure and pain that I am not merely present in the body like a sailor in a ship, but that I am very closely conjoined and intermingled with it so that I and the body form a unit' (Sixth Meditation). But the difficulty is to see how two utterly alien and incompatible substances, mind and body, can be united in this way. Descartes wrote in correspondence with Princess Elizabeth of Bohemia that whereas the distinction between mind and body could be grasped by our reason, the 'substantial union' between them just had to be experienced. Yet this seems tantamount to admitting that what we experience undermines the distinction which reason (allegedly) perceives.

In his last work, the *Passions of the Soul*, composed shortly before his ill-fated visit to Sweden in the winter of 1649–50 (where he contracted pneumonia and died just short of his fifty-fourth birthday), Descartes examines the physiological basis for our feelings and sensations. Although the mechanisms of the body are no part of our nature as 'thinking beings', Descartes none the less maintains that there is a 'naturally ordained' relationship whereby physiological events automatically generate certain psychological responses; learning about these responses, and about the conditioning process which can allow us to modify them in certain cases, is the key to controlling the passions 'so that the evils they cause become bearable and even a source of joy' (*Passions*, art. 212). Descartes thus holds out the hope that a proper understanding of our nature as human beings will yield genuine benefits for the conduct of life—a hope which accords with the early ambition, which he had voiced in the *Discourse*, to replace the 'speculative' philosophy of scholasticism with a practical philosophy that would improve the human lot.

For all his ambitions to ameliorate the human condition, Descartes's account of that condition as depending on a mysterious fusion of incorporeal self and mechanical body remains deeply unsatisfying. But the so-called 'mind–body problem' which continues to engage the attention of philosophers today bears witness to the compelling nature of the issues with which Descartes wrestled. The relationship between the physical world as described in the objective language of mathematical physics, and the inner world of the mind, of which each of us has a peculiarly direct and intimate awareness, involves difficulties which even now we seem far from being able to resolve. But the reason why these problems so fascinate us is precisely that they represent the ultimate test case for that all-embracing model of scientific understanding which Descartes himself so spectacularly and so successfully inaugurated.

BARUCH SPINOZA (1632–1677)

T. L. S. SPRIGGE

THE Dutch Jewish philosopher Baruch (or Benedictus) Spinoza's family were Portuguese Judaizing Marranos (forced converts to Christianity living secretly as Jews). His father had emigrated to Amsterdam to avoid persecution, where he built up a successful merchant business. Spinoza's mother died when he was 6 and his father when he was 22. Spinoza continued for a time as a respected member of his synagogue, running the family business with his brother. However, a crisis arose when he would not renounce the heterodox opinions he had been heard to voice, and, after unsuccessful efforts to buy his silence, he was cursed and excommunicated from the Jewish community. Opinions differ over why such strong action was taken against him. One view is that the peculiar religious position of the Marranos had encouraged scepticism and laxity in Jewish practice and that the rabbis felt that they must affirm the religious unity of their community (there were some other similar 'herems'). Others emphasize the need to reassure the city fathers that the Jewish community was committed to the same basic theism as Christianity.

A few years after the ban Spinoza (with the family business wound up) left Amsterdam and lived for some years in Rijnsburg, near Leiden, lodging with a member of the Collegiant sect, with which he was developing an association. After four years he moved to Voorburg and then to The Hague, living in modest lodgings. (The houses at Rijnsburg and The Hague now contain the library and offices of the Dutch Spinoza society, the *Vereniging het Spinozahuis*.) He was a skilled optical lens grinder and some of his income came from this, though he also accepted some small financial support from his followers. He acquired international fame, and, with the publication of the *Tractatus Theologico-Politicus* in 1670, notoriety. Among his friends and frequent correspondents was Henry Oldenburg, Secretary of the Royal Society in London. Oldenburg and some other Christians may have hoped that Spinoza would lead that mass conversion of the Jews to Christianity which their millenarian beliefs led them to expect. However, Spinoza conceived Jesus as at most the last of the great Jewish prophets.

Spinoza only published two books in his lifetime: *The Principles of Descartes's Philosophy* (written initially for a young man he was informally tutoring, published 1663) and the *Tractatus Theologico-Politicus*. The latter was published anonymously at Amsterdam, though for reasons of prudence with a falsely titled frontispiece and binding. It soon became explosively infamous and Spinoza, once he became known as the author, much reviled for it.

It is part biblical study, part political treatise. Its overriding goal is to recommend full freedom of thought and religious practice, subject to behavioural conformity with the laws of the land. As virtually the first examination of the Scriptures (primarily the Pentateuch) as historical documents, reflecting the intellectual limitations of their time, and of problematic authorship, it opened the so-called higher criticism. What is important, claims Spinoza, is the Bible's moral message; its implied science and metaphysics can stand only as imaginative adjuncts for teaching ethics to the multitude. Though Spinoza unobtrusively identifies God and nature, one of the opinions leading to his excommunication (as he was already doing in his work in progress on the *Ethics*), he writes in a seemingly more orthodox vein, even while denying the genuinely supernatural character of reported miracles. It is much debated whether this shows that those who now read the *Ethics* in too secular a way are misunderstanding it, or whether Spinoza was adapting his presentation not indeed to the masses, but to conventionally religious intellectuals of his time, among whom he wished to promote tolerant liberal ideals. The study of the Bible is designed to show that there is nothing in it which should sanction intolerance within Judaism or Christianity, or between them, and to illustrate certain political facts by reflections on Jewish history, such as the desirable relations between Church and State. Spinoza's political theory owes a good deal to Hobbes, utilizing similarly the idea of a social contract, but deriving a more liberal and democratic lesson from it. Spinoza was personally committed to the republican policies of the De Witt brothers in Amsterdam, was outraged at their murder, and was against the royalist ambitions of the House of Orange.

Shortly after his death *Opera Postuma* was published by his friends, containing the *Ethics*, one of the major and most influential works of Western philosophy, the unfinished *Tractatus Politicus*, some lesser works, and some important correspondence. So notorious had Spinoza's opinions become that they still only gave the name of the author as B.D.S. (Two other works have come to light since.)

Spinoza has been more variously interpreted than most philosophers. Perhaps this only shows his system's resemblance to the universe it mirrors. A less contentious explanation is that, depending on the reader's starting-point, it may come either as a call to abandon traditional Jewish or Christian religious belief and practice, or as a revitalization of the conception of a God who seemed to be dying. In the seventeenth and eighteenth centuries he was widely regarded with horror as a scarcely covert atheist, in the nineteenth as a precursor of absolute idealism. Some twentieth-century thinkers interpret him, rather one-sidedly, as a precursor of a 'cognitive science' interpretation of mind, others almost as a logical atomist, while others again hail his pantheism as providing a metaphysical foundation for 'deep ecology'. Among the many very different thinkers who have either regarded themselves as, in a broad sense, Spinozists, or as strongly influenced by him, are Goethe, Lessing, Heine, Nietzsche, George Eliot, Einstein, Freud, Bertrand Russell, and George Santayana, while Hegel saw Spinoza's philosophy as a particularly important dialectical stage on the road to his own absolute idea. Historically, Spinoza was strongly influenced by Descartes, though the upshot of his thought is markedly different, and, to a debatable degree, by various Jewish thinkers.

Spinoza's great work, the *Ethics*, is presented as a deductive system in the manner of Euclid. Each of its five parts ('Concerning God'; 'On the Nature and Origin of the Mind'; 'Concerning the Origin and Nature of the Emotions'; 'Of Human Bondage, or the Strength of the Emotions'; 'Of the Power of the Intellect, or of Human Freedom') opens with a set of definitions and axioms and is followed by a series of theorems proved upon the basis of what precedes them, with more informal remarks in scholia and appendices.

In part I Spinoza proves (understand henceforth: or intends to prove) that there is only one substance (in the sense of genuinely individual thing with an intelligibility not derivative from that of other things), and this answers both to the traditional meanings of 'God' (for example, its existence follows from its essence) and of 'nature' (that of which the laws of nature are the operations). (Thus God did not create but *is* nature.) Spinoza derives this claim by pushing the traditional notions of an individual substance to its limit in a complex argument roughly as follows.

1. First we must note some of his opening definitions: 'By substance I understand what is in itself and is conceived through itself, i.e. that whose concept does not require the concept of another thing, from which it must be formed.' 'By attribute I understand what the intellect perceives of a substance, as constituting its essence.' 'By mode I understand the affections of a substance or that which is in another thing through which it is also conceived.' 'By God I understand a being absolutely infinite, i.e. a substance consisting of an infinity of attributes, of which each one expresses an eternal and infinite essence.'

2. After certain initial moves Spinoza proves proposition 5, 'In the universe there cannot be two or more substances of the same nature or attribute', by considering what could possibly distinguish two such substances. It could not be their affections or modes, because they must be different in order to have different affections (just as two men could not be distinguished by the fact that one was angry and the other not, for this possibility rests upon their being different men—compare some recent arguments for bare particulars). However, on the only alternative, that they are distinguished by their natures or attributes, they would not be instances of what is denied. Why Spinoza did not consider the apparently obvious objection (noted by Leibniz) that they might share one but not all their attributes has been debated. The solution recommended here is that, since an attribute is simply a way of conceiving the essence or nature of a substance, any shared attribute implies a shared essence which in turn implies the same set of attributes as ways of conceiving it.

3. The next crucial proposition (part 1, proposition 11) affirms the necessary existence of God as we have seen him (or it—to say 'her' would be wildly anachronistic) defined. Spinoza's ontological argument for this is derived with peculiar abruptness from proposition 7, according to which existence appertains to the nature of substance (and so must pertain to the divine substance), this being derived in turn from the impossibility, established in previous propositions, of one substance producing another (because such causation requires a community of nature that is impossible granted that two substances cannot share their nature).

One might think that this only shows that if a substance exists at all, then it must exist of its own nature, and does not tell us which if any substances do exist. However, the underlying thought seems to be that any coherently conceivable substance (with a possibly actualizable essence) must exist, since the conception of it cannot be derived from anything but its own existing self. In the case of that which could only exist as the modification of something else, the case is different, for the conception of it may be derived from the conception of that of which it is a possible modification. Thus (my examples) the conception of Horatio's bravery in some non-actual situation may be derived from a proper conception of Horatio himself, and the conception of a unicorn may be derived from the conception of the universal space within which it could figure as a possible form. But in the case of a coherently conceivable substance, such as God, there can be no such derivation, and its coherent conceivability must derive from its own actual being. (Leibniz's claim that the ontological argument should first establish the coherent conceivability of God is apt here. In fact in the course of the first of two further proofs Spinoza does try to show this.)

4. Since a perfect substance exists possessing all attributes, and since there cannot be more than one substance possessing the same attribute, it follows that this perfect substance is the only substance, since there are no attributes left for any other substance. Thus (part 1, proposition 14) 'Except God, no substance can be or be conceived.'

We must continue in even less detail. All ordinary finite things are modes of this one substance, that is, stand to it as, say, an emotion pertains to a person or a movement to a moving thing. Thus the existence of a person consists in the one substance being in a certain state, just as the existence of my anger consists in my being in a certain state. (This traditional reading of Spinoza is sometimes challenged.) In effect, my anger is the mode (Spinoza says 'affection') of a mode.

Some commentators resist the usual idea that for Spinoza God simply is the universe, insisting that he is rather the one substance in which all natural phenomena inhere. But though we should distinguish between the essence-and-attributes-of-God and his modes, that still leaves all natural phenomena as his states just as my moods are mine. However, certainly God is not merely the physical universe for Spinoza. (Though that God was, among other things, physical, was, indeed, one of his most shocking claims.) For the essence of God is expressed in an infinite number of attributes of which physical extension is just one. Thus the physical world is God's body, God in his physical aspect, rather than the totality of what God is. Humans, as it happens, only know of one other of these attributes, namely thought. God or the universe is thus both an infinite physical thing and an infinite thinking thing (as well as an infinite number of other infinite things the nature of which is hidden from us).

The one substance and its modes exhaust the things which are. But where does that leave the essence and attributes of the one substance and the essences-of-its-modes (of which Spinoza also makes much)? On the face of it, these seem additional sorts of entity. However, this is not really so.

(i) The essence of a finite thing (that is, a finite mode) is simply the thing itself (or rather that core thereof which must endure so long as the thing exists at all) *qua* possibility whose actualization constitutes it an existent or whose non-actualization leaves it merely as something which might exist (so far at least as the general character of the universe goes). The essence of the one substance is similarly one with the substance itself, that core of the universe which must endure so long as anything does and of which all finite things are passing states. However, there is no question of its ever having or having had status as a mere possibility and it is a necessarily actualized essence. That something is possible but non-existent must be a fact about something which does exist. The non-existence of unicorns is the fact that nature has no place for them, but there is nothing which could have no place for Nature, that is, the one divine substance. There is an implied further proof of God's existence here.

(ii) Much discussion has centred on how Spinoza conceived the relation between the essence of the one substance and its attributes. The 'subjective' interpretation regards them as the subjective appearances to a mind of some unknown ultimate noumenal essence. Modern commentators mostly prefer the objective interpretation according to which they are genuine constituents of the essence rather than a veil behind which it hides. There are difficulties in both accounts, both as interpretation and as philosophy. This writer holds the intermediate position that each attribute is one of various alternative ways of conceiving the essence correctly. (Among other reasons for this are the justification we have seen that it provides of part 1, proposition 5.) Thus the world can be truly seen either as a physical system (the attribute of extension) or as a mental system, that is, a system of ideas (the attribute of thought) while there are other in principle possible ways of seeing it (the unknown attributes) beyond human mental capacity.

In short, neither the essence of substance nor its attributes are items in addition to substance itself.

Qua system of thought God, or Nature, is the idea of itself *qua* physical system, and every finite thing, as mode of the one substance, is both a physical thing and the idea of that physical thing, that is, that component of God's mind which is his awareness of it. Thus every genuine unit in physical nature, animal, plant, or ultimate particle, has its mental counterpart, that is, may be conceived not as a physical thing but as the idea of a physical thing. The human mind is the idea of the human body (of how it functions as a whole, rather than of its every detail). Here again commentators interpret Spinoza somewhat divergently, but most agree that this implies that every physical thing has some kind of sentience. However, it is only in so far as a physical thing has a certain wholeness to it that its mental counterpart constitutes a mind with much distinctness from the rest of cosmic mentality.

Every finite thing has a built in *conatus* (striving or endeavour) to persist in its own being, that is, to keep its own essence actualized (in fact, the *conatus* simply is the essence with its own tendency to persist) until it is defeated in so doing by external causes. This produces self-preserving behaviour suited, to the extent that it can internally register them, to current circumstances. The human mind–body is especially apt in such registration, which constitutes its own ideas of its current environment. (Its ideas of its environment are part of God's current idea of it as affected by this.) Pleasure and pain are the mental analogues of an increase or decrease in the effectiveness of its *conatus*, differing in character with the thing's essence. Spinoza defines all the emotions in terms of pleasure, pain, and the basic *conatus* they manifest. He aims to study human psychology dispassionately 'just as if it were an investigation into lines, planes, or bodies', in contrast to those 'who prefer to abuse or deride the emotions and actions of men rather than to understand them'. For only by understanding ourselves can we win freedom in Spinoza's sense.

Spinoza is an uncompromising determinist. Everything that happens is determined by two factors, in the manner of Hempel's account of scientific explanation, the standing nature of God, that is, the laws of nature, and previous conditions likewise determined back through infinite time. There is no human 'freedom of indifference' but there are various degrees of human freedom in a more worthy sense. The physical and mental behaviour of a human being (or, in principle, of any other finite thing) may be active or passive to various degrees. The more it stems distinctively (or creatively) from its own *conatus*, the more active it is; the more it is merely acted on by external things, the more passive it is. The active behaviour of the mind consists in what Spinoza calls adequate ideas, the passive behaviour in inadequate ideas; adequate ideas necessarily constitute more genuine knowledge. Knowledge has three main grades, in order of its adequacy: (1) knowledge by hearsay and vague experience; (2) knowledge by general reasoning; (3) intuitive rational insight. The first type of knowledge yields emotion and activity of an essentially enslaved sort; human liberation consists in movement through the second to the third type of knowledge. Only at that level do we cease to be victims of emotions which we do not properly understand and cannot control. The third type of knowledge ultimately yields the 'intellectual love of God', Spinoza's version of salvation.

More informally put, Spinoza regards us in bondage so far as we are under the control of external things (in a sense which includes especially mental processes of our own which we do not properly understand) and as free to the extent that we meet life with creative understanding of what will best serve the purposes that adequate ideas will determine in us.

One may still wonder how far Spinoza is really committed to what one might call a religious view of the world.

Well, he was certainly against all forms of religion which he regarded as life-denying and which view the present life as a mere preparation for a life to come; rather, our primary aim should be joyous living in the here and now. This, however, should ideally culminate in that quasi-mystical grasp of our eternal place in the scheme of things, and oneness with God, or nature, which he calls the intellectual love of God. Love of God, in this sense, should be the focal aim of the wise man's life.

So far as religion, as most people conceive it, goes, he clearly thought that a good deal of it was mere superstition, fomenting intolerance and in many ways unhelpful as a basis for a genuinely good life. But he also thought that for the mass of people, who are incapable of the philosopher's intellectual love of God, a good popular religion could act as a morally worthy substitute, providing a less complete form of salvation available to all who live morally and love God, as they conceive him, appropriately, provided only that their love of God is of a type which promotes obedience to the basic commands of morality.

Spinoza is arguably the only really great 'modern' Western philosopher who develops what can be properly called a personal philosophy of life.

JOHN LOCKE (1632–1704)

ROGER WOOLHOUSE

THE foremost English philosopher of the early period of modern post-Cartesian philosophy was educated at Westminster School and Christ Church, Oxford. Besides studying, and then teaching, subjects such as logic, moral philosophy, rhetoric, and Greek, he had a deep and abiding interest in medicine, which brought him into the service of the Earl of Shaftesbury. As secretary to Shaftesbury he became involved in Protestant politics. This involvement resulted in an exile in Holland from 1683 to 1689, when, shortly after William of Orange took the throne, he returned to England and a life of private study and public service.

He wrote widely—not only on various branches of philosophy, but also on education, economics, theology, and medicine. He is best known for his anonymously published *Treatises of Government* (1690) and his *Essay Concerning Human Understanding* (1690).

The *Treatises*, which contain Locke's political philosophy, were composed in the years of the Exclusion Crisis, during which Locke's patron, Shaftesbury, and others, sought to exclude James, then Duke of York, from the succession to the throne, and argued for government by consent and for the right to religious dissent.

The *First Treatise*, less studied now than the second, consists mainly of criticism of Robert Filmer's theory (*Patriarcha* (1680)) of absolute monarchy and the divine right of kings. Locke found this account of political authority, according to which God granted Adam absolute and total political authority, unworkable. It could not be used to justify any actual political authority, since it is impossible to show of any particular ruler that he is one of Adam's heirs. In an alternative account the *Second Treatise* argues that though subjects do have a duty to God to obey their ruler, their ruler's power is not God-given or absolute, and it goes along with duties to his subjects. If a ruler's commands do not deserve obedience, resistance to them might be justified.

Locke develops his account from the idea of people living in a state of nature, free from external authority, in families and loose groups. In this state each person has a duty to God not to 'harm another in his life . . . liberty, or . . . goods' (sect. 6), and so has a parallel right to defend against such attack. But it does not follow that these rights and duties are actually respected and obeyed. Someone may lack the power to defend his rights, or he may go too far in his own defence. For such reasons people agree to unite, and to 'enter into society to make one people, one body politic, under one supreme government' (sect. 89). Leaving the state of nature, they 'set up a judge . . . with authority to determine all the controversies and redress the injuries that may happen to any member of the commonwealth' (sect. 89). But this authority is not absolute in his dealings and decisions; he is answerable to 'the will and determination of the majority' (sect. 96). The views and wishes of the people form a possible court of appeal against the ruler. Popular consent not only creates, but also produces, the continued existence of a Lockean political society.

A distinction between tacit and explicit consent provides Locke's answer to the objections that there is no historical evidence for his account of the creation of political authority, and that people are simply born into civil societies and come under their laws and authority without choice. By remaining in society, one gives one's tacit consent to it. Locke's suggestion that one is always 'at liberty to . . . incorporate himself into any other community, or . . . to begin a new one' (sect. 121) is even less plausible now than then. But his whole account can be seen as a picturesque way of analysing the structure of legitimate political authority, and of revealing it to be essentially based on the consent of the governed. The notion of tacit consent is given further substance by Locke's allowing the possibility of legitimate resistance or revolution. 'The community perpetually retains a supreme power of saving themselves from . . . their legislators, whenever they shall be so foolish or so wicked, as to lay and carry on designs against the[ir] liberties and properties' (sect. 149).

Turning now from Locke's political philosophy to his epistemology or theory of knowledge we must look at the work for which he is best known, his masterpiece *An Essay Concerning Human Understanding*.

Devoutly believing that we have been put in this world by God with some expectation of an afterlife in another, Locke's aim in the *Essay* is to discover what kind of things God has fitted us to know, and so how we should direct and use our intellect and understanding. 'My purpose', he tells us, is 'to enquire into the original, certainty, and extent of human knowledge; together, with the grounds and degrees of belief, opinion, and assent' (II. i. 2).

He maintains from the outset that none of our ideas or knowledge (whether theoretical or ethical) is 'native' or innate: the mind at birth, he says, is like 'white paper' (II. i. 2) and all our ideas are derived from experience. But such experience-based ideas are only 'the materials of reason and knowledge' (II. i. 2). Knowledge itself is *not* 'made out to us by our senses' (Draft A, 157). It is a product of reason working out the connections between those ideas. Locke's empiricism about ideas is combined with a rationalism about knowledge. For him, without reason all we have is belief, not knowledge. 'Reason must be our last judge and guide in everything' (IV. xix. 14).

His claim that all our ideas, all the materials of knowledge, come from experience is facilitated by a distinction between simple and complex ideas—the former being unanalysable and indefinable, the latter being mentally constructible out of simples. Complex ideas are of various sorts: substances (e.g. gold, lead, horses), which represent things in the material world; modes (e.g. triangle, gratitude), which are 'dependences on, or affections of substances' (II. xii. 4); and relations (e.g. parent, whiter). He defends his view that all our ideas derive from experience by consideration of such cases as 'space, time, and infinity, and some few others' (II. xii. 8) such as perception, solidity, memory, number, volition, pure substance in general, cause and effect, identity. Besides offering these as difficult test cases, Locke obviously finds these philosophically important ideas intrinsically interesting too.

Locke's discussion of 'pure substance in general' (II. xxiii. 2) became notorious and there are different accounts of what he means. Often he is taken to be rejecting the kind of view which was later held by Bertrand Russell according to which a material thing is no more than 'a bundle of properties'. He is often, that is, supposed to be saying that, in addition to properties, things have a 'substratum' which 'supports' their properties. According to another interpretation of it, Locke's 'substratum' should not be seen in the context of abstract logical questions about the difference between 'things' and 'properties'. It should be identified simply with matter as understood by the 'corpuscularians' of his century, who revived classical Greek atomism, or, more specifically, with particular arrangements of corpuscles of that matter, arrangements which Locke calls the real essences of material things.

His discussion of identity is of perennial interest too. There is, he points out, a relativity about identity. 'Is this what was here before?' It depends what kind of thing *this* is meant to be. If a mass of matter, it is the same if it consists of the same particles; if a living body, this need not be so: 'a colt grown up to a horse . . . is all the while the same . . . though there may be a manifest change of the parts' (II. xxvii. 3). Identity consists here in matter's being continuously arranged in a similar way so that it 'partakes of the same life' (II. xxvii. 4). The point is important for his distinction, made in connection with personal identity, between the idea of 'man' and that of 'person'. A man's identity is basically no different from that of any other animal: 'participation of the same continued life, by constantly fleeting particles of matter, in succession vitally united to the same organised body' (II. xxvii. 6). But a person is not simply a living body. Identity here is that of 'a thinking intelligent being, that has reason, and reflection, and can consider itself as itself, the same thinking thing in different times and places' (II. xxvii. 9). Locke's description of a person as 'a thinking intelligent being' does not mean that the continuity of self-consciousness which constitutes personal identity is the continuity of some immaterial substance, which is self-conscious, for he is clearly unhappy with this view of Descartes's.

In fact the *Essay* contains a fair amount of criticism of Descartes: the identification of extension as the whole essence of material substance, and the claim that the mind is always thinking, are further examples of things to which he objects. Nevertheless, it was that 'justly-admired gentleman' Descartes who rescued Locke from the obscurantism (as it seemed) of the then-prevailing Aristotelian scholasticism to which he had been exposed as a student. To him he owed 'the great obligation of my first deliverance from the unintelligible way of talking of the philosophy in use in the schools' (*Works*, iv. 48). It was Descartes too from whom Locke takes his central and hard-worked notion of an 'idea' ('whatsoever is the object of the understanding when a man thinks' (*Essay*, I. i. 8)) as an essentially mind-dependent thing, rather than a Platonic entity with a reality of its own quite independent of any relation it might have to our minds.

Locke refers to the 'vague and insignificant forms of speech' of the scholastics in his 'Epistle to the Reader'. They come in for criticism in book III, 'On Words', where he rejects the idea that the classificatory words in our language stand for 'real essences' understood, not as Locke prefers (as corpuscular constitutions), but as so-called 'substantial forms' which, by being embodied in things, make them to be of one sort or another. Instead, he argues that classification is a matter of human interests and convenience, and that general words stand for 'nominal essences', mental abstract ideas which we ourselves construct. Generality and universality, he says, 'belong not to the real existence of things; but are the inventions and creatures of the understanding, made by it for its own use' (III. iii. 11).

In book IV, knowledge is defined as 'the perception of the connection and agreement, or disagreement . . . of any of our ideas' (IV. i. 2). Some propositions are true because the relevant ideas are connected and related in such a way as to make them true. Any number is even or odd by virtue of there being a connection between the idea of 'number' and those of 'evenness' and 'oddness'. It is by 'perceiving' these relations by the light of our reason that we come to have knowledge. Sometimes the perception of connection between two ideas is direct, and we have 'intuitive knowledge'. At other times it is indirect, via the medium of other connections and ideas, and then our knowledge is 'demonstrative'. Where either intellectual incapacity or lack of any actual connection means we can perceive no connection then, 'though we may fancy, guess, or believe, yet we always come short of knowledge' (IV. i. 2).

The definition of knowledge as the perception of connections *between ideas* is ill suited to a third degree of knowledge, our 'sensitive knowledge' of the existence of *things* 'without us' *which correspond to our ideas* (IV. ii. 14). Moreover, though the certainty of sensitive knowledge is not so great as that of the other two degrees, it still, Locke says, deserves the name of knowledge; and he is dismissive about those who might be sceptical about the existence of an external world. Because of his talk of a correspondence between external things and our ideas Locke has usually been taken to be a representational realist about perception; but in recent years, and despite his saying that the mind 'perceives nothing but its own ideas' (IV. iv. 3), some have interpreted him as a direct realist.

Locke's definition of knowledge seems perfect for our a priori knowledge in a subject such as geometry, which deals with modes such as 'triangle'. But what of our knowledge in the area of what was known as 'natural philosophy', for example our knowledge that the substance gold is malleable and graphite not? This is surely based on observation and experience and not on intellectual perception of any connection between ideas. Locke recognizes such cases where, because there is 'a want of a discoverable connection between those ideas which we have . . . we are . . . left only to observation and experiment' (IV. iii. 28) and explicitly says that they do not constitute 'knowledge', but what he calls belief or opinion.

The contrast between knowledge proper and belief or opinion is inherited from the scholastics. But Locke does not, like them, think that 'opinion' or 'belief' about the properties and behaviour of substances in the material world is not worth having. He clearly aligns himself with the idea of a systematic observationally and experimentally based study of nature, a study of the kind being pursued by his colleague and friend, the chemist Robert Boyle, whom he refers to in his Epistle to the Reader as one of the 'master builders' of the 'commonwealth of learning'.

The reason why 'natural philosophy is not capable of being made a science' (IV. xii. 10), i.e. into a systematic body of *knowledge* as Locke defines it, is that we do not know the real essences, the corpuscular constitutions, of the substances with which it is concerned. The fact that *we* can perceive no connection between being gold and being malleable does not mean that there is not one. The properties of gold depend on or result from its corpuscular constitution, and if we knew just how its corpuscles are structured and arranged we would be able to see just why it has those properties. If, that is to say, our idea of gold were an idea of its real essence we might see a connection between being gold and being malleable.

But this limitation on our knowledge, that natural philosophy is not capable of being made a science, is no cause for pessimistic concern. The 'belief' and 'opinion' we have about the properties of substances in the world are sufficient for daily practicalities. 'Men have reason to be well satisfied with what God hath thought fit for them, since he has given them . . . whatsoever is necessary for the conveniences of life' (I. i. 5).

Unlike 'natural philosophy', geometry is a science and falls on this side of the horizon of our knowledge. This is because it deals not with substances (e.g. gold, lead) but with modes (e.g. the triangle), whose real essences we know. As with a substance such as gold, it is because a mode such as a triangle is what it is that it has the properties it has; but whereas in the first case we do not know the real essence, in the second, Locke says, we do. It is because it is a figure of three lines enclosing a space that a triangle's external angle equals its internal opposites; and because our idea of a triangle is an idea of that real essence we can see a connection between being a triangle and having angles like that.

Our knowledge is bounded by our ideas, and, in general, extends only so far as they are ideas of real essences. But geometrical figures are not alone in being modes, and so are not the only things whose real essences we might know. The ideas of morality are modes too, and Locke thinks that, with proper application, a systematic science of ethics similar to that of geometry could be developed. But though human reason has gone some way in 'its great and proper business of morality' (*Works*, vii. 140), the progress has been slow.

Yet though moral principles are neither innate nor easy to acquire by reason, no one need remain ignorant of his duties and obligations; for the Bible teaches us them too. This need not mean taking things on authority and abandoning all thought of moral knowledge. We can in hindsight find rationally justifying arguments for what the Bible first suggests. Nevertheless, some people, 'perplexed in the necessary affairs of life' (I. iii. 25) may have no time for this and their morality must be a matter of 'faith' or 'belief'.

Locke's general conclusion concerning the extent of our knowledge is, then, that not only has God 'put within the reach of [our] discovery [beliefs sufficient for] the comfortable provision for [this] life' (I. i. 5), he has also put within the grasp of our rationality 'the way that leads to a better' and given us the means to acquire knowledge of 'whatsoever is necessary for . . . the information of virtue' (I. i. 5).

Many of the early reactions to the *Essay* were critical, and he was sometimes supposed to be a sceptic. But though he does put limits on our ability to know and understand, he is hardly pessimistic about the human situation. He explicitly aimed to defeat the despairing idea 'that either there is no such thing as truth at all; or that mankind hath no sufficient means to attain a certain knowledge of it' (I. i. 2). Nevertheless, his polemic against innate ideas was taken to have dangerous consequences for religion and morality, the role he allotted to reason in religion was taken to imply an impersonal deism, and his suggestion that matter might think (despite his stress that 'all the great ends of morality, and religion, are well enough secured, without philosophical proofs of the soul's immateriality' (IV. iii. 6)) was pointed to with horror. Berkeley, the first great British philosopher after Locke, reacted against what he saw as the sceptical and atheistical consequences of Locke's philosophy.

The framework of Locke's approach to the human mind influenced psychology and epistemology for a long time. David Hartley (1705–57), Joseph Priestley (1733–1804), Francis Hutcheson (1694–1747), James Mill (1733–1836), and Étienne Condillac (1715–80) all approached this problem by analysing experience, after the manner of Locke, into elements and their combinations and associations.

Many of the ideas in the *Essay* (the stress on observation and the corpuscular theory of matter, the attack on the scholastics, the place of reason in religion) can be found in Locke's lesser contemporaries too. But he
was a powerful and vigorous spokesman for them. Along with his friend
and Royal Society colleague, Isaac Newton, he became one of the figure-
heads of the Age of Enlightenment. Both then, and in our own century,
he is valued for a judicious, sober reasonableness, and an individualistic
insistence that opinions are to be weighed carefully on their merits by
each of us, independently of what others, particularly those in majority
or authority, say. 'Trial and examination must give [truth] price.'

GOTTFRIED WILHELM LEIBNIZ (1646–1716)

R. C. SLEIGH, Jr.

E MINENT rationalist philosopher, born in Leipzig, died in Hanover. Leibniz was acquainted with all the major scientific developments of the second half of the seventeenth century. He made important contributions in geology, linguistics, historiography, mathematics, and physics, as well as philosophy. His professional training was in the law; he earned his living in the Court of Hanover by combining the roles of councillor, diplomat, librarian, and historian. He did his philosophy (as well as his physics and mathematics) in his spare time. Although the vast bulk of Leibniz's writings remained unpublished at his death, and a considerable amount is still unpublished, his contributions in the law, mathematics, physics, and philosophy were known and appreciated by his educated European contemporaries in virtue of what he did publish and in virtue of his vast correspondence with intellectuals in a variety of fields. He was best known in his lifetime for his contributions to mathematics, especially to the development of the calculus. The debate concerning to whom priority of discovery should be assigned—Newton or Leibniz—captured the attention of their contemporaries. Current scholarly opinion seems to have reached the conclusion that each discovered the basic foundations of the calculus independently, that Newton's discovery preceded that of Leibniz's, but Leibniz's publication of the basic theory of the calculus preceded that of Newton.

Although Leibniz published only one book on philosophy in his lifetime—*The Theodicy* (1710)—he did publish considerable philosophical work in the leading learned European journals of the time; for example, 'Meditations on Knowledge, Truth, and Ideas' (1684), 'Brief Demonstration of a Notable Error of Descartes' (1686), 'Whether the Essence of Body Consists in Extension' (1691), 'New System of Nature' (1695), and

'On Nature Itself' (1698). He also wrote a book-length study of John Locke's empiricism, *New Essays on Human Understanding*, but decided not to publish it when he learned of Locke's death.

Leibniz's philosophical thinking underwent significant development; the mature metaphysics, presented in bare-bones form in the *Monadology* (1714), is strikingly different from his early work on the nature of bodies. None the less, certain themes persist—the requirement that the basic individuals of an acceptable ontology (the individual substances) satisfy the most rigorous standards of substantial unity, and the requirement that individual substances be endowed with causal powers and, hence, be centres of genuine activity. In the *Monadology* Leibniz presented the main outlines of his mature metaphysical system unaccompanied by much in the way of argumentation in favour of the conclusions therein presented. Consider, for example, the first two paragraphs of the *Monadology*:

1. The Monad, which we shall discuss here, is nothing but a simple substance that enters into composites—simple, i.e. without parts.

2. And there must be simple substances, since there are composites; for the composite is nothing more than a collection, or aggregate, of simples.

These are striking doctrines. If true, the consequence would seem to be that there are no spatially extended substances. But surely the argument of paragraph 2 is in need of considerable support. Perhaps the most complete formulation of the relevant doctrines, and Leibniz's reasons for accepting these doctrines, occurs in his correspondence (1698–1706) with Burcher de Volder, a professor of philosophy at the University of Leiden. In this correspondence Leibniz formulated his basic ontological thesis in the following passage:

considering matters accurately, it must be said that there is nothing in things except simple substances, and, in them, nothing but perception and appetite. Moreover, matter and motion are not so much substances or things as they are the phenomena of percipient beings, the reality of which is located in the harmony of each percipient with itself (with respect to different times) and with other percipients.

In this passage Leibniz claimed that the basic individuals are immaterial entities lacking spatial parts whose properties are a function of their perceptions and appetites. In the correspondence with de Volder, as in the *Monadology*, Leibniz presented his major metaphysical theses concerning these simple immaterial substances. With respect to causality he held the following theses. God creates, conserves, and concurs in the actions of each created substance. Each state of a created monad is a causal consequence of its preceding state, except for its initial state at creation and any other states that result from miraculous divine intervention. While intrasubstantial causality is the rule among created substances, according to Leibniz, he denied the possibility of intersubstantial causal relations among created substances. In what he denied, he agreed with Malebranche, but in affirming spontaneity, i.e. that each individual substance is the cause of its own states, he separated himself from Malebranche's occasionalism. The doctrine of the spontaneity of substance ensured for Leibniz that created individual substances were centres of activity, a feature he took to be a necessary condition of genuine individuality.

Leibniz was sensitive to the idea that this scheme is at odds with common sense—that there appear to be material entities that are spatially extended, existing in space, causally interacting with each other and with us. More than some of his rationalist contemporaries, Leibniz took the claims of common sense seriously. In the second sentence of the passage quoted above Leibniz outlined his way of 'saving the appearances' that are sufficiently well-founded to deserve saving. Two theses are at the heart of his effort: (1) the thesis that each created monad perceives every other monad with varying levels of distinctness; (2) the thesis that God so programmed the monads at creation that, although none causally interacts with any other, each has the perceptions we would expect it to have, were they to interact, and each has the perceptions we would expect it to have, were there extended material objects that are perceived. The first is the thesis of universal expression; the second, the thesis of the pre-established harmony. In the case of material objects, Leibniz formulated the rudiments of a version of phenomenalism, based on the pre-established harmony among the perceptions of the monads. In the case of apparent causal interactions among monads, Leibniz proposed an analysis according to which the underlying reality is an increase in the clarity of the relevant perceptions of the apparent causal agent, accompanied by a corresponding decrease in the clarity of the relevant perceptions of the entity apparently acted upon.

Leibniz's mature metaphysics includes a threefold classification of entities that must be accorded some degree of reality: ideal entities, well-founded phenomena, and actual existents, i.e. monads with their perceptions and appetites. Material objects are examples of well-founded phenomena, according to Leibniz, while space and time are ideal entities. In the following passage from another letter to de Volder, Leibniz formulated the distinction between actual and ideal entities:

in actual entities there is nothing but discrete quantity, namely, the multitude of monads, i.e. simple substances . . . But continuous quantity is something ideal, which pertains to possibles, and to actuals, insofar as they are possible. Indeed, a continuum involves indeterminate parts, whereas, by contrast, there is nothing indefinite in actual entities, in which every division that can be made, is made. Actual things are composed in the manner that a number is composed of unities, ideal things are composed in the manner that a number is composed of fractions. The parts are actual in the real whole, but not in the ideal. By confusing ideal things with real substances when we seek actual parts in the order of possibles and indeterminate parts in the aggregate of actual things, we entangle ourselves in the labyrinth of the continuum and in inexplicable contradictions.

Leibniz's consideration of the labyrinth of the continuum was one source of his monadology. Ultimately, he reached the conclusion that whatever can be infinitely divided without reaching entities that cannot be further divided is not a basic individual in an acceptable ontology. In part, Leibniz's reasoning here turns on his beliefs that divisible entities of the sort noted can not satisfy the standards for substantial unity required of basic individuals. The originality and complexity of Leibniz's reasoning concerning these topics is on display in his correspondence with de Volder, and in his correspondence with Arnauld. In the process of refining the metaphysical considerations that shaped the monadology, Leibniz formulated and defended the following doctrines: the identity of indiscernibles—the thesis that individual substances differ with respect to their intrinsic, non-relational properties; the theory of minute perceptions—that each created monad has some perceptions of which it lacks awareness; as well as the theses of universal expression, the pre-established harmony, and spontaneity, previously mentioned.

An important element in Leibniz's treatment of entities he regarded as ideal is his treatment of space and time, which is formulated in his correspondence with Samuel Clarke. Leibniz set out to explicate the notion of place and space in terms of the spatial relations among material objects, thereby avoiding commitment to space as an independent entity.

Another route to Leibniz's monadology may be traced beginning from some of his conclusions concerning certain of the well-founded phenomena, in particular, material objects. He argued that a correct application of Galileo's discoveries concerning the acceleration of freely falling bodies to the phenomena of impact established that force is not to be identified with quantity of motion, i.e. mass times velocity, as Descartes had held, but is to be measured by mass times the velocity squared. From these physical results, Leibniz drew important metaphysical conclusions—that force, unlike quantity of motion, cannot be identified with some mode of extension and that, therefore, Descartes was mistaken in identifying matter with extension and its modifications. He concluded that each material substance must have an immaterial component, a substantial form, which accounts for its active force.

The labyrinth of the continuum, previously noted, is one of two labyrinths that, according to Leibniz, vex the human mind. The second concerns the possibility of free choice. The nub of this problem for Leibniz is to explain how things might have been otherwise than they are. Leibniz was committed to the concept-containment account of truth, i.e. that a proposition is true just in case the concept of its predicate is contained in the concept of its subject. But that seems to imply that all true propositions are conceptually true, and, hence, necessarily true, and that, therefore, things could not have been otherwise than they are. Leibniz denied that all conceptually true propositions are necessarily true, employing the doctrine of infinite analysis, affirming that in the case of contingent truths, the subject concept contains the predicate concept, but there is no finite analysis of the relevant concepts that establishes that fact. By contrast, Leibniz argued that in the case of necessary truths there is always a finite analysis of the relevant concepts that constitutes a proof of the proposition in question.

Leibniz made important contributions to philosophical theology. The *Theodicy* contains his solution to the problem of evil, i.e. to the question how the facts concerning evil in this world can be consistent with the conception of God as omnipotent, morally perfect, and creator—a conception to which Leibniz was committed. One basic element in his answer to this question is his thesis that this is the best possible world. In outline, Leibniz reached this conclusion in the following manner. He was totally committed to the principle of sufficient reason, i.e. the thesis that for every state of affairs that obtains there must be a sufficient reason why it obtains. Applied to God's choice of a possible world to create, the principle of sufficient reason implies that God must have a sufficient reason for creating just this world, according to Leibniz. But, given God's moral perfection, this reason must have to do with the value of the world selected. Hence, the world selected must be the best possible.

Leibniz also made what he took to be a significant contribution to the formulation of the ontological argument for the existence of God. He claimed that the ontological argument, as formulated by Descartes, for example, proved that a perfect being exists, with one crucial proviso, namely, the premiss that a perfect being is possible. Leibniz believed that none of his predecessors had shown this premiss to be true, and so he set out to do so. The basic idea of his purported proof is this. A perfect being is a being with every perfection. A perfection is a simple, positive property. Therefore, there can be no demonstration that there is a formal contradiction involved in supposing that one and the same entity has all the perfections. Since there can be no demonstration of a formal contradiction, it must be possible for one and the same being to have them all. Such a being would be a perfect being. Hence, a perfect being is possible.

Although Leibniz was not as taken with epistemological problems as Descartes or the British Empiricists, none the less he made significant contributions to the theory of knowledge. In his commentary on John Locke, the *New Essays on Human Understanding*, Leibniz argued forcefully for the thesis that the mind is furnished with innate ideas. Leibniz summarized his debate with Locke on this point as follows:

Our differences are on matters of some importance. It is a matter of knowing if the soul in itself is entirely empty like a writing tablet on which nothing has as yet been written (tabula rasa) . . . and if everything inscribed there comes solely from the senses and experience, or if the soul contains originally the sources of various concepts and doctrines that external objects merely reveal on occasion.

The claim that some concepts and doctrines are innate to the mind is important for Leibniz's metaphysics as well as his theory of knowledge, because he held that some of the central concepts of metaphysics, e.g. the concepts of self, substance, and causation, are innate.

Throughout his career, Leibniz developed various systems of formal logic, most based on the concept containment account of truth, previously mentioned. Some of those systems provide the elements of an approach to formal logic that is a genuine alternative to Aristotelian logic and contemporary quantification theory.

GEORGE
BERKELEY (1685–1753)

GEOFFREY WARNOCK

BERKELEY is a most striking and even unique phenomenon in the history of philosophy. There have been many philosophers who have constructed bold and sweeping, often strange and astonishing, metaphysical systems. Some, particularly in the English tradition—for example, Thomas Reid in the eighteenth century or G. E. Moore in the twentieth—have been devoted to the clarification and defence of 'common sense'. And some have made it their chief concern to defend religious faith and doctrine against their perceived enemies. It is the peculiar achievement of Berkeley that, with high virtuosity and skill, he contrived to present himself in all these roles at once. His readers have differed in their assessments of the relative weights to be accorded to these not clearly compatible concerns. It is easy to read him as primarily a fantastic metaphysician—a line taken, to his baffled chagrin, by almost all his own contemporaries. More recently some, by reaction against this, have perhaps tended to overstress his credentials as the champion of common sense. His religious apologetics, if scarcely his dominant interest, were unquestionably sincere. But mainly one should try to see how, not merely temperamentally but as a lucid theorist, he really did contrive to make a coherent whole of his diverse concerns.

The works on which Berkeley's fame securely rests were written when he was a very young man. Born and educated in Ireland, he first visited England in 1713, when he was 28, and his *Three Dialogues between Hylas and Philonous* was published in that year. But he had by then already published his *Essay towards a New Theory of Vision* (1709) and his major work *A Treatise Concerning the Principles of Human Knowledge* (1710). His later philosophical writings do little more than defend, amplify, and in one or two respects amend the comprehensive views thus early arrived at. It is, in fact, evident from his correspondence that in his later years concern with philosophical issues was for long periods wholly displaced by other interests. In this respect he differs markedly from John Locke—the chief target of his criticism—whose *Essay Concerning Human Understanding* (1690), long meditated and much revised, did not appear till its author was nearly 60. The young Berkeley was apt to commend Locke's thoughts, not without irony, as quite creditable for one so far advanced in years.

A major motive of Locke's philosophy—with which Berkeley was well acquainted in his student days—was to work out the implications of the great achievements of seventeenth-century science. It had been established beyond all question, he took it, that the material universe was really, essentially a system of bodies mechanically interacting in space—bodies 'made', so to speak, of matter, and really possessing just those qualities (*primary* qualities) required for their mechanical mode of operation—'solidity, figure, extension, motion or rest, and number'. This was the bedrock of Locke's position. These bodies operate on, among other things, the sense-organs of human beings—either through actual contact with the 'external object' or, as in vision, by 'insensible particles' emitted or reflected from it. This mechanical stimulation in due course reaches the brain, and thereupon causes 'ideas' to arise in the mind; and these are the items of which the observer is really aware. In some respects these ideas faithfully represent to the mind the actual character of the 'external world'—bodies really do have 'solidity', etc.—but in others not; ideas of, for instance, sound, colour, and smell have no real counterparts in physical reality, but are merely modes in which a suitably constituted observer is affected by the appropriate mechanical stimuli.

Berkeley came very early to regard this picture of the world as at once absurd, dangerous, and repulsive. It was absurd, he argued, because it implied a fantastic scepticism, plainly intolerable to good common sense. For how could an observer, aware only of his own ideas, know *anything* of Locke's 'external world'? Locke himself had insisted that colour, for example, is only an apparent, not a real, feature of that world; but how, in fact, could he know that our ideas correctly represent to us, in any respect, the world's actual character? A sceptic has only to suggest that our ideas perhaps mislead us not merely in some ways, but in every way, and it is evident that Locke is left helpless before that suggestion—unable, indeed, even to assure himself that any 'external' world actually exists. That is surely, for any person of good sense, an intolerable position.

But it is also dangerous, Berkeley holds. For—besides this general lean-ing towards an absurd scepticism—the 'scientism', as one may perhaps call it, of Locke's doctrine seemed to lead naturally towards materialism and, by way of universal causal determinism, to atheism also, and there-fore, in Berkeley's view, to the subversion of all morality. God is brought in by Locke as the designer, creator, and starter of the great Machine; but could he show that matter itself was not eternal, with no beginning and no creator? Might God turn out to be superfluous? Again, though Locke himself had made the supposition that minds are 'immaterial substances' and no doubt hoped to sustain a Christian view of the soul, he had confessed that he could not disprove the counter-suggestion that consciousness might be merely one of the properties of matter, and so wholly dependent on the maintenance of certain purely physical conditions. Thus Locke's theories at best permit, at worst positively encourage, denial of God's existence and the soul's immortality; with that denial religion falls and, in Berkeley's view, drags morality after it.

Finally, it is clear from, though less explicit in, Berkeley's words that he was simply oppressed and repelled by the notion of the universe as a vast machine. Locke loved mechanisms. He delighted in metaphors of clocks and engines, springs, levers, and wheels, and indeed took mechanics to be the paradigm of satisfactory intelligibility. All this Berkeley detested. God's creation, he was sure, could not really be like that—particularly if, in order to maintain that it is, we have to assert that its actual appearance is delusive, that 'the visible beauty of creation' is to be regarded as noth-ing but 'a false imaginary glare'. Why, to embrace such a nightmare, should we deny the evidence of our senses?

What then was to be done? Berkeley thought that the solution of all these perplexities was obvious, luminously simple, and ready to hand. As he wrote in his notebook, 'I wonder not at my sagacity in discovering the obvious though amazing truth, I rather wonder at my stupid inadver-tency in not finding it out before.' The solution was *to deny the existence of matter*.

First, Berkeley insists, this odd-looking denial is wholly supportive of common sense. On Locke's own admission we are never actually aware of anything but our own ideas; to deny the existence, then, of his 'exter-nal objects', material bodies, is not to take away anything that has ever entered into our experience. But not only so; it must also put an end to all sceptical questioning. For Locke was obliged to concede to the sceptic that our ideas might mislead us about the real character of things, precisely because he had regarded things as something other than, merely 'represented' by, our ideas. But if, eliminating the supposed material body, we adopt the view that the ordinary objects of experience simply *are* 'collections of ideas', it will be plainly impossible to suggest that things may not be as they appear to us—even more so, to suggest that their very existence might be doubted. If an apple is not an 'external' material body, but a collection of ideas, then I may be entirely certain—as of course, Berkeley says, any person of good sense actually is—both that it exists, and that it really has the colour, taste, texture, and aroma that I find in it. Doubt on so simple a matter could only seem to arise as a result of the quite needless assertion that things exist, distinct from and in superfluous addition to the ideas we have.

But surely, it may be objected, our ideas have causes. We do not generate our own ideas just as we please; they plainly come to us from some independent source; and what could this be, if not the 'external world'? But this point redounds wholly, Berkeley claims, to his own advantage. For to cause is to *act*; and nothing is genuinely active but the will of an intelligent being. Locke's inanimate material bodies, therefore, could not be true causes of anything; that ideas occur in our minds as they do, with such admirable order, coherence, and regularity, must be by the will of an intelligent being. And of course we know that there is such a Being— God, eternal, omnipresent, omnipotent, 'in whom we live, and move, and have our being', 'who works all in all, and by whom all things consist'. Berkeley wonders at the 'stupidity and inattention' of men who, though every moment 'surrounded with such clear manifestations of the Deity, are yet so little affected by them, that they seem as it were blinded with excess of light' (*Principles*, para. 149).

Finally—and certainly, for Berkeley, most satisfactorily—he finds himself in a position to put the physical scientist firmly in his place. For if there is no matter, no material bodies, there are no 'corpuscles', no 'insensible particles'; that whole corpus of mechanistic physical theorizing in which Locke delighted cannot possibly be true, for there is simply nothing for it to be true *of*. At first, in his early (though major) work the *Principles*, Berkeley embraced this position in the most unqualified form. There is a modest role for the scientist, he there argued, in observation and description of the objects of experience, in the search for true generalizations about the course of our ideas, that is, of natural phenomena; but all reference to items supposedly 'underlying'—supposedly explanatory of, and according to Locke more 'real' than—human experience, must be dismissed as moonshine, the product of mere confusion. But later—regarding, perhaps, as over-drastic this wholesale dismissal of not only Locke but also, for example, Gassendi, Newton, and Boyle—he devised a strikingly ingenious variant position in which, though running hopelessly against the main tendency of his age, he foreshadowed the ideas of many contemporary philosophers of science. In his pamphlet *De Motu* of 1721, he still maintained that corpuscular theories of matter, for example, or the particle theory of light could not be true; but they may nevertheless be allowed, not indeed as truths, but as useful fictions. The 'theory' of the corpuscular structure of matter makes possible the exact mathematical expression of formulae, by which we can make very valuable calculations and predictions; but there is no need to make the supposition that the corpuscles and particles of that theory actually exist. So long as it is useful to us to speak and to calculate *as if* they exist, let us so speak and calculate. Such intellectual dodges 'serve the purpose of mechanical science and reckoning; but to be of service to reckoning and mathematical demonstrations is one thing, to set forth the nature of things is another'. It is Locke's concession, one might say, to the physical scientist of metaphysical *authority* that Berkeley, at every stage, implacably opposes.

Two of Berkeley's later works may be mentioned briefly. His *Alciphron* (1732) is a long work in dialogue form, in which the tenets of Anglican orthodoxy are defended against various types of 'free-thinking' and deism. Though able enough, it suffers from the artificiality of the convention, and has limited interest now that the controversies which prompted it are moribund. His last work was *Siris* (1744), a very strange, even baffling production, in which a most uncharacteristically rambling, ponderous, and speculative statement of some part of his earlier opinions leads on to an inquiry into the virtues of tar-water, a medicine which Berkeley made popular, and for the promotion of which he worked in his later years with surprising zeal.

Berkeley's main work was slow to exert any influence on philosophy, though his limited early *Essay* on vision became fairly well known. His criticism of Locke, though not always ideally fair, was for the most part powerful and well taken; and the transition to his own remarkable doctrine of a wholly non-material, theocentric universe, whose *esse* was *percipi*, and in which human 'spirits' were conceived of as conversing directly with the mind of God, was at least a feat of dazzling ingenuity.

Geoffrey Warnock   99

But this doctrine was too extraordinary to be taken quite seriously. The fact that, so far as the course of actual experience went, he could insist that it coincided with the customary views of ordinary life was felt, rightly, to be not enough to make it actually the same—he was far indeed from being accepted as the friend of common sense. His strikingly original philosophy of science—really *the* fundamental area in which he dissented from Locke—was also much less persuasive then than it would be if it were propounded today. In the early eighteenth century it was still possible, even natural, to regard physical theory as merely a kind of extension of ordinary observation, offering—or at any rate aiming at—literal truths of just the same kind, and couched in much the same terms, as those of everyday experience. Today the sophistication of physical theory has made this difficult, or indeed impossible, to believe; but to deny it then was probably felt not only to be perverse and unnecessary, but also—entirely rightly, in Berkeley's case—to constitute an attempt to undermine the physicist's prestige. It was his misfortune that he opposed, even hated, the 'scientific world-view' at a time when that view was in the first flush of its general ascendancy.

Berkeley was born near Kilkenny, and educated at Kilkenny College and, from 1700, at Trinity College, Dublin. He was a Fellow of that college—though often absent—from 1707 to 1724. Ordained in 1709, he was appointed Dean of Derry in 1724, and Bishop of Cloyne in 1734. He married in 1728, and died at his lodgings in Holywell Street, Oxford, in 1753, while overseeing the introduction of his son George to Christ Church. Berkeley's life, apart from his philosophical writings, is remarkable chiefly for his curious attempt in middle life to establish a college in Bermuda. The purpose of this project was mainly missionary. Berkeley's hope was to attract to his college both the colonial settlers of America and the indigenous American Indians, so that they would in due course return to their communities as ministers of religion and purveyors of enlightenment. As Dean of Derry he devoted to this scheme his considerable energies, powers of persuasion, and personal charm, and at first succeeded in securing for it both private and official backing. He was granted a charter, raised substantial funds by private subscription, and was even promised an ample parliamentary grant. But the scheme was really impracticable, and was in the end recognized to be so. Bermuda—as he was perhaps not clearly aware—is far too distant from the American mainland to have been an attractive location for his institution. Berkeley himself set out boldly for America in 1728, but in his absence doubts and hesitations began to prevail in London. He waited nearly three years for his promised grant to be paid over, but in 1731 the Prime Minister, Walpole, discreetly indicated that there was no prospect that his hopes would be gratified. The house at Newport, Rhode Island, which Berkeley built and inhabited is still preserved.

DAVID HUME (1711–1776)

JUSTIN BROACKES

SCOTTISH philosopher, essayist, and historian. Perhaps the greatest of British philosophers since Locke, Hume aimed to place 'Logic, Morals, Criticism, and Politics' on a new foundation: the 'science of man' and the theory of human nature. Famous for his scepticism in metaphysics, Hume also emphasized the limits that human nature places on our capacity for scepticism. In morals, Hume insisted on the reality of moral distinctions, though our judgements are ultimately founded only in human sentiment. In these and other areas, his concern was to expose the limitations of reason, and to explain how we none the less make the judgements we do, careless of the absence of rational support.

Life

Hume was the second son in a strict Presbyterian family that was a minor branch of the line of the Earls of Home. After two or three years at the University of Edinburgh, Hume began to study for a legal career, but soon discovered that his interests lay elsewhere. Immersing himself in the classics (with a particular love of Cicero's philosophical works), he decided that the existing philosophy contained 'little more than endless disputes', and set out to find 'some medium by which truth might be established'. About the age of eighteen, there finally seemed to open up to him 'a new scene of thought', which made him 'throw up every other pleasure or business to apply entirely to it.' He decided on the life of 'a scholar and a philosopher'.

After four years of intense study overshadowed by something like a nervous breakdown, Hume left Scotland in 1734. He settled in France, at La Flèche, a town in Anjou at whose Jesuit school Descartes had studied a century before. He conceived his general plan of life 'to make a very rigid frugality supply my deficiency of fortune, to maintain unimpaired my independency, and to regard every object as contemptible, except the improvement of my talents in literature'.

It was mostly at La Flèche that Hume wrote *A Treatise of Human Nature*, the most widely studied of his works today. He returned to London in 1737, at the age of 26, and the work appeared in 1739 and 1740. It was soon a disappointment to the author. 'Never literary attempt was more unfortunate than my Treatise of Human Nature. It fell *dead-born from the press*, without reaching such distinction, as even to excite a murmur among the zealots.' Hume had hopes for a second edition, but the work was not reprinted in England until 1817.

Hume had some success with two volumes of *Essays: Moral and Political* (1741, 1742). But he failed in an attempt at the Chair of Ethics and Pneumatical Philosophy in Edinburgh, and turned in his mid-thirties to less literary activities. He was tutor for a year to a mad nobleman, and secretary to General St Clair on an abortive attempt to invade France. Hume seems to have appreciated these activities mainly for the contribution they made to his precarious finances.

The neglect of the *Treatise*, Hume believed, arose from going to press too early, 'carried away by the heat of youth and invention'. He reworked book I, and restored a discussion of miracles that he had cut from the earlier work. The result was a slim volume of *Philosophical Essays Concerning Human Understanding* (1748)—known after 1758 as *An Enquiry Concerning Human Understanding*. He developed book III into a parallel volume, *An Enquiry Concerning the Principles of Morals* (1751). Hume later asked that his philosophical views should be judged on the basis of the *Enquiries*, rather than the *Treatise*. They are the works that spread his philosophy most widely—and in due course roused Kant from his 'dogmatic slumber'.

A draft of the *Dialogues Concerning Natural Religion* existed by 1751, though for reasons of expediency Hume kept this dangerously sceptical work unpublished. In his forties, Hume's main energy turned from philosophy to politics and history. The *Political Discourses* (1752) contain important essays on money and interest. Having failed again to get an academic post (this time at Glasgow), in 1752 Hume became Librarian to the Faculty of Advocates in Edinburgh. With his own library, he worked fast on a *History of England*, publishing volumes on the Stuarts (1754, 1756), the Tudors (1759), and the period from Julius Caesar to Henry VII (1762). Persuaded at first that he was of 'no party' and 'no bias', he found himself a determined opponent of the Whig interpretation of history. The *History* earned Hume a great following and royalties far larger, he said, than 'anything formerly known in England'.

Hume wrote little of note in his fifties. He lived in Paris for a while (1763–6), where he became the darling of the philosophical salons. He returned to England accompanied by Rousseau, who promptly quarrelled with him, imagining that Hume was plotting to ruin his reputation. Hume served for two years in London as under-secretary in the Northern Department—a position which, ironically, gave him responsibility for ecclesiastical preferment in Scotland. He returned to Edinburgh finally in 1769.

The death of Hume earned him something of the status of a secular saint. Knowing that his disease of the bowel was incurable, he faced death with equanimity, cheerfulness, and resignation. His persistence in irreligion shook the conviction of Boswell, and provoked some particularly unpleasant comments from Dr Johnson.

Hume died on 25 August 1776. Some months before, he had written a few pages of autobiography under the title 'My Own Life'. Besides his frugality and need for independence, he stressed the 'great moderation' in his passions. 'Even my love of literary fame, my ruling passion, never soured my temper, notwithstanding my frequent disappointments.' Adam Smith commented: 'Upon the whole, I have always considered him, both in his lifetime and since his death, as approaching as nearly to the idea of a perfectly wise and virtuous man, as perhaps the nature of human frailty will premit.'

Logic and Metaphysics

Hume divides the contents of the mind into *impressions* and *ideas*. Impressions are our 'sensations, passions and emotions'; ideas are 'the faint images of these' in thought, reflection, and imagination. Complex ideas may be formed out of simpler ideas; but simple ideas can enter the mind in only one way, as 'copies of our impressions'.

Causal Reasoning. How do we acquire beliefs about things we are not currently experiencing? We see a flame, for example, and conclude that it is hot. Hume notes that we start from a present impression—the sight of the flame—and suppose a causal relation—between flames and heat. But how do we come to believe in that causal relation?

Hume's great claim is that it is not because of reason. *Reason alone* cannot tell us that flames are hot: it is conceivable that a fire might be cold, and therefore possible. *Reason and experience together* cannot produce the belief either. Our experience has been confined to certain tracts of space and time. Within those reaches, we have found flames to be hot. But there is a gap between 'Observed flames have been hot' and 'All flames are hot'. To reach the second, we would need to add the principle that nature is uniform, that the future resembles the past. But how could we ever establish the uniformity principle?

Hume claims that there are only two kinds of reasoning, 'demonstrative' and 'probable', and neither can do the job. Demonstrative reasoning (such as deduction) cannot establish the uniformity of nature—for non-uniformity is conceivable, and therefore possible. 'Probable' reasoning—or causal reasoning from the observed to the unobserved—cannot establish the uniformity either. Probable reasoning itself presupposes the uniformity of nature, so to employ it in support of that principle would be circular. As Russell later explained, even if experience has told us that past futures resembled past pasts, we cannot conclude that future futures will resemble future pasts—unless we already assume that the future resembles the past.

If reason does not give us our beliefs about the unobserved, what does? Simply 'custom or habit', trading on two fundamentally non-rational processes. Repeated experience of the conjunction of flames and heat creates an *association of ideas*—so if we see a flame, by sheer habit an idea of heat will come to mind. A belief differs from a mere conception by being 'lively or vivid'; so when *vivacity* from the impression of the flame is *transferred* to the associated idea of heat, the idea becomes a belief in the presence of heat. Our beliefs are the product not of reason but of these mechanisms of 'the Imagination'.

Does this make Hume a sceptic about induction? He says that we have 'no reason' to believe that the sun will rise tomorrow. On the other hand, he believes that our inductive reasoning processes are genuinely 'correspondent' to the natural processes in the world; he describes induction as 'essential to the subsistence of human creatures'; and he even says that causal conclusions have their own kind of certainty, 'as satisfactory to the mind . . . as the demonstrative kind'. Perhaps the way to reconcile these claims is to remember that 'reason' is for Hume 'nothing but the comparing of ideas and the discovery of their relations'; so discovering that 'reason', in this sense, is not the source of our inductive beliefs is very different from claiming that induction is, in a more general sense, unreasonable.

Hume's account of causal power builds on his account of causal inference. In accord with the empiricist principle that ideas are derived from impressions, Hume explains that to clarify our idea of necessity we must find and examine the impression that has given rise to it. This proves surprisingly hard. Necessity cannot be found in our experience of any *individual* cases of causation. 'We are never able, in a single instance, to discover any power or necessary connexion'; we simply see one event follow another. The idea arises instead from our experience of a *multiplicity* of similar cases. The *constant conjunction* (say, of flames and heat) produces, as we have seen, an association of ideas. Hume now adds that 'this connexion . . . which we feel in the mind' is the true source of our idea of necessity, and therefore all we can be talking about when we talk about power, connection, or necessity.

Hume's view here is not entirely clear. He has really indicated not one source for the idea of necessity, but a chain of three—conjunction in the objects, association in the mind, and a feeling of connection. Of these, the first and the second tend to weigh most with him, and it is unsurprising, therefore, to find them at the heart of his definitions of cause.

Hume accordingly gives two definitions of causation. The notion of cause contains the notions of *priority* and *necessary connection*. (The *Treatise* treats *contiguity* as a third constituent.) On the view of necessity as constant conjunction, therefore, a cause will be 'an object, followed by another, and where all the objects similar to the first are followed by objects similar to the second'. This is the famous definition of causation as regular succession. On the view of necessity as connection in the mind, a cause will be 'an object followed by another, and whose appearance always conveys the thought to that other'—a rather different account, and less influential upon Hume's followers.

Does Hume deny the existence of power and necessity? Certainly not—any more than Berkeley denies the existence of tables and trees. 'Necessity, according to the sense in which it is here taken, has never yet been rejected, nor can ever, I think, be rejected by any philosopher.' Far from rejecting necessity, Hume is attempting a reductive explanation of it. There is something, however, that Hume does deny, namely, necessity as misconceived. The mind has a 'propensity to spread itself on external objects': we are apt to treat the feeling of connection, which is really only in the mind, instead as a feature of external objects. This is a mistake—the mistake made by rationalists who believe in an intelligible connection between cause and effect.

External World. The final part of book I of the *Treatise* purports to be a study of 'the sceptical and other systems of philosophy'—as if scepticism were a malady to be studied in other people. In the course of discussion, however, it becomes clear the malady is one that Hume himself has caught, and only the strongest instincts can save him from being overcome by it. Hume discusses two versions of the belief in external objects or the external world, the 'vulgar' and the 'philosophical', and finds both of them unjustified. The vulgar or common-sense belief is, on Hume's view, a belief in the 'continued and distinct existence' of the 'interrupted images' of sense. (This attributes to common sense a view like that which Berkeley held—and also, surely implausibly, attributed to common sense.) The 'vulgar' view is false. ' 'Tis a gross illusion to suppose, that our resembling perceptions are numerically the same' after a gap—an illusion due to the *constancy* and *coherence* of our perceptions.

The 'philosophical' or Lockean view does no better, in holding that our impressions are only *representations* of external objects, resembling and caused by them. For 'as no beings are ever present to the mind but perceptions', we can never observe a causal relation (or indeed a similarity) between perceptions and external objects thus conceived.

Hume implies that the 'necessary consequence' is, strictly, to reject 'the opinion of a continued existence' altogether—and believe in nothing but fleeting and 'dependent' ideas and impressions. But nature saves us from this fate: 'The sceptic must assent to the principle concerning the existence of body, tho' he cannot pretend by any arguments of philosophy to maintain its veracity. Nature has not left this to his choice.' Hume's arguments may have produced in the reader a moment of philosophical doubt, but an hour hence he will again be 'persuaded there is both an external and internal world.'

Personal Identity. Hume rejects the view, apparently shared by philosophers and the vulgar, that we are conscious of a self, simple in itself, and identical from one time to another. We have no impression of a simple, identical self; so we can have no idea of any such thing. Hume's own view is that mankind 'is nothing but a bundle or collection of different perceptions, which succeed each other with an inconceivable rapidity, and are in a perpetual flux and movement.' The common mistake arises, Hume thinks, from a tendency to confuse related perceptions with identical.

Hume maintains a more steady scepticism about personal identity than about the external world. In the latter case nature saves us from the hard conclusions of 'intense reflection'; with personal identity, on the other hand, Hume thinks he can live with his own deflationary conclusions. This later proved to be an exaggeration. In an appendix, he admits to feeling confused about his account of personal identity, though for reasons few readers find clear.

Scepticism. The concluding section of the *Treatise*, book I, depicts a battle between reason and nature. Hume has exposed the weakness of the human mind—where what passed for reason turns out to be 'imagination', and even the most plausible inference can be made to seem uncertain. In the face of this weakness, Hume is 'ready to reject all belief and reasoning, and can look upon no opinion even as more probable or likely than another'.

Human nature saves him. 'Most fortunately it happens, that since reason is incapable of dispelling these clouds, nature herself suffices to that purpose.' A few hours of good company and backgammon make his melancholy and sceptical conclusions seem ridiculous. What is more, 'amusement and company' lead Hume to a third phase—of curiosity and constructive philosophical ambition. Following his own nature, Hume finds a place after all for philosophy and the modest pursuit of science.

Hume here reconciles scepticism and naturalism. It is not merely that scepticism is a natural attitude. Rather, the best expression of scepticism is one where we follow our nature without pretending we have an independent justification; in doing so we may even contribute to the 'advancement of knowledge'.

Theory of the Passions, Moral Philosophy

Like Hutcheson before him, Hume models his theory of morality on a theory of aesthetic judgement, linked with an account of the passions. The picture is roughly this. Finding something beautiful is deriving a certain sort of pleasure from it; and that pleasure is a 'calm passion'. Similarly, approving of someone's character, or finding it virtuous, is simply 'feeling that it pleases' in a certain way; and that feeling is a calm passion, though it is liable to be confused with a 'determination of reason'. Like beauty, morality 'is more properly felt than judged of'.

Hume seems himself to have become less confident of the details of his theory of the passions after the *Treatise*, and he never reworked book II as he did books I and III. He is both acute in analysing the conditions necessary for the various passions and resolute in tracing them to associative mechanisms in the mind.

Hume starts with pride and humility. 'Every thing related to us, which produces pleasure or pain, produces likewise pride or humility.' A beautiful house produces pleasure in anyone who looks at it; but it produces pride only in someone *related* to it, for example, as designer or owner. Hume explains this by two mechanisms. The house is related to the owner, so—by an association of ideas—the idea of the house produces in him the idea of himself. (This contributes to pride, because the self is 'the object of pride'.) At the same time, the house produces pleasure, and—by an association of impressions—pleasure produces pride. By two associative processes, the house produces the feeling of pride.

Hume treats love and hatred in a similar fashion, except that whereas the 'object' of pride and humility is oneself, the object of love and hate is another person. Book II also contains an important argument that determinism is compatible with a form of liberty.

Moral Theory. Book III of the *Treatise* begins with a spirited rejection of the view that moral distinctions are derived from reason. 'Morals excite passions, and produce or prevent actions.' By contrast, 'Reason is perfectly inert,' and can never produce or prevent an action. So the rules of morality are 'not conclusions of our reason'—and the rationalist theories of Clarke and Wollaston must be rejected. Moral distinctions are derived from a 'moral sense', not from reason.

Since approval and blame are, respectively, 'agreeable' and 'uneasy', they may be described as varieties of pleasure and pain. By producing pleasure therefore, a virtue will tend (in accordance with the theory of the passions) to produce pride in the possessor, and love in other people. (Pride of this kind, therefore, is no sin.) Hume's remaining task is to explain exactly which characteristics produce that variety of love which is the discerning of virtue.

The answer is easy in the case of 'natural' virtues—characteristics which we approve of because of natural instinct. Hume places in this category those features of a person's character that are '*useful* or *agreeable* to the *person himself* or to *others*'; and he invokes *sympathy*, probably the central notion of his whole moral theory, to explain their operation. Qualities that are useful or agreeable to others will directly elicit pleasure and approval in them. Qualities that are useful or agreeable primarily to the possessor—like good sense or a cheerful character—are approved of because of *sympathy*. We have a natural propensity 'to sympathize with others, and to receive by communication their inclinations and sentiments'. This process—given a complex mechanistic explanation in the *Treatise*, but treated as an ultimate principle in the second *Enquiry*—explains how qualities that give pleasure to one person can inspire pleasure (and hence approval) in others.

The 'artificial' virtues pose a greater problem. An individual act of justice may be approved of, though it benefits no one. Why do we approve of paying back a debt to 'a profligate debauchee, [who] would rather receive harm than benefit from large possessions'? The answer is that we have a conventional or 'artificial' system of rules of property, which as a whole provides security, in an environment where goods are scarce and people are greedy. Even if 'single acts of justice may be contrary, either to public or private interest', the whole scheme is 'absolutely requisite, both to the support of society, and the well-being of every individual'.

Hume's moral theory is in many ways parallel to his general epistemology: he shows the limits of reason, and then explains, in the naturalistic spirit of an empirical student of the mind, how we reach the judgements (or rather, feelings) that we do. But the consequences are less sceptical in the case of morals. To discover that morality is only a matter of feeling, informed by instincts of sympathy, modulated in accord with conventions of justice, and regulated by general rules, is not, it seems, to discover that moral judgement is any less than it could properly be expected to be. On the other hand, to learn that causal judgements are only the effects of habit, to learn that our beliefs in external objects and in the self are false, even if inescapable—all this, Hume seems to think, exposes a tear in the fabric of belief. We may continue to do philosophy, with a kind of confidence that consists in following human nature and being diffident even of our doubts. But Hume does not pretend that to philosophize in that 'careless manner' is to philosophize with no sense of loss.

Philosophy of Religion

The *Dialogues Concerning Natural Religion* appeared in 1779, three years after Hume's death. They present fundamental objections to the ontological and, above all, the cosmological arguments for the existence of God.

It is absurd, Hume suggests, to attempt to demonstrate the existence of God a priori; since the issue is a matter of fact. An a posteriori argument from order in the world to the existence of a designer, however, is also unpersuasive. We can infer only those characteristics which are precisely necessary to produce the features we find in the world; and the only licence we can use in our inference comes from regularities which we have observed. If we agree that order in the world has a cause, the question remains whether 'the cause or causes of order in the universe probably bear some remote analogy to human intelligence'. If the answer is Yes, the analogy with human intelligence may still be quite remote; and in any case this gives us no licence to attribute to the cause any particular moral qualities.

The first *Enquiry* brought Hume notoriety for its argument against believing in miracles. On all topics, 'A wise man . . . proportions his belief to the evidence.' Hence: 'No testimony its sufficient to establish a miracle, unless the testimony be of such a kind, that its falsehood would be more miraculous, than the fact, which it endeavours to establish.' Hume adds reasons to suppose that the latter condition has never been met: witnesses have never been of 'unquestioned good-sense' and learning; human nature takes a misleading delight in things that amaze; moreover, the miracles that supposedly support one religion must in the same way undermine other religions. 'Upon the whole,' Hume concludes, 'the *Christian Religion* not only was at first attended with miracles, but even at this day cannot be believed by any reasonable person without one.'

Having concluded that the source of religion can hardly be reason. Hume gives his own anthropological account of it—in the irreverent essay *The Natural History of Religion*, which appeared in the *Four Dissertations* of 1757.

IMMANUEL KANT (1724–1804)

HENRY E. ALLISON

PERHAPS the most important European philosopher of modern times, Kant was born, spent his entire life, and died in Königsberg in East Prussia. After studying at the University of Königsberg from 1740 to 1746, he worked for a time as a private tutor. In 1755 he returned to the University, received his master's degree, and began lecturing. In 1770 he was appointed professor and he continued to lecture on a wide variety of subjects, including mathematics, physics, anthropology, pedagogy, and physical geography, as well as the central fields in philosophy, until his retirement in 1796. Although he never married or travelled outside of East Prussia and led a highly regimented existence, he was no recluse. On the contrary, he was known as a brilliant lecturer and conversationalist, had a wide circle of friends, and was keenly interested in the intellectual and political issues of the day.

Kant's philosophical career is conventionally divided into three periods. The first, or 'pre-critical period', runs from 1747, the year of his first publication, 'On the True Estimate of Living Forces', to 1770, when he published his inaugural dissertation, *On the Form and Principles of the Sensible and the Intelligible Worlds*. In spite of significant shifting of views, the writings of this period are unified by Kant's abiding concerns with foundational questions in science and the search for the proper method in metaphysics. The middle period (1771–80), called the 'silent decade' because Kant published virtually nothing, was devoted to the study and reflection that led eventually to the *Critique of Pure Reason*. The third, or 'critical period', dates from the publication of the first edition of the *Critique* in 1781. This was followed by the *Prolegomena to any Future Metaphysic* (1783), the *Groundwork to the Metaphysic of Morals* (1785), the *Metaphysical Foundations of Natural Science* (1786), a second edition of the *Critique of Pure Reason* (1787), the *Critique of Practical Reason* (1788), the

Critique of Judgement (1790), *Religion within the Limits of Reason Alone* (1793), and the *Metaphysic of Morals* (1797), as well as many important essays on topics in metaphysics, science, morals, legal and political theory, and the philosophy of history. In addition, he published compilations of his lectures on anthropology, logic, and pedagogy. In his last years he devoted himself to a major revision of some of his basic views on metaphysics and the foundations of science. The work remained uncompleted at his death, but has been edited and published under the title *Opus Postumum*.

The central concern of Kant's greatest masterpiece, the *Critique of Pure Reason*, is with the possibility of metaphysics, understood as philosophical knowledge that transcends the bounds of experience. For Kant, such knowledge claims to be both synthetic and a priori. In other words, metaphysics purports to provide necessary truths, which, as such, cannot be based on empirical evidence (their apriority), but which also claim more of their referents than can be derived from an analysis of their concepts (their syntheticity). The propositions 'God exists' and 'Every event has a cause' are examples of such claims. By contrast, propositions which merely explicate what is already thought in the concept of a subject, e.g. 'God is omnipotent', are termed analytic. Since the truth of the latter can be ascertained merely by appealing to accepted meanings and logical considerations, Kant thought that these were non-problematic. Accordingly, the fundamental philosophical task is to account for the possibility of synthetic a priori knowledge; and since Kant also believed that mathematical propositions are of this nature, accounting for their possibility likewise became an integral part of his project.

The second aspect of Kant's concern with metaphysics is with the problem of the antinomies. As a result of his reflections on the concept of a world, he became convinced that reason inevitably falls into contradiction with itself when it endeavours to 'think the whole', that is, when it ventures beyond experience in order to answer such questions as whether the universe has a beginning in time, limit in space, or first cause, or is, rather, infinite in these respects. The contradiction or antinomy arises because it is possible to construct valid proofs for each of the two conflicting positions: the universe has a beginning in time; the universe has existed for an infinite period of time; etc. He also thought that, if unresolved, this problem would lead to a hopeless scepticism, which he termed the 'euthanasia of pure reason'. Consequently, Kant came to see the 'fate of metaphysics' as crucially dependent on a successful resolution of the antinomies as well as an account of the possibility of synthetic a priori knowledge.

Kant thought that he could deal with both problems at once by means of what is usually called his 'Copernican revolution in philosophy', since he compared his innovation to the 'first thoughts of Copernicus'. This involves reversing the usual way of viewing cognition and instead of thinking of our knowledge as conforming to a realm of objects, we think of objects as conforming to our ways of knowing. The latter include 'forms of sensibility', through which objects are given to the mind in sensory experience, and pure concepts or categories, through which they are thought. Since objects must appear to us in accordance with these sensible forms in order to be known, it follows that we can know them only as they appear, not as they may be in themselves. Accordingly, for Kant human knowledge is limited to appearances or phenomena, whereas things-in-themselves or noumena are thinkable but not actually knowable. Kant termed this doctrine transcendental idealism; and, given this idealism, which he distinguished sharply from that of Berkeley, the possibility of synthetic a priori knowledge of objects of possible experience is easily explicable, since such objects must necessarily conform to the conditions under which they can become objects for us.

This whole project assumes, however, that the human mind is, in fact, endowed with such conditions, and demonstrating this is the main task of the Transcendental Aesthetic and the Transcendental Analytic. In the former, Kant argued that space and time are subjective forms of human sensibility, through which the manifold of sense is given to the mind, rather than either self-subsisting realities (Newton) or relations between self-subsisting things (Leibniz). He also argued that only this conception of space is capable of accounting for the possibility of geometry. In the latter, he first tried to establish by means of a 'transcendental deduction' that certain pure concepts or categories, including substance and causality, are universally valid with respect to possible experience, since they are necessary conditions of the empirical thought of an object. On the basis of these results, he then argued for a set of synthetic a priori principles regarding nature, considered as the sum total of objects of possible experience. Prominent among these are the principles that substance in nature remains permanent throughout all change and that every alteration has a cause.

The immediate consequence of Kant's limitation of knowledge is to rule out virtually all traditional metaphysics, which is concerned precisely with such 'transcendent' questions as the existence of God, the immortality of the soul, and the freedom of the will, which cannot be resolved by any appeal to possible experience. Kant spells out the negative implications of this result in his Transcendental Dialectic, which provides a systematic account of metaphysical illusion. Nevertheless, this limitation also enables him to resolve the problem of the antinomies. Since the appearance of contradiction arises from considering the spatio-temporal world as if it were a self-contained realm of things-in-themselves, once this assumption is rejected, it can be seen first that the sensible world is neither finite nor infinite in the relevant respects and second that it is possible to reconcile the causal determinism operative in nature with the freedom required for morality. Although everything in the realm of appearance, including human actions, is subject to the category of causality and thus causally determined, it remains at least conceivable that human beings, considered as things-in-themselves or noumena, are free; and this conceivability, according to Kant, is sufficient for morality.

Kant's moral theory centres around the categorical imperative 'Act only on that maxim which you can at the same time will to be a universal law'. Maxims are the general rules or principles on which rational agents act and they reflect the end that an agent has in view in choosing actions of a certain type in given circumstances. Thus, maxims are principles of the form: When in an S-type situation, act in an A-type manner in order to attain end-E. For example, I might make it my maxim always to pay my debts as soon as possible so as to avoid incurring unnecessary obligations. The categorical imperative tests maxims by prescribing a thought experiment in which one asks oneself whether one could consistently will one's maxim as a universal law, that is, one on which all other agents would also choose to act. The idea is to determine not simply whether the imagined universal law is consistent with itself, but whether its universal adoption is consistent with the agent's own ends and, therefore, something that the agent could consistently will. A maxim which passes this test is morally permissible, whereas one which does not is forbidden. Consider the maxim of borrowing money by falsely promising that one will repay. This maxim, Kant argues, conflicts with itself when universalized because it assumes a state of affairs in which promises to repay would not be believed and, therefore, the agent's project of profiting by false promising could not succeed. Consequently, policies such as false promising succeed only in so far as they are not universally adopted, so that in choosing them one makes an exception of oneself to a rule that one wills to hold for others.

The whole issue of the categorical imperative is extremely controversial, however, and there are a large number of interpretations and objections in the literature. The basic problem is that the test seems to yield both false positives such as 'I shall smother infants who keep me awake at night by crying', which is clearly immoral but does not seem to be ruled out by the test, and false negatives such as 'I shall play tennis on Sunday mornings when courts are available since everyone else is in Church', which seems both to fail the test and to be morally permissible. Although there have been many attempts to deal with these problems, it is not clear that any has been entirely satisfactory.

A second key notion in Kant's moral theory is that of autonomy, understood as the capacity of the will to legislate to itself, that is, to choose maxims for itself independently of desires stemming from one's nature as a sensuous being. Since the categorical imperative demands that we select maxims on the basis of their conformity to universal law, which presupposes that we are able to disregard our inclinations and the thought of our own happiness in choosing a course of action, Kant claimed that morality presupposes autonomy. But since he also thought that autonomy, so conceived, itself presupposes freedom in the sense of independence from causal determination by anything in the phenomenal world, he concluded that the possibility of morality rests ultimately on the assumption of such freedom. Thus, the project of grounding or justifying morality for Kant (as opposed to merely analysing its presuppositions) turns crucially on the possibility of establishing our noumenal freedom. This poses a problem, since Kant denied that we can have any theoretical knowledge of noumena; but he thought that a way out was provided by the fact that the resolution of the antinomy established at least the conceivability of noumenal freedom. In the *Groundwork*, Kant appealed to this result and argued, in effect, that we must assume the reality of freedom from a 'practical point of view', if we are to regard ourselves as rational agents capable of reasoned choice; and from this he inferred the validity of the categorical imperative or moral law as the 'law of freedom'. He appears to have changed his mind on this point, however, for in the *Critique of Practical Reason* he argues instead that the reality of the categorical imperative is immediately guaranteed as a 'fact of reason', from which the reality of freedom may be inferred.

But morality for Kant involves not only a law (the categorical impera-tive) and the autonomy of the will but also an object, that is, an ultimate end at which all action is directed. This object is defined as the 'Highest good', consisting of the perfect union of virtue and happiness; and this provides the basis for his moral arguments for God and immortality as 'postulates of practical reason'. The basic idea is that, since a just appor-tionment of happiness to virtue is inconceivable according to the laws of nature, we are constrained to assume the reality of a noumenal ground, that is, God, as its guarantor. Interestingly enough, Kant does not argue for immortality on the grounds that we must assume an afterlife in order to account for the reward of the virtuous and the punishment of the wicked, but claims instead that it is necessary in order to conceive of the possibility of the attainment of the moral perfection that is commanded by the categorical imperative yet unattainable in this life. In neither case, however, does Kant claim that this amounts to a theoretical proof; it is rather that God and immortality must be assumed as conditions of the full realization of the goals of morality. This reflects the principle of the 'primacy of practical reason', which is the central doctrine of the *Critique of Practical Reason*.

The *Critique of Judgement*, or third *Critique*, is an extraordinarily complex work in which Kant attempts to complete his critical programme by finding an a priori principle for judgement. In the first *Critique*, Kant had regarded judgement as essentially 'determinative', that is, as a capacity to subsume sensibly given particulars under the concepts and principles sup-plied by the understanding. From that perspective there is no basis for attributing to judgement any principle of its own. Now, however, Kant affirms a distinct function for judgement ('reflection') and argues that with respect to that function it does have a separate a priori principle: namely, the purposiveness of nature. The function of judgement in its reflective capacity is to find concepts and laws in terms of which nature can be cog-nized in a scientific manner. This requires concepts, such as those of nat-ural kinds, through which it is possible to represent real connections and distinctions in things rather than merely accidental similarities and differ-ences. Since the first *Critique* argued only that nature necessarily conforms to the universal principles of the understanding, it left open the possibility that the true order of nature might be so complex as to be incapable of discovery by the human mind. Thus, Kant now argues that it is necessary to assume, as a distinct principle, that nature is ordered in such a way as to be intelligible, which means that we are constrained to think of it as if it were designed by a supreme intelligence with our cognitive requirements in view. To think of nature in this way is to regard it as purposive. Naturally, Kant denies that this entitles us to assume that nature really is so designed, but he insists that the necessity of thinking of it in this manner suffices to give to the principle of purposiveness a regulative function.

After discussing this general principle of purposiveness in the introduction, Kant turns in the first part of the *Critique of Judgement* to judgements regarding the beautiful and the sublime, both of which are 'aesthetic' because they are based on feeling rather than concepts of their objects. Confining ourselves to judgements of beauty, with which Kant was primarily concerned, the problem is that, although based on feeling, which is essentially private or subjective, such judgements claim to be universally valid, just as if they were ordinary cognitive judgements. In other words, when I claim that an object is beautiful I am saying not merely that it pleases me but also that it must please any other observer who views it in the appropriate manner. The main task, then, is to account for the possibility of such judgements, just as the central task of the first *Critique* was to account for the possibility of synthetic a priori judgements. Not surprisingly, Kant's solution to this problem bears a certain similarity to his solution of the earlier one. Very roughly, the claim is that the peculiar pleasure in the beautiful consists in a feeling of the 'subjective purposiveness' of an object, that is, the accord of its form, which is apprehended in an act of aesthetic reflection, with the general requirements of judgement. Since these requirements hold for all subjects, the liking for the beautiful may be required of everyone. The second part of the third *Critique* is concerned with teleological judgement, particularly its role in biology. It also includes a lengthy appendix, however, in which Kant articulates his views on the relationship between teleology, theology, and morality and sketches his philosophy of history, together with his views on culture and its relation to the moral development of the human race. Thus, taken as a whole, the *Critique of Judgement* is an extremely rich and important, if frequently perplexing, work, which exhibits virtually the full range of Kant's interests as a philosopher.

JEREMY BENTHAM (1748–1832)

ROSS HARRISON

E NGLISH philosopher who dreamed at a young age of founding a
sect of philosophers called utilitarians and who lived to see his dream
fulfilled. He also planned that his body when he died should be made into
what he called an 'auto-icon' (that is, a representation of itself) so that it
could be used as a monument to the founder of the sect. This intention
was also fulfilled, so that to this day meetings of Benthamites sometimes
take place in the actual presence of Bentham himself (who spends the rest
of his time sitting in a glass box in University College London).

Bentham was the son and grandson of lawyers working in the City of
London and was intended by his father to follow and surpass them as a
practising lawyer. However, while following his legal studies, Bentham
became disgusted with the current state of English law and so, rather
than making money by the practice of the law as it is, he turned instead to
a study of what the law might be. This study formed the centre of his long
life, during which he wrote an enormous amount of manuscript material on law, economics, politics, and the philosophy which naturally arises
from these subjects.

In his earlier years Bentham turned some of this manuscript into books,
such as his *Fragment on Government* of 1776, or his *Introduction to the Principles
of Morals and Legislation* of 1789 (although, as the titles indicate, both of
these were in fact only parts of projected works). Later on, even the fragments tended not to be published by him and were left for others to edit. In
this manner, the first work which made his name was produced in French
and published in Paris by his disciple Étienne Dumont of Geneva (the
Traités de législation civile et pénale of 1802). Dumont subsequently edited
other works; these were translated into English by disciples, who also edited
others directly. Therefore much of the published text of Bentham has
passed through the hands of others, and also sometimes been translated or

retranslated prior to its publication. In fact, Bentham's greatest work on the philosophy of law was not published until the present century (in its latest version, edited by H. L. A. Hart, under the title *Of Laws in General*).

Bentham's grand project was for legislation: the exploration and theoretical foundations of a perfect system of law and government. For this he needed a measure of perfection, or of value; and this for Bentham was the principle of utility, otherwise known as the greatest happiness principle. In his already mentioned *Introduction* to the subject, Bentham starts chapter 1 with the rousing declaration that 'Nature has placed mankind under the governance of two sovereign masters, *pain* and *pleasure*.' This first paragraph ends with the statement that 'the *principle of utility* recognizes this subjection, and assumes it for the foundation of that system, the object of which is to rear the fabric of felicity by the hands of reason and of law'. Bentham's aim is to produce felicity, happiness. The means to be employed are 'reason and law': the right law will produce happiness, and the right law is one in accordance with reason. This means one in accordance with the principle of utility. In Bentham's draft codes of law, each particular law was attached to a 'commentary of reasons on this law'. The commentary demonstrated its value and also, Bentham hoped, improved its effect. For, as he says elsewhere, 'power gives reason to law for the moment, but it is upon reason that it must depend for its stability'.

Bentham explicitly says in the *Introduction* that by 'utility' he means 'that property in any object, whereby it tends to produce benefit, advantage, pleasure, good, or happiness . . . or . . . to prevent the happening of mischief, pain, evil, or unhappiness'. The rightness of actions depends on their utility; and the utility is measured by the consequences which the actions tend to produce. Of all these varying terms describing the consequences, the most important for Bentham are the ones with which he began the *Introduction*, pleasure and pain. For Bentham thinks that these are clear, easily understandable terms, which can therefore be used to give precise sense to the others. So the good, for Bentham, is the maximization of pleasure and the minimization of pain. Otherwise, as he puts it in the *Introduction*, we would be dealing 'in sounds instead of sense, in caprice instead of reason, in darkness instead of light'. For Bentham the principle of utility, interpreted in terms of pleasure and pain, is the only appropriate measure of value because it is the only comprehensible one.

Bentham's aim of increasing happiness is a practical one; and he had many purely practical proposals, such as for trains of carts between London and Edinburgh, or a Panama canal, or the freezing of peas. But the most famous and important of these particular practical proposals was for a prison which he called the 'panopticon'. It was to be circular so that the warders could sit in the centre and observe all the prisoners. It was also going to be privately run, by contract management with Bentham as its manager. Bentham therefore not only intended to produce what he called a 'mill for grinding rogues honest' but also to make money in the process. In fact, blocked by the interests of the landowners whose property abutted the site of the proposed prison (now occupied by the Tate Gallery in London), he lost both money and time until, after twenty years' struggle, he was compensated by Parliament. Bentham took his winnings, rented a house in Devon, and instead of grinding rogues chopped logic, producing his most profound work on the philosophy of language.

In his more general theory of government, just as in his more particular prison proposals, Bentham needed to rely on a psychology. This is that people tend to act in their own interests, where these are again understood in terms of pleasure and pain. People are understood to be seekers after pleasure and avoiders of pain. Given this knowledge of people's psychology, the benign legislator can so arrange his system of law that people, seeking only their own interests, will in fact be led into doing what they are meant to do, which is to promote the general interest (or the greatest happiness for all).

From this follows the Benthamite theory of punishment. It is a deterrent account. The proper aim of punishment, as of anything else, is to produce pleasure and prevent pain. Now all punishment is in itself a pain. Therefore, for Bentham, all punishment is in itself a harm. Therefore it can only be justified if this particular pain is outbalanced by the reduction in pain (or increase of pleasure) it causes. If people are deterred by punishment from doing things which would produce more pain (such, for example, as rape, theft, or murder), then the punishment will be justified. If not, not: there is no point in punishment or retribution for its own sake. This defence of punishment not only justifies punishment but also enables in principle the precise calculation of how much punishment is appropriate. It is that amount whose pain is outweighed by the pains of the actions it deters.

Bentham's general account of law and punishment and his use of the principle of utility as a means of providing reasons for his particular codes of law is constant through his life. However, his ideas about the particular political system which should be the source of this law developed. At the start he thought that he only needed to appeal to enlightened governments for such obviously beneficial arrangements to be put into effect. When he found that this did not happen (or that he was blocked in his own proposals, such as that for the panopticon), he became a supporter of democracy. Not just the law had to be changed but also the system of government. He was accordingly active in the movement for the extension of the parliamentary franchise, which finally came into effect in the year he died (although Bentham wanted something considerably more radical than the extension which actually happened: he wanted one man, one vote; and a secret ballot).

Such democratic proposals were in any case much more in accord with his general theories. If, according to the psychological theory, everyone acts in their own interests, so also do governments or governors. The classic eighteenth-century figure of the benevolent, semi-divine legislator has to be dispensed with. Dictators (supposedly enlightened or otherwise), kings, oligarchies can not be trusted. The appropriate end of government, popularly sloganized by Bentham as 'the greatest happiness of the greatest number', is only safe in the hands of the greatest number themselves. If the people as a whole are granted political power, they will, merely by following their own interests, promote what is also the appropriate end. Just as in the right system of law, so in the right system of politics or government, actual and appropriate action will coincide.

It can be seen that Bentham's project was centrally a project of clarification. He wanted to clarify values, to show at what we ought to aim. He wanted to clarify psychology, to show at what people actually do aim. He wanted to devise the appropriate systems of government, law, or punishment so that these two things could be placed in step. However, his interest in clarification went further. He also wanted to clarify the very idea of law; both as a whole and also in its central terms. It was in this project that he was led into his most original thought.

Understanding the law involves understanding such things as rights and duties. In the empiricist tradition, to which Bentham was loosely attached, understanding is provided by perception. Locke and, following him, Hume made a distinction between simple and complex ideas which allowed them to understand things which were not directly perceived. Complex ideas, such as that of a golden mountain, can be understood because they can be analysed into their simple constituents, of which we have experience. However, this technique does not work for the terms which Bentham wished to analyse, such as obligation or right. So here he was forced into a wholly new technique, which he called 'paraphrasis'.

This technique anticipates twentieth-century methods of analysis as does Bentham's related claim that the primary unit of significance is a sentence rather than a word. His idea in paraphrasis is not to translate the problematic word into other words. Rather, 'some whole sentence of which it forms a part is translated into another sentence'. So in the analysis of what Bentham called 'fictional entities' (such as right, duty, property, obligation, immunity, privilege—the whole language of the law), he uses his technique of paraphrasis to place these terms in sentences for which he then gives substitute sentences not containing the offending term. For example, sentences about rights are explained by Bentham in terms of sentences about duties. A particular right is for him the benefit which is conferred on someone by the imposition of duties on others. With duties we still, of course, have fictional entities. But these, in turn, can be placed in sentences which are translated into sentences about the threat of punishment. Punishment is, for Bentham, the threat of the imposition of pain. So here, at last, we reach what Bentham calls real entities. We reach clear, simple ideas, which can be directly understood by perception. As Bentham says in the *Fragment on Government*, '*pain* and *pleasure* at least are words which a man has no need, we may hope, to go to a Lawyer to know the meaning of'. With them the law can be clarified; for lawyers and others. The ultimate clarifier of value, of what the law should be, will also work as a clarifier of what the law actually is.

These projects are projects for change: current conditions are criticized. However, although Bentham's goals were the same as many of the contemporary movements for change, his foundations were not. Bentham was on the side not just of the struggle for reform of the franchise in England but also of the American and French Revolutions. The central contemporary justification for these revolutions was in terms of natural rights. However, Bentham was consistently opposed to the use of natural rights and he therefore criticized the rhetorical justification of both of these revolutions.

Bentham thinks that a natural right is a 'contradiction in terms'. He thinks that they are 'nonsense', fictitious entities. However, as has been seen, Bentham produced a new engine of analysis in his technique of paraphrasis precisely to make sense of fictitious entities. So it might be thought that he could make sense in the same way of natural rights. However, comparing a natural right with a legal right exposes the difference. Both can be analysed in terms of corresponding duties. However, as seen, Bentham analyses a legal duty in terms of the law (or threat of punishment) which creates it. There is no corresponding law, he holds, with respect to supposed natural duties. Hence he holds that natural rights are just imaginary rights by contrast with the real rights produced by actually existing systems of law. As he puts it, 'from real law come real rights . . . from imaginary laws come imaginary ones'. The so-called rights of man are in fact merely 'counterfeit rights'.

Bentham's most famous slogan expressing this view is 'nonsense on stilts'. This comes from his critical analysis of the French Declaration of the Rights of Man and Citizen in a work usually known as *Anarchical Fallacies* (which, in fact, is Dumont's title). Bentham's claim is that language which looks as if it is describing what rights there actually are is in fact suggesting what rights there ought to be. That is, instead of citing existing rights, the French Declaration is giving reasons why there ought to be rights. As Bentham puts it in *Anarchical Fallacies*, 'a reason for wishing that a certain right were established, is not that right; want is not supply; hunger is not bread'. So to suppose that such rights actually exist is nonsense. Even worse is to suppose that we can be sure that the correct rights have been found for all time. For Bentham is a promoter of experimentation. We have to keep seeing what utility is actually produced by particular systems of rights. Hence it is an additional mistake to think that any rights are unalterable (indefeasible, imprescriptible). This mistake was also made by the French. Hence the famous slogan. The complete remark from which it comes is 'natural rights is simple nonsense: natural and imprescriptible rights, rhetorical nonsense, nonsense upon stilts'.

Natural rights was one attempted answer to the question of the source of obedience to the state and the conditions for legitimate revolution. Another attempted answer also popular in Bentham's day was the original, or social contract. This device, founding obedience on agreement, was used by the leading contemporary defender of British law William Blackstone. Bentham ridicules such a defence in his *Fragment on Government*. For Bentham, justification of obedience to government depends upon utility, that is upon calculation of whether the 'probable mischiefs of obedience are less than the probable mischiefs of resistance'.

A contract will not work here for Bentham because, just like rights, all real contracts are legal contracts. Hence they are produced by law and government; and cannot therefore be used to provide a foundation for law and government. Even if its force is not supposed to be the force of a proper contract but merely that of a promise, or agreement, this again will not help to provide justification. For whether someone (government or people) should keep their agreements has, again, for Bentham to be tested by the calculation of utility. Yet if utility is to be the ultimate justification of promise-keeping, it would have been better to have started there in the first place, rather than (like Blackstone) traversing a tortuous path through contracts, original contracts, and largely fictional agreements. Again Bentham designates the supposed alternative source of justification to be merely a fiction and, as he puts it in the *Fragment*, 'the indestructible prerogatives of man-kind have no need to be supported upon the sandy foundation of a fiction'.

Although all justification comes from utility, this does not mean that Bentham can not support secondary ends; that is, things which, if promoted, will normally tend to increase utility. He lays down four such intermediate ends which should be promoted by the right system of law and government: subsistence, abundance, security, equality. These form two pairs so that subsistence (the securing to people of the means to life) takes precedence over abundance; and securing people's expectations takes precedence over equality. The utilitarian argument for this depends upon the psychological claim that deprivation of the former member of each pair causes more pain than the latter.

Psychological assumptions also lie behind Bentham's promotion of equality. He claims that (in general) equal increments of a good will not produce equal increments of utility. (That is, he claims that there is diminishing marginal utility.) Therefore, in general, provision of a particular good will provide more utility for those who already have less than those who already have more; hence a general tendency towards providing goods for the less well-off; or equality.

Bentham's is a consequentialist ethic. It looks towards actual and possible future states of affairs for justification of right action, not to what happened in the past. (For example, punishment is not retribution for past action, but prevention of future harms; obedience to the state is not because of some past promise, but to prevent future harms.) This is for Bentham the right, indeed the only possible, way of thinking correctly about these matters. It explains his central stance with regard to reform of the law. The law he found was common law, made by judges, based on precedent and custom. It came from history. For this he wanted to substitute statute law, made by democratic parliaments, and founded on reason. These reasons would be independent of history and would be in terms of future benefit.

GEORG WILHELM FRIEDRICH HEGEL (1770–1831)

PETER SINGER

O F all the major Western philosophers, Hegel has gained the reputation of being the most impenetrable. He was a formidable critic of his predecessor Immanuel Kant and a formative influence on Karl Marx. Through his influence on Marx, Hegel's thought has changed the course of nineteenth- and twentieth-century history.

Hegel lived and worked in what we now know as Germany, although in his time the many independent states of the region had not been united into one nation. He came of age at the time of the French Revolution, sharing what he later called 'the jubilation of this epoch'. His career included periods as a private tutor, and nine years as the headmaster of a secondary school, before his growing reputation gained him a university chair. He ended his days as Professor of Philosophy at the University of Berlin, which under the reformed Prussian monarchy was becoming the intellectual centre of the German states.

Hegel wrote several long and dense books, of which the most important are *The Phenomenology of Mind*, *The Science of Logic*, and *The Philosophy of Right*. His *Encyclopedia of the Philosophical Sciences* is a summary version of his philosophical system. A number of other works were delivered as lectures, and in some cases published after his death from his lecture notes. These include his *Lectures on the Philosophy of History*, *Lectures on Aesthetics*, *Lectures on the Philosophy of Religion*, and *Lectures on the History of Philosophy*.

Hegel is a difficult thinker because all his work reflects a systematic view of the world, and he makes few concessions to those not familiar with his way of thinking. In addition his style is anything but 'user-friendly'; at first glance most readers will find his sentences simply incomprehensible. This has led some to denounce him as a charlatan, hiding an emptiness of thought behind a deliberate obscurity of expression in order to give an air of profundity. Yet the meaning of Hegel's writing does, eventually, become apparent after careful study. Though his philosophical system as a whole finds few adherents today, his writings yield original insights and arguments that illuminate many philosophical, social, and political issues.

The easiest point of entry to Hegel's thought is his *Lectures on the Philosophy of History*. One of Hegel's greatest contributions to our intellectual heritage is—as Marx appreciated—his grasp of the historically conditioned nature of our thinking. One might ask why a philosopher should write a work that is, in one sense, a brief outline of the history of the world, from ancient times to his own day. The answer is that for Hegel the facts of history are raw material to which the philosopher must give some sense. For Hegel thought that history displays a rational process of development, and, by studying it, we can understand our own nature and place in the world. This idea of history having meaning can be interpreted as a reworking of the religious idea that the world was created by a being with some purpose in mind; but it may also be understood in a more limited way, as a claim that history has a direction that we can discern, and is heading to a goal that we can welcome.

Hegel presents his view of the direction of history in a famous sentence from the introduction to *The Philosophy of History*: 'The history of the world is none other than the progress of the consciousness of freedom.' The remainder of the work is a long illustration of this thought. Hegel begins with the ancient empires of China, India, and Persia. Here, he says, only one individual—the ruler—is free. The subjects of these oriental despots, Hegel thought, lacked not merely political freedom, but even the very awareness that they are capable of forming their own judgements about right or wrong. It was only in ancient Greece that the principle of free individual thinking developed, and even then Hegel saw the Greeks as so closely identified with their city-state, and so much ruled by its habits and customs, that they did not see themselves as independent individuals in the modern sense. Though the spark of individuality was lit by the critical thinking of Socrates, individuality did not triumph until the Protestant Reformation recognized that each individual can find his or her own salvation, and gave the right of individual conscience its proper place.

For Hegel the course of history since the Reformation has been governed by the need to transform the world so as to reflect the newly recognized principle of individual freedom. The era of the Enlightenment, culminating in the French Revolution, was an attempt to abolish every institution that depended on mere custom, and instead ensure that the light of reason, to which every individual can freely assent, guides every aspect of our political and social lives. To Hegel this attempt was based on a 'glorious mental dawn': the understanding that thought ought to govern reality, instead of the other way around. Yet the French revolutionaries misunderstood reason, taking it in too abstract a way, without considering the nature of existing communities and the way in which these communities have formed their inhabitants. Thus the abstract universalism of the Enlightenment led to the excesses of the guillotine. Yet now that we understand what is needed, Hegel concluded, a fully rational organization of the world—and hence a truly free community—is ready to unfold.

Hegel's conception of freedom is central to his thought, but it often misleads modern readers brought up on a conception of freedom made popular through the writings of such classical liberal thinkers as John Stuart Mill. According to the standard liberal conception, I am free when I am left alone, not interfered with, and able to choose as I please. This is, for example, the sense of freedom used by economists who picture consumers as free when there are no restrictions on the goods and services they can choose to buy in a free market. Hegel thought this an utterly superficial notion of freedom, because it does not probe beneath the surface and ask *why* individuals make the choices they do. Hegel saw these choices as often determined by external forces which effectively control us. He even anticipates, by more than a century, the modern critique of the consumer society as creating needs in order to satisfy them: he points out that the need for greater 'comfort' does not arise within us, but 'is suggested to you by those who hope to make a profit from its creation'.

Behind such insights lies Hegel's grasp of history as a process that shapes our choices and our very nature. So to be left alone to make our own choices without interference by others is not to be free; it is merely to be subjected to the historical forces of our own times. Real freedom begins with the realization that instead of allowing these forces to control us, we can take control of them. But how can this happen? As long as we see ourselves as independent beings with conflicting wills, we will always regard the existence of other human beings as something alien to ourselves, placing limits on our own freedom. In the classical liberal tradition, that is simply the way the world is, and there is nothing that can be done about it. For Hegel, however, the problem is overcome when we recognize that all human beings share a common ability to reason. Hence if a community can be built on a rational basis, every human being can accept it, not as something alien, but as an expression of his or her own rational will. Our duty and our self-interest will then coincide, for our duty will be rationally based, and our true interest is to realize our nature as a rational being.

In his belief that we are free only when we act in accordance with our reason, Hegel is in agreement with Kant; and so too when he sees our duty as based on our reason; but Hegel criticized Kant's notion of morality, based as it is on a categorical imperative derived from pure reason, as too abstract, a bare formal framework lacking all content. Moreover, on Kant's view human beings are destined for perpetual conflict between duty and interest. They will always be subject to desires that they must suppress if they are to act as the categorical imperative commands. A purely rational morality like Kant's, Hegel thought, needs to be combined in some way with the ethical customs that are part of our nature as beings of a particular time and place. Thus Hegel sought a synthesis between our concrete ethical nature, formed in a specific community, and the rational aspect of our being. When this synthesis was achieved, we would have a community in which each of us would find our own fulfilment, while contributing to the well-being of the whole. We would be free both in the subjective sense, in that we could do as we wished to do, and in the objective sense, in that we would rationally determine the course of our history, instead of being determined by it. This would then be a truly rational state, reconciling individual freedom with the values of community.

In *The Philosophy of Right*, Hegel describes this rational community in a manner that parallels—though is not identical with—the Prussian monarchy of his own day. For this he was accused by Schopenhauer of selling himself to his employer. After Hegel's death, the Young Hegelians, a group of young radicals that for a time included Marx among its members, thought that in *The Philosophy of Right* Hegel had betrayed the essence of his own philosophy. They determined to develop his ideas in a way that was truer to the core of his thought than Hegel himself had been. From this group arose the criticism of religion developed by Bruno Bauer and Ludwig Feuerbach, Max Stirner's individual anarchism, developed in his *The Ego and its Own*, and such early writings of Marx as *The Economic and Philosophical Manuscripts of 1844* and *The German Ideology*.

More recently Karl Popper has seen Hegel as a precursor of the modern totalitarian state. Popper argues that by exalting the rational state and using the concept of freedom in a way that denies that irrational choices are truly free, Hegel made it possible for later authoritarian rulers to justify their tyranny by saying that they must force their citizens to be free. It may be true that Hegel's philosophy is open to this misreading, but it *is* a misreading. The real Hegel supported constitutional monarchy, the rule of law, trial by jury, and (by the standards of his day) considerable freedom of expression. He would never have regarded the kind of state set up by Hitler or Stalin as a rational state with free citizens.

Yet Popper has touched on a real problem in Hegel's philosophy. Hegel was driven by an extraordinary optimism about the prospects of overcoming conflict between human beings, and hence of bringing about a rational and harmonious community. The roots of this optimistic view lie in his metaphysics, and especially in his concept of *Geist*. This German word can be rendered in English, according to the context, either as 'spirit' or as 'mind'. In the former sense it can have religious connotations; in the second it is the normal word used to describe the mental or intellectual side of our being, as distinct from the physical. Because the German term covers both these meanings, Hegel is able to use it in a way that suggests an overarching collective Mind that is an active force throughout history, and of which all individual minds—that is, all human beings, considered in their mental aspect—are a part. Thus Hegel sees the study of history as a way of getting to know the nature of *Geist*, and sees the rational state as *Geist* objectified. Since there is no ideal English translation, I shall henceforth use the capitalized term 'Mind' to express Hegel's concept of *Geist*.

Hegel's greatest work is his *The Phenomenology of Mind* (sometimes referred to in English as *The Phenomenology of Spirit*), described by Marx as 'the true birthplace and secret of Hegel's philosophy'. In it Hegel seeks to show that all human intellectual development up to now is the logically necessary working out of Mind's coming to know itself. The logic of this process is, however, not the traditional logic of the syllogism, but rather Hegel's own dialectical logic. In dialectical logic, we start from a given position—as an example, we might take the customary ethics of ancient Greece. Then we find that this position contains within itself the seeds of its own destruction, in the form of an internal contradiction. The questioning of a Socrates leads eventually to the downfall of customary ethics, for example, and its replacement during the Reformation by a morality based on individual conscience alone. Yet this too is one-sided and unstable, and so we must move to a third position, the rational community. This third position combines the positive aspects of its two predecessors.

This dialectic is sometimes referred to as a movement from *thesis* to *antithesis* to *synthesis*. In the example given, the customary morality of ancient Greece is the thesis, the Reformation morality of individual conscience its antithesis, and the rational community is the synthesis of the two. This last is, in Hegel's philosophy of history, the final synthesis, but in other instances, the synthesis of one stage of the dialectic can serve as the thesis for a new dialectical movement. In *The Science of Logic*, Hegel applies the same method to the abstract categories with which we think. Here Hegel starts with the bare notion of existence, or being, and argues that since this bare notion of being has no content at all, it cannot be anything. Thus it must be nothing, the antithesis of being. Being and nothing, however, are opposites, constantly moving in and apart from each other; they require to be brought together under the synthesis, becoming. Then the dialectic moves on, through many more obscure stages, until in the end Hegel claims to be able to demonstrate the necessity of absolute idealism: that is, that the only thing that is ultimately real is the absolute idea, which is Mind, knowing itself as all reality.

Absolute idealism seems a strange doctrine, but it was by no means unique to Hegel. Kant had already argued that the mind constitutes the known universe because we can only know things within a framework of our own creation, namely the categories of time, space, and substance. Yet Kant thought that beyond these categories there must be the 'thing-in-itself', forever unknowable. In doing away with the 'thing-in-itself', and saying that all we know is also all that there is, Hegel was following the line of Kantian criticism developed earlier by Johann Fichte.

Both *The Phenomenology of Mind* and *The Science of Logic*, then, have the same process as their subject, the process of Mind coming to know itself as ultimate reality. In the *Phenomenology* this process is presented by an attempt to show the logical necessity inherent in the historical development of human consciousness. In the *Logic* it is shown as a pure dialectical necessity, as (Hegel tells us) showing 'God as he is in his eternal essence, before the creation of nature and of a finite mind'. The *Logic* is, therefore, by far the more abstract and difficult work. The *Phenomenology* is, by comparison (but only by comparison), a gripping account of how the finite minds of human beings progress to a point at which they can see that the world beyond them is not alien or hostile to them, but a part of themselves. This is so, because Mind alone is all that is real, and each finite mind is a part of Mind.

One curious aspect of the enterprise of the *Phenomenology* is that it seeks to understand a process that is completed by the fact that it is understood. The goal of all history is that mind should come to understand itself as the only ultimate reality. When is that understanding first achieved? By Hegel himself in the *Phenomenology*! If Hegel is to be believed, the closing pages of his masterpiece are no mere description of the culmination of everything that has happened since finite minds were first created: they *are* that culmination.

In the light of Hegel's belief that all finite minds share in a greater underlying reality, we can appreciate why he should have believed in the possibility of a form of society that transcended all conflicts between the individual and the collective, and was truly free while at the same time in no sense anarchic. We can also see why this belief should have made it possible for Hegel's ideas to lead some of his successors, Marx among them, to a similarly misplaced optimism about the possibility of avoiding such conflicts. For while Marx claimed to have rejected the 'mysticism' in which Hegel enveloped his system, Marx never freed himself from the conviction that history is tending toward a final destination in which there will be complete harmony between the interests of the individual and the common interests of the community. That is why he believed that communism would be a condition in which everyone freely advanced the common interests of all.

ARTHUR SCHOPENHAUER (1788–1860)

T. L. S. SPRIGGE

GERMAN philosopher of inherited independent means, who gained distinction only towards the end of his life as a result, partly, of the notice taken of him in the British utilitarian journal the *Westminster Review*. His mother, who thoroughly disliked her son for his gloomy outlook, ran a literary salon in Weimar, frequented by Goethe, and this led to a short period of intellectual friendship during Schopenhauer's youth, as Goethe initially thought Schopenhauer's philosophy relevant for his own theory of colours. Schopenhauer arrived at his general philosophical position very early and all his works are developments of the same basic initial ideas. His chief inspirations were Plato, Kant, and the Upanishads. He is, in fact, the first (and remains among the few) Western philosophers to have related his thought to Hindu and Buddhist ideas. However, his most distinctive contribution to philosophy is in his insistence that Will is more basic than thought in both man and nature.

1

Schopenhauer's starting-point for his solution to 'the riddle of the world' is a form of transcendental idealism which he owes to Kant, though he seeks to establish it in a less contorted way. The physical world is phenomenal and exists only for 'the subject of knowledge'. Only by recognizing this can we explain how we know certain necessary synthetic a priori truths about it. Our cognitive faculties construct the world on the basis of four versions of the 'principle of sufficient reason', to which all phenomena must conform. (This is elaborated most fully in the book of his early youth, *On the Fourfold Root of the Principle of Sufficient Reason* (1813).) Our *sensibility* operates with the principle that everything is situated in a space of which the parts are mutually determining according to Euclidean geometry, and a time the mutual conditioning of whose moments is the topic of arithmetic (via the temporal nature of counting); our *understanding* works with the law of causality, and yields perception of a physical world which it pictures as the cause of our sensations. Our *reason*—whose conceptual representations (*Vorstellungen*) are quite secondary to the representations which understanding produces in perception and from which they are abstracted (Schopenhauer particularly scorns the many philosophers who confuse these or, like Hegel, treat concepts as primary)—works on the principle that every judgement must have its justification. A fourth principle bids us conceive of human action as necessarily determined by *motive*. The world constructed on these principles can only exist for the subject of knowledge to whose faculties they correspond.

2

Matters are taken further in Schopenhauer's *magnum opus The World as Will and Representation (Die Welt als Wille und Vorstellung* (1818)). Kant's greatest merit, for Schopenhauer, was the distinction of the phenomenon from the thing-in-itself. He was also right (though not consistently) that the thing-in-itself is not the cause of our sensations or of phenomena, since causation applies only within the phenomenal world and cannot relate it to something else. But that, for Schopenhauer, does not mean that we can form no idea of the nature of the thing-in-itself. For our perceptual experience of the phenomenal world of things in space and time is not our only experience. We are aware of ourselves, both in the perceptual fashion by which we know external things, and, quite differently, 'from within' as Will, more specifically as Will to Live. So our behaviour presents itself to us not only as the movements of a physical object but more intimately as the phases of a Will. The latter is not, and is not felt to be, the cause of the behaviour; rather, these are the same thing known outwardly and inwardly.

From knowledge of my own nature as thing-in-itself I can infer something of the nature of the physical world in general. For while I cannot prove that the rest of nature is more than mere appearance, namely the appearance of something in itself, to deny this would be a form of solipsism, something which belongs only to the madhouse. If we are to look upon the world sanely, we must suppose that everything in it is the appearance of what in itself is Will in basically the same sense as is my body and its behaviour. This argument is treated by some commentators with less respect than it deserves. If it is true that my body is Will in its real inner being, then, since the physical world outwardly seems homogeneous with it, and belongs to the same unitary interacting system, it is reasonable to suppose that the same is true of physical nature, not only in other humans and animals, as is quite easily granted, but throughout. The reasonable doubt is whether Schopenhauer has shown that Will is the inner being of my organism and behaviour, rather than the justification of extending this conclusion to the world at large.

3

The natural world, then, is the appearance of Will to itself, when this generates the subject of knowledge as an affection of itself. But is it one Will or many which appears to itself as the organic and inorganic world? Schopenhauer takes the former view (as Nietzsche was later to take the latter). For, so he argues, number, as an operation of the human intellect, only applies to the world of representation and cannot be relevant to reality as it is in itself. This cannot, then, be many, but must be one, not, indeed, in the sense that this would be the upshot of a count, but in the sense that number is inapplicable. (Whether this gives him the oneness he requires is doubtful.) He could have argued more effectively, however, that since causality cannot apply to reality in itself, it cannot figure there as 'the cement of the universe' (in Mackie's phrase) and that the unity of the cosmos must not depend upon such external relations between its parts.

But if what each of us experiences as his own inner being is Will at all, surely it is Will as a series of acts of willing, something both temporal and plural? Schopenhauer, more especially in the greatly enlarged second edition (1844) of his great work, is alert to this problem. It only shows, he says, that the thing-in-itself is still revealing itself incompletely, and has divested itself only of the more external garments in which it is dressed by consciousness. In fact, there seems some oscillation between the claim (characteristic later of Nietzsche) that introspectible processes of desire, pleasure and pain, and so forth are what I find as the inner being of myself and the claim that I can detect at the core of my being a dim unvarying drive to satisfaction. No reading of the text makes him altogether consistent on such matters. But the general upshot, that the universe is a single, 'vast', cosmic Will to Exist which experiences itself through an apparent diversity of conscious beings in a spatio-temporal and deterministic world, is clear enough and strongly argued. This Will is said to be unconscious in inanimate nature, but it is hard to see how one can understand

Schopenhauer unless it is supposed that it has some sort of dumb feeling of itself, even if there is not the contrast between subject and object required for consciousness in any full sense.

4

More than anything else, Schopenhauer is famous as the philosopher of pessimism. The wretchedness of the world (with whose horrors he became obsessed early in life) and the nastiness of human nature, he contends, with many striking examples, is evident enough empirically. But it is also a necessary truth, following from the very nature of its underlying reality, the Will. Will seeks constantly for a quietus which from its very nature as striving it could only reach by forfeiting its main goal, existence; indeed pleasure has really only a negative character as the relief from the suffering which is its normal state. Moreover, in its apparent pluralization, each part of the phenomenal world is powered by a drive to survive at the expense of others, so that there is a universal and appalling war of all against all. This is no time to consider the psychological sources of Schopenhauer's extreme pessimism, nor weigh its pros and cons empirically; we remark only that, central as it was to his philosophy as he conceived it, it does not seem entailed by his most interesting metaphysical conclusions. It is not so obvious as he thought that a world of Will *must* have been one of misery, while some have found it possible to delight in a world thus conceived even with the miseries actually pertaining to it.

5

Glum as his view of the world is, Schopenhauer offers two ways of escape from its horrors, one temporary, the other in principle permanent.

First, there is aesthetic experience, Schopenhauer's detailed and brilliant account of which has had considerable influence. Here our faculty of knowledge, in particular perception, normally only an instrument to the Will's satisfaction, gains a certain independence as pure will-less contemplation for its own sake, freeing us briefly from our misery, while the veil which hides the true nature of reality from us is partially rent. We no longer experience ourselves as one individual standing in contrast to others, but rather as the impersonal and universal pure subject of knowledge. And with this change in our experience of ourselves goes a change in the character of the object presented to us. It is no longer particular things in space and time which present themselves, but rather the basic types and principles by which the Will manifests itself, types and principles which Schopenhauer identifies with the Platonic Ideas, believing that he is uncovering the true significance of Plato's doctrine. There is a distinct law, or system of laws, of nature which is the phenomenal manifestation of each of these (the laws of physics, of chemistry, of biology, etc., and of each animal species, a partially distinct one also for every human being constituting his innate character). The artist produces a perceptual representation which yields us awareness of these Ideas (*Ideen*) rather than of the particular thing before us. (Music alone depicts the Will in its various grades as it is in itself rather than as manifested in the phenomenal world.)

Aspects of this account are puzzling. Why are aesthetic contemplation, and its peaceful objects, so free of the travails essential to Will, if they really bring us closer to the reality underlying phenomena? And in what sense does the Will objectify itself in these different grades? Schopenhauer often writes as though this objectification was a kind of real entry into all the variety of the world's phenomena, but he should be referring not to a real pouring of itself into an external world, but to the way in which the one Will manifests itself to itself, *qua* subject of knowledge.

The only lasting solution, however, to our misery comes when people become so aware of the necessary wretchedness of life, of the misery of existing as futile manifestations of the cosmic Will to Live, that they lose all wish for existence and gratification. This is what happens in the case of the genuine saint, an ascetic who has no concern with living and prospering. In him the Will to Live has denied itself. Or rather, there is only a faint twinkling of it left, hardly enough to sustain the picture of a world of things in space and time. When he dies this twinkling will utterly cease, and with it the world of which he was conscious, since this consisted in nothing but his picture of it. For Will and its picture of the world cannot continue to be when it no longer desires, and the world cannot be when the Will ceases, since it is only the Will's own delusive picture of itself.

But surely the Will as personalized in me, and the world for me, end equally, when I die, whether I have reached will-denying sainthood or not, while in both cases the Will continues its life in others and in nature? The answer seems to be that, when the saint dies, his particular grade or type of Will is at an end, whereas when the ordinary man dies, though he is at an end, his type is not. (Thus suicide is self-defeating, a mere complaint over current conditions on the part of one particular grade of Will.) Moreover, universal sainthood would somehow bring everything to an end (though the real truth here must be somehow non-temporal). Will anything be left at all? Yes, Schopenhauer darkly hints, something inconceivable by us but experienced by the saint in mystic contemplation. For what is *nothing* from one point of view must always be *something* from another. The analysis of *nothing* here is similar to Bergson's.

Schopenhauer's ethics (*On the Freedom of the Will* and *On the Basis of Morality*, published together in 1841) is closely related to his metaphysics. It is prefaced by a critique of Kant's account of morality. For Schopenhauer the very idea of a categorical, as opposed to a hypothetical, imperative, is an absurdity. An intelligible imperative is normally an order given by someone who can impose sanctions on those who do not conform to it, and has the form of 'Do this . . . or else'. Schopenhauer believed that the categorical imperative only seemed to make sense to Kant because unconsciously he took it as the command of God. Moreover, in spite of himself Kant comes too near to giving ethics an egoistic foundation, effectively basing it, claims Schopenhauer, on our concern with how it would affect us personally if everyone acted according to our example.

In contrast, moral goodness is identified by Schopenhauer with unselfish compassion for others. The good man is one who, not making the usual distinction between himself and others, is filled with universal compassion. Thus he acts on the principle 'Injure no one; on the contrary, help everyone as much as you can'. In doing so, he is concretely aware of what metaphysics teaches in the abstract, the oneness of the Will in all its manifestations. Thus this principle is not really an imperative but rather a description of how the good man acts. As an instruction it would really be useless, because each man acts according to his innate character anyway. So-called moral education may make men more tolerable by pointing out the advantages of co-operation with others, but our behaviour can only possess true moral worth if it stems from a moral goodness which cannot be taught. That moral worth consists in this capacity for compassion has hardly been recognized by most official moralists, but all over the world nothing is really admired in a morally relevant way except genuine concern with the welfare of others.

The compassion which constitutes moral worth manifests itself in its lesser form in justice based on the principle of non-interference with anyone's obtaining by their activity what they would otherwise legitimately achieve by it. By an illegitimate achievement is meant one made at the expense of someone else's achieving what they would otherwise—judged by the same criterion—legitimately achieve by their action. It manifests itself in a fuller form, as the loving kindness which inspires an active concern to help others in their need. It should be noted that for Schopenhauer the goal of compassion is the relief of misery and does not include the creation of positive happiness. This is partly because his pessimistic view of life implies that positive happiness, as opposed to relief from the worst sort of unhappiness, is impossible, and partly because he thinks that the kind of identification with others which constitutes compassion can only occur when one becomes aware of another as a fellow sufferer.

Schopenhauer's treatment of the freedom of the will is a brilliant (if ultimately implausible) development of Kant's. For Schopenhauer universal determinism holds necessarily for the phenomenal world. This follows from the fact that consciousness constructs the world on the principle of sufficient reason, in particular in its causal form. However, the thing-in-itself has freely chosen to manifest itself as a phenomenal individual answering to the particular Platonic Idea which constitutes each human being's character. This character (just like one of the laws of nature) settles just what he will do in every possible empirical circumstance. Each action is causally determined in that it flows necessarily from the combination of the agent's character and his beliefs about the consequences of acting in one way rather than another. The beliefs are the cause of the action, but, like all other causes, they operate because they affect something with a determinate nature. At the level of causation specific to physics it is only the determinate nature of matter in general that is involved, while chemistry and biology explore the type of causation which arises in matter which has reached a higher level of complexity. The causation of human activity is just as inevitable, but there is no one single set of causal laws, because each single human has a quite unique determinate nature. This is his moral character, the special quality of his will. It is this which is the ultimate possessor or otherwise of moral worth. A man is blamed not so much for what he does, but for what his action shows that he is. This cannot change, because all change in a man's outward behaviour arises from causes which can only operate on him in consequence of his unchanging basic character. Causes only affect him as they do in virtue of his character and therefore cannot act on it. Nevertheless, *qua* the thing-in-itself or Will which has chosen to manifest itself in an individual with my particular character, I am to blame for what I am and do, and deserve whatever fate this brings me. The only behaviour which does not thus follow deterministically from an individual's innate character, operating in particular conditions, occurs in those rare cases when a saint reaches liberation; while his character and its consequences manifested the Will's futile but free assertion of itself, his liberation manifests the Will's wiser and equally free return to the mysterious Nothingness whence it emerged thereby.

SØREN AABYE KIERKEGAARD (1813–1855)

ALASTAIR HANNAY

DANISH writer and social critic widely credited with setting the stage and providing the conceptual tools for modern existentialism. Kierkegaard was also one of Hegel's most devastating critics. The formative years in Copenhagen were marked by personal dependence on an oppressively religious father and by the deaths, before he reached the age of 21, of his mother and five of the family of seven of which he was the youngest. Kierkegaard spent ten years at the university before completing his dissertation *On the Concept of Irony with Constant Reference to Socrates* (1841) preliminary to a career in the Church. His second major work *Either/Or* (1843) marked a postponement of that career and was the outcome of the fateful decision to break off an engagement and disappointment at not finding in Schelling's Berlin lectures a philosophical alternative to established Hegelianism. The work portrays two life-views, one consciously hedonistic, the other ethical in a way which Hegelians would recognize except that the choice of the ethical is a personal one, not the outcome of a philosophical insight. The hedonistic or 'aesthetic' alternative is presented by a gifted essayist, and member of a society called 'companions of the deathbound', who applies it as a consistent principle in his own life, while the ethical perspective is conveyed in two extended admonitory letters addressed to the hedonist by a friend, a state functionary who urges him to admit that his situation is one of despair so that he can then 'choose himself' in ethical categories, these providing the true fulfilment of the aesthetic values he prizes. Kierkegaard's own intentions are concealed behind an elaborate barrage of *noms de plume* (the work is published by a pseudonymous 'editor' who tells how he has come upon the papers quite by accident).

The impression given by the title that the aesthetic and ethical life-views represent an exhaustive choice is disturbed by a concluding sermon passed on to the hedonist by the functionary on the theme that before God we are always in the wrong. Kierkegaard claimed later that at the time he himself had despaired of finding fulfilment in marriage but said that he had portrayed marriage as a form of fulfilment because it struck him as being 'the deepest form of revelation'. Unable to reveal himself in that way, Kierkegaard embarked on a series of 'edifying' works under his own name. These works, though on the surface in a conventionally religious vein, convey deep moral-psychological insight and it would not be improper to refer to them as philosophical.

The practice of concealment was continued, however, in a parallel series of pseudonymous works which include those more usually regarded as philosophical. These include, already in 1843, two works written largely in Berlin, *Repetition* and *Fear and Trembling*, followed in 1844 by *Philosophical Fragments* and *The Concept of Anxiety*, and in 1845 by *Stages on Life's Way*, in which a religious stage is distinguished from *Either/Or*'s ethical alternative.

The pseudonymous authorship was to have ended with the publication of the *Concluding Unscientific Postscript to Philosophical Fragments* (1846), Kierkegaard having in mind to resume his intention to enter the priesthood. Instead, however, he wrote further non-pseudonymous works on specifically Christian themes motivated in part by the thought that he was better able to serve the truth as a writer. Among them are *Purity of Heart is to Will One Thing* (1847) with its account of double-mindedness and the formidable *Works of Love* (1847). But at the same time, virtually ostracized by a feud he had himself provoked with a satiric weekly and which left him a figure of public ridicule, Kierkegaard's plans for at least partial self-revelatory absorption into society had given way to an urge to reveal to society its errors. The popular monarchy and people's Church, newly established in the aftermath of 1848, and which Kierkegaard saw as merely finite institutions catastrophically usurping the true role of religion, provided the political target. Deciding to announce that his intentions as an author had been religious all along, Kierkegaard now planned a second (unrevised) edition of *Either/Or* together with an explanation (*The Point of View of my Work as an Author*) of the relation of that and the subsequent pseudonymous works to the Christian themes of his non-pseudonymous production. For a variety of reasons detailed in his journals the explanation was withheld (but published posthumously by his brother in 1859), and instead Kierkegaard gave out two further works under a new pseudonym.

The first of these, *The Sickness unto Death* (1849), followed hard upon the second edition of *Either/Or*. It typologizes forms of despair as failures to sustain a 'synthesis' which expresses the structure of selfhood. The work introduces a non-substantial but normative concept of the self or 'spirit'. The most common and dangerous form of despair is one which people fail to recognize in themselves and even mistake for its opposite. In a spiritless society whose institutions have taken over spirit's functions also in name, no real basis for spirit, or true selfhood, remains in the established forms of life. Spiritual possibilities then tend to find their outlets outside such forms in madness, religious intoxication, the cult of the aesthetic, or in utopian politics. This, from the individual's perspective, is one way of failing to maintain the synthesis. The other is for the individual to duck below the level of its own spiritual possibilities and lead a spiritually emasculated life of worldliness. The solution which *The Sickness unto Death* prescribes for despair is faith, or willing acceptance of the task of becoming a self 'posited' not by itself but by a transcendent power.

In the final pseudonymous work, *Training in Christianity* (1850), Kierkegaard readdresses themes raised in the earlier *Philosophical Fragments*, in particular the individual's relation to Christ as one not of history but of contemporaneity and of shared human degradation. In the five years remaining until his early death at 42, Kierkegaard lived in increasingly straitened (though never degrading) circumstances, expending the remainder of a considerable inheritance on an explosive broadsheet (*The Instant*), in which, under his own name, he savagely satirized the State Church, its dignitaries, and minions.

According to the withheld explanation the pseudonymous ('aesthetic') works deliberately adopt an aesthetic point of view in order to loosen the grip on their readers of a falsely 'aesthetic' picture of religious fulfilment. They can also be read as mirroring their true author's own struggles as a social outsider playing with the thought that his literary talents and situation might have marked him out for a specifically religious mission. In *Either/Or* human fulfilment, corresponding to the second, 'ethical' stage in the progression from the aesthetic to the religious, meant choice of a self wedded in a conventionally Hegelian way to shared social norms. The subsequent pseudonymous works, beginning with *Repetition* and *Fear and Trembling*, present the radically anti-Hegelian idea that the ethical component in the individual's life is established first in a psychologically unmasked and socially unmediated relation to God. The slim but elegantly crafted *Philosophical Fragments* contrasts an idealist view, identified with Plato's Socrates but clearly to be construed as a progenitor of Hegel, with one where the relationship to truth depends on faith. The massive *Postscript* is described by Kierkegaard as a turning-point in the 'aesthetic' works, since it clearly identifies the latter view with Christianity and raises explicitly the question of what it means to be a Christian. The Christian's proper relation to the 'absolute object of worship' is inwardness, or a 'passionate' interest in a transcendentally grounded fulfilment, the more passionate because the individual is aware that no empirical or rational inquiry can support acceptance of an assurance based exclusively on the belief that some other existing individual has been the eternal in time (the God-man). This is literally unthinkable and therefore immune to argument or evidence one way or the other. The principal target is Hegel's 'System', which, by treating matters requiring personal choice as topics for a shared rational insight, turns living issues into matters for a generalized curiosity. In fact there are two opposed objections to a scientific approach to the question of personal fulfilment. In Hegelian science the matter is decided already by the truth of being which will emerge as the system of thought develops, but that abstracts from your own existence which 'keeps thought and being apart' and therefore fails to capture the forward movement of the individual's own life. And treating the issue as a scientific matter in a general sense to be decided collaboratively in the light of evidence not all of which is (or ever will be) in, ignores the urgency of the Christian message which stands there, as William James would say, as a 'forced' option that brooks no delay.

Some see in Kierkegaard's philosophical pseudonym (Johannes Climacus) an assassin hired to deal with the Hegelians, so that the absurdity and paradox of Christianity arise only for the misguided 'systematizer'. Wittgensteinians have interpreted the *Postscript* as a demonstration of what happens if you apply the rules of one language-game inappropriately to another, but this inner relativism fits ill with Kierkegaard's emphasis on the 'crucifixion' of reason in faith. In his journals Kierkegaard says that paradox and absurdity are the negative conditions of faith—guarantees, as it were, that the assurance sought in faith is not being treated as though it were achievable through the exercise of some human capacity. That capacity need not be cognitive; the distinction between Religiousness A and Religiousness B is between, on the one hand, a view which interprets what the pseudonymous author calls 'dying from immediacy' procedurally, as if a relationship with the object of worship can be established simply by subordinating all 'relative' ends to an 'absolute' end, and on the other hand a non-immanentist view and the 'Christian' view in which human capacities as such extend no further than to history so that a historical event, the Incarnation, offers our only relation to the Absolute. From this point of view the Absolute lies beyond the reach of any kind of natural relationship.

What then is the positive content of faith? The pseudonymous works do not say; their 'dialectic' is, as some have said, merely 'negative'. But the final pseudonymous work, *Training in Christianity*, can be read together with parts of the non-pseudonymous 'religious' corpus as indicating that the saving truth can be grasped in a moral agent's sense, in imitating the example of Christ, of acting out this truth in the form of Christian love. The earlier *Works of Love* presents the Christian ideal of love of one's neighbour in the form of a generalized selflessness. Part of what emerges is that it is only by removing personal preferences that values inherent in other persons, but also in nature, can be truly acknowledged and allowed their fulfilment. This assumes that the value or worth of persons and things is neither, as Hobbes has it, their price nor any degree of natural attachment to them. Values, on this view, reside in possibilities inherent in the persons and things themselves independently of human interests, and indeed these interests stand in the way of those values both in the sense that they do not become visible and in the sense that they fail to be elicited. The inner consistency of the view as a generally applicable ethics depends at least in part on how far the sacrifice of human desires or interests is compatible with the sacrificer's own personal or human fulfilment.

Kierkegaard detects in social forms, and in patterns of human behaviour in general, a pervasive disinclination to face live issues in their appropriately living form. In this respect Hegelianism is not simply a failed attempt to capture the forward movement of life, but part of a general contempt for the individual, evident also in the conflation of the truism that human life is impossible without political groupings with the pernicious idea that the individual's fulfilment can come to expression only in the form of political association or religious community (see *Literary Review: The Two Ages* (1846)). Kierkegaard's writings are profitably grasped in the light of his sense of a prevailing flight from subjectivity and of society's need to divest itself of protective self-images. The more scandalous views attributed to Kierkegaard, such as the arbitrary defeasibility of shared norms, the subjectivity of truth, and the supposed foundational role assigned to criterionless choice, often vanish on a closer reading of the texts, which in context lend themselves to more readily acceptable readings. Thus the notorious teleological suspension of the ethical in *Fear and Trembling* can be seen as part of Kierkegaard's now-adays uncontroversial insistence that systems of shared social norms are purely historical phenomena set against his championing of the view that a true system of values derives directly from an unconditioned transcendent source, unmediated by contingent and merely finite facts of preference. His target is the common assumption in his time that facts of preference are both historical and expressions of an unfolding Absolute. The claims in the *Postscript* for the subjectivity of truth can be read as the requirement that the relation to the unconditional source of value be one of inwardness and personal devotion both to the source itself and, through it, though distributively rather than collectively, to mankind. As for the rumour of a criterionless choice, in Kierkegaard there is little or no evidence for this idea as distinct from that of the notion of personal commitment and choice. At least the reader of *Either/Or*, the most widely cited source for the rumour, cannot fail to detect signs of dialogue in that work, objections to the ethical life-view implicit in the first part which are then made explicit and countered in the second part, which is also in itself a sustained argument in favour of the ethical alternative. Failure to choose the ethical alternative is presented as more in the nature of a motivated rejection of a form of human fulfilment that the hedonist is already in a position to acknowledge but refuses so to do, than a choice made in a vacuum between two quite independent and equally valid ways of life.

The tendency to ascribe extreme views to Kierkegaard may be due in part to the fanatical anti-humanism of his later rejection of all bourgeois forms of human association, including marriage and the family. Kierkegaard himself remarks on how the original either/or becomes radicalized so that in the end both ethics and institutional religion (castigated as the fraud of 'Christendom') end up on the aesthetic side as merely forms of self-indulgence, while self-abnegation, suffering, and devotion to God now form the saving option. This could be seen as a pattern set from the start; Lukács suggests it is the outcome of Kierkegaard's life-long tendency to spite reality. Or perhaps the extremity was one that Kierkegaard was driven to by circumstances. The radical stance might also, however, at a pinch be interpreted as prescribed by the *Postscript*'s insistence that Religiousness A is a necessary prolegomenon to Religiousness B. The later Kierkegaard may be insisting that the institutions of a spiritless society must be comprehensively vacated before creative alternatives based on true selfhood can replace them. We note that Kierkegaard describes *The Sickness unto Death* as containing a polemic directed at that 'altogether un-Christian conception', Christendom. Regarding the establishment's scorn of sects, he said there was 'infinitely more Christian truth' in the errors of their ways than in 'the mawkishness, torpor, and sloth of the establishment'. The trick is to be rid of the errors of the pagans without losing, as in a spiritless society which shuns true selfhood, their 'primitive' spiritual impetus.

For obvious reasons rationalists and, because of his attitude to shared norms, Hegelians have dismissed Kierkegaard as an *ir*rationalist; while what in Kierkegaard's writings repels rationalists and Hegelians alike has drawn sympathy from circles later stigmatized as fascist. Equally, democrats are put off by Kierkegaard's contempt for public opinion, the crowd, and parliamentary institutions, and although Marcuse saw 'traits of a deep-rooted social theory' in Kierkegaard, the Christian framework and the focus on the individual make Kierkegaard an obvious target for the Marxist. Eagerly read in German academic circles at the beginning of the twentieth century, and heralded by theologians as the provider of a radical Christian apologetic, Kierkegaard also influenced agnostic and atheist thinkers of such divergent political sympathies as Heidegger and Lukács. The enormous extent of the former's debt to Kierkegaard is still to be appreciated. The latter in his pre-Marxist days admired what he saw as the tragic heroism with which Kierkegaard, by exalting the notion of choice, vainly defied the necessities of life by seeking, first in his own life, to impose on them a poetic form. The later Lukács blamed Kierkegaard for the 'bourgeois' philosophy of post-war existentialism and even saw in him a source of modern nihilism and decadence. As if in confirmation of this latter charge some post-modern writers, notably Jean Baudrillard, focus on Kierkegaard the 'aesthetic' author and see in this complex man a pre-incarnation of the modern existentialist. Adorno, sympathizing with Kierkegaard's campaign against the tyranny of the universal over the particular though not with the resort to religious concepts, found in Kierkegaard's experimental 'aesthetic' writings the makings of a new style of reasoning which elicits rather than buries the truth of the particular. Many modern philosophers have found in the religious framework of Kierkegaard's writings an impediment to any serious appreciation of his thought. Wittgenstein, however, once referred to Kierkegaard as 'by far the most profound thinker of the last century'.

JOHN STUART MILL (1806–1873)

JOHN SKORUPSKI

JOHN Stuart Mill, the son of James Mill, was the greatest British philosopher of the nineteenth century, bringing Britain's traditions of empiricism and liberalism to their Victorian apogee.

The *System of Logic*, a product of his thirties, published in 1843, made his reputation as a philosopher. The *Principles of Political Economy*, of 1848, was a synthesis of classical economics which defined liberal orthodoxy for at least a quarter of a century. His two best-known works of moral philosophy, *On Liberty* and *Utilitarianism*, appeared later—in 1859 and 1861. In the 1860s he was briefly a Member of Parliament, and throughout his life was involved in many radical causes. Among them was his enduring support for women's rights—see *The Subjection of Women* of 1869.

The leading element in Mill's thought is his lifelong effort to weave together the insights of enlightenment and romanticism. He subscribed unwaveringly to what he called the 'school of experience and association'. He denied that there is knowledge independent of experience and held that attitudes and beliefs are the products of psychological laws of association. His view of human beings is naturalistic and his ethics is utilitarian. But he redesigned the liberal edifice built on these foundations to the romantic patterns of the nineteenth century. For these he was himself one of the great spokesmen. He learned much of the historical sociology which was so important to his liberalism from Frenchmen; but it was to German romanticism, via his Coleridgean friends, that he owes his deepest ethical theme—that of human nature as the seat of individuality and autonomy, capable of being brought to fruition through the culture of the whole man.

The controversy over Mill's achievement has always centred on whether the synthesis he sought, of enlightenment and romantic-idealist themes, is a possible one. Kant had argued that the naturalism of the

Enlightenment subverted reason, and idealist philosophers of the nine-teenth century followed him in that. Kant and Mill do in fact agree on a vital aspect of this question. They agree that if the mind is only a part of nature, no knowledge of the natural world can be a priori. Either all knowledge is a posteriori, grounded in experience, or there is no know-ledge. Any grounds for asserting a proposition that has real content must be empirical grounds. However, much more important is the difference between them: whereas Kant thought knowledge could not be grounded on such a basis, and thus rejected naturalism, Mill thought it could. This radically empiricist doctrine is the thesis of the *System of Logic*.

There Mill draws a distinction between 'verbal' and 'real' propos-itions, and between 'merely apparent' and 'real' inferences. The distinc-tion corresponds, as Mill himself notes, to that which Kant makes between analytic and synthetic judgements. But Mill applies it with greater strictness than anyone had done before, insisting with greater reso-lution that merely apparent inferences have no genuine cognitive con-tent. He points out that pure mathematics, and logic itself, contain real propositions and inferences with genuine cognitive content. This clear assertion is central to the *System of Logic*, and the basis of its continuing importance in the empiricist tradition. For if Mill is also right in holding that naturalism entails that no real proposition is a priori, he has shown the implications of naturalism to be radical indeed. Not only mathemat-ics but logic itself will be empirical.

His strategy is a pincer movement. One pincer is an indirect argument. If logic did not contain real inferences, all deductive reasoning would be a *petitio principii*, a begging of the question—it could produce no new knowledge. Yet clearly it does produce new knowledge. So logic must contain real inferences. The other pincer is a direct semantic analysis of basic logical laws. It shows them to be real and not merely verbal. The same strategy is applied to mathematics. If it was merely verbal, math-ematical reasoning would be a *petitio principii*. But a detailed semantic analysis shows that it does contain real propositions.

Why do we think these real propositions in logic and mathematics to be a priori? Because we find their negations inconceivable, or derive them, by principles whose unsoundness we find inconceivable, from pre-misses whose negation we find inconceivable. Mill thought he could explain these facts about unthinkability, or imaginative unrepresentabil-ity, in associationist terms. His explanations are none too convincing, but his philosophical point still stands: the step from our inability to represent to ourselves the negation of a proposition to acceptance of its truth calls for justification. Moreover, the justification *itself* must be a priori if it is to show that the proposition is known a priori. (Thus Mill is prepared, for example, to concede the reliability of geometrical intuition: but he stresses that its reliability is an empirical fact, itself known inductively.)

All reasoning is empirical. What then is the basis of reasoning? Epistemologically, historically, and psychologically, Mill holds, it is *enumerative induction*, simple generalization from experience. We spontaneously agree in reasoning that way, and in holding that way of reasoning to be sound. The proposition 'Enumerative induction is a valid mode of reasoning' is not a verbal proposition. But nor is it grounded in an a priori intuition. All that Mill will say for it is that people in general, and the reader in particular, in fact agree on reflection in accepting it. It is on that basis alone that he rests its claim.

He does not take seriously Hume's sceptical problem of induction; his concern in the *System of Logic* is rather to find ways of improving the reliability of inductive reasoning:

if induction by simple enumeration were an invalid process, no process grounded on it would be valid; just as no reliance could be placed on telescopes, if we could not trust our eyes. But though a valid process, it is a fallible one, and fallible in very different degrees: if therefore we can substitute for the more fallible forms of the process, an operation grounded on the same process in a less fallible form, we shall have effected a very material improvement. And this is what scientific induction does.

So Mill's question is not a sceptical but an internal one—why is it that some inductions are more trustworthy than others? He answers by means of a natural history of induction, which traces how enumerative induction is internally vindicated by its actual success in establishing regularities, and how it eventually gives rise to more searching methods of investigation.

The origins are 'spontaneous' and 'unscientific' inductions about particular unconnected natural phenomena. They accumulate, interweave, and are not disconfirmed by further experience. As they accumulate and interweave, they justify the second-order inductive conclusion that *all* phenomena are subject to uniformity, and, more specifically, that all have discoverable sufficient conditions. In this less vague form, the principle of general uniformity becomes, given Mill's analysis of causation, the law of universal causation. This conclusion in turn provides (Mill believes) the grounding assumption for a new style of reasoning about nature—*eliminative induction*.

Here the assumption that a type of phenomenon has uniform causes, together with a (revisable) assumption about what its possible causes are, initiates a comparative inquiry in which the actual cause is identified by elimination. Mill formulates the logic of this eliminative reasoning in his 'methods of empirical inquiry'. The improved scientific induction which results spills back on to the principle of universal causation on which it rests, and raises its certainty to a new level. That in turn raises our confidence in the totality of particular enumerative inductions from which the principle is derived. This analysis of the 'inductive process' is one of Mill's most elegant achievements.

Mill and Hume then are both naturalistic radicals, but in quite different ways—Hume by virtue of his scepticism, Mill by virtue of his empiricist analysis of deduction. The only cognitive dispositions which Mill recognizes as primitively legitimate are the disposition to rely on memory and the habit of enumerative induction. The whole of science, he thinks, is built from the materials of experience and memory by disciplined employment of this habit.

This is Mill's *inductivism*—the view that enumerative induction is the only *ultimate* method of inference which puts us in possession of new truths. Is he right in thinking it to be so? In his own time the question produced an important, if confused, controversy between him and William Whewell. Whewell argued that fundamental to scientific inquiry was the hypothetical method, in which one argues to the truth of a hypothesis from the fact that it would explain observed phenomena. Mill, on the other hand, could not accept that the mere fact that a hypothesis accounted for the data in itself provided a reason for thinking it true. The point he appealed to is a powerful one: it is always possible that a body of data may be explained equally well by more than one hypothesis.

What he does not see, and this is one of the points of weakness in his philosophy, is how much must be torn from the fabric of our belief if inductivism is applied strictly. Thus, for example, while his case for empiricism about logic and mathematics is very strong, it is his methodology of science which then forces him to hold that we know basic logical and mathematical principles only by an enumerative induction. That is desperately implausible; accepting the hypothetical method would be one, though only one, possible remedy.

Inductivism also plays a key role in Mill's metaphysics. He sets this out in his *Examination of Sir William Hamilton's Philosophy* (1865)—a detailed criticism of the Scottish philosopher who had attempted to bring together the views of Reid and Kant. Here Mill endorses a doctrine which was then accepted, as he says, on all sides (though it would now be treated with greater mistrust). The doctrine is that our knowledge and conception of objects external to consciousness consists entirely in the conscious states they excite in us, or that we can imagine them exciting in us.

This leaves open the question whether objects exist independently of consciousness. It may be held that there are such objects, although we can only know them by hypothesis from their effects on us. Mill rejects this view—as, given his inductivism, he must. Instead he argues that external objects amount to nothing more than 'permanent possibilities of sensation'. The possibilities are 'permanent' in the sense that they obtain whether or not realized; they would occur if an antecedent condition obtained. (As well as 'permanent' Mill uses other terms, such as 'certified' or 'guaranteed'.)

Our knowledge of mind, like our knowledge of matter, Mill thinks to be 'entirely relative'. But he baulks at resolving it into a series of feelings and possibilities of feeling. For 'the thread of consciousness' contains memories and expectations as well as sensations. To remember or expect a feeling is not simply to believe that it has existed or will exist; it is to believe that *I* have experienced or will experience that feeling. Thus if the mind is to be a series of feelings, we would, he thinks, be forced to conclude that it is a series that can be aware of itself as a series. This drives him to recognize in mind, or self, a reality greater than the existence as a permanent possibility which is the only reality he concedes to matter. He fails to note that the doctrine that mind resolves into a series of feelings need not literally *identify* selves with series: it paraphrases talk of selves in terms of talk of series.

Discounting this uncertainty about what to say of the self, all that ultimately exists in Mill's view is experience in a temporal order. But he claims this to be consistent with common-sense realism, and he continues to see minds as proper parts of a natural order. The difficulties of this begin to emerge when we ask whether the experiences referred to in Mill's metaphysics are the very same as those referred to by common sense—and explained by physical antecedents. The same difficulties emerge for later phenomenalists, but Mill never addresses them.

To the succeeding generation of philosophers, who took Kant's philosophy seriously, Mill's naturalism seemed thoroughly incoherent. He fails to see the need for a synthetic a priori to render any knowledge possible, even though he gives an account of real propositions and inferences which agrees in essentials with Kant. On top of that, in accepting phenomenalism he accepts a doctrine which must lead to a transcendental view of consciousness, yet he remains determinedly naturalistic in his view of the mind. Perhaps present-day naturalism is finding ways of avoiding this second impasse, by being more rigorously naturalistic about experience than Mill was. But it has yet to cope clearly with the first.

In ethics and politics Mill's premises remain those of enlightenment humanism. Value resides in the well-being achieved within individual lives; the interests of all make an equal claim on the consideration of all. Happiness is most effectively attained when society leaves people free to pursue their own ends subject to rules established for the general good. A science of man will ground rational policies for social improvement.

His reason for thinking that happiness is the only ultimate human end is just like his reason for thinking enumerative induction is the only ultimate principle of reasoning. He appeals to reflective agreement, in this case of desires rather than reasoning dispositions: 'the sole evidence it is possible to produce that anything is desirable, is that people do actually desire it. If the end which the utilitarian doctrine proposes to itself were not, in theory and in practice, acknowledged to be an end, nothing could ever convince any person that it was so.'

But do we not, in theory and in practice, desire things under ends other than the end of happiness, for example under the idea of duty? Mill's response to this question has strength and subtlety. He acknowledges that we can will against inclination: 'instead of willing the thing because we desire it, we often desire it only because we will it'. There are, he agrees, conscientious actions, flowing not from any unmotivated desire but solely from acceptance of duty. But his point is that when we *un*motivatedly desire a thing we desire it under the idea of it as pleasant. He further distinguishes between desiring a thing as 'part' of our happiness and desiring it as a means to our happiness. Virtuous ends can be a part of happiness: consider, for example, the difference between a spontaneously generous man and a conscientious giver. The first wants to give because he takes pleasure in giving. The second gives from a 'confirmed will to do right'. The benefit of another is for the first, but not the second, a 'part' of his own happiness.

The virtues can become a part of our happiness, and for Mill they ideally should be so. That ideal state is not an unrealistic one, for the virtues have a natural basis and a moral education can build on it by association. More generally, people can come to a deeper understanding of happiness through education and experience. Mill holds that some forms of happiness are inherently preferred as finer by those able to experience them fully—but these valuations are still in his view made from within the perspective of happiness, not from outside it.

So Mill deepened the Benthamite understanding of happiness; however, he never adequately examined the principle of utility itself. It was a philosopher of the generation after Mill's, Henry Sidgwick, who probed its groundings most deeply. But when we turn to Mill's conception of the relationship between the utility principle and the texture of norms by which day-to-day social life proceeds, we find him at his most impressive. His ability to combine abstract moral theory with the human understanding of a great political and social thinker here comes into its own. Benthamite radicalism lacks historical and sociological sense. The philosophes of the eighteenth century, 'attempting to new-model society without the binding forces which hold society together, met with such success as might have been expected'.

The utilitarian, he says, need not and cannot require that 'the test of conduct should also be the exclusive motive of it'. This historical and concrete aspect of Mill's utilitarianism is the key to his view of the institutions of justice and liberty; though his analysis of rights follows Bentham. A person has a right to a thing, he holds, if there is an obligation on society to protect him in his possession of that thing. But the obligation itself must be grounded in general utility.

The rights of justice reflect a class of exceptionally stringent obligations on society. They are obligations to provide to each person 'the essentials of human well-being'. The claim of justice is the 'claim we have on our fellow-creatures to join in making safe for us the very groundwork of our existence'. Because justice-rights protect those utilities which touch that groundwork they take priority over the direct pursuit of general utility as well as over the private pursuit of personal ends.

With liberty we find again that Mill's liberalism is grounded on a utilitarian base. He appeals to 'utility in the largest sense, grounded on the permanent interests of man as a progressive being'. In that respect, his liberalism stands opposed to the classical natural-rights liberalism of Locke. The famous principle which Mill enunciates in his *On Liberty* is intended to safeguard the individual's freedom to pursue his goals in his private domain: 'the only purpose for which power can be rightfully exercised over any member of a civilised community, against his will, is to prevent harm to others. His own good, either physical or moral, is not a sufficient warrant.'

Mill magnificently defends this principle of liberty on two grounds: it enables individuals to realize their individual potential in their own way, and, by liberating talents, creativity, and dynamism, it sets up the essential precondition for moral and intellectual progress. Yet the limitations of his Benthamite inheritance, despite the major enlargements he made to it, residually constrain him. His defence of the principle would have been still stronger if he had weakened (or liberalized) its foundation—by acknowledging the irreducible plurality of human ends and substituting for aggregate utility the generic concept of general good.

KARL MARX (1818–1883)

ALLEN WOOD

RADICAL social theorist and organizer of the working class, whose thought is widely regarded as the chief inspiration for all forms of modern social radicalism. Born 5 May 1818 in the Rhenish city of Trier, Karl Heinrich Marx was son of a successful Jewish lawyer of conservative political views who converted to Christianity in 1824. He studied law at the University of Bonn in 1835 and at the University of Berlin in 1836, changing his course of study in that year to philosophy, under the influence of Ludwig Feuerbach, Bruno Bauer, and the Young Hegelian movement. Marx completed his doctorate in philosophy in 1841. With the accession of Friedrich Wilhelm IV in 1840, however, the Young Hegelians came under attack from the government, and Marx lost all chance of an academic career in philosophy. Between 1842 and 1848 he edited radical publications in the Rhineland, France, and Belgium. He married his childhood sweetheart, Jenny von Westphalen, in 1843; despite their exceedingly hard life after 1850, the marriage was a happy one, and lasted until her death in 1881. (While in London the Marxes' family servant, Helene Demuth, gave birth to an illegitimate child; during the present century it was believed for a time that Marx was the father, but it is now widely held that he was not.)

In 1844, while in Paris, Marx was introduced both to the working-class movement and to the study of political economy by his former fellow student at Berlin, Friedrich Engels, with whom he began a lifetime of collaboration. While in Brussels, he formulated the programme of historical materialism, first expounded in the unpublished manuscript *The German Ideology*. Marx returned from Belgium to Paris in 1848 after the revolution, and then went back to the Rhineland where he worked as a publicist on behalf of the insurrection there. In the same year Marx and Engels played a key role in founding the Communist League (which lasted until 1850); the *Communist Manifesto* was part of their activity in the League. After successfully defending himself and his associates in a Cologne court on charges of inciting to revolt, Marx was expelled from Prussian territories in 1848. After a brief stay in Paris, he took up residence in London. The first years in England were a time of bitter, brutal poverty for the Marx family: three of their six children died of want and Marx's health suffered a collapse from which it never fully recovered. For much of the 1850s his only regular income was from Horace Greeley's *New York Tribune*, for which he served as European correspondent, receiving a fee of £1 per article. Throughout the 1850s and 1860s, when not confined to bed by illness, Marx regularly spent ten hours of every day in the library of the British Museum studying and writing. His first scientific work on political economy, *Contribution to a Critique of Political Economy*, was published in 1859; the Preface to this work contains a succinct statement of the materialist conception of history, usually regarded as the definitive formulation of that doctrine. This was only a prelude to Marx's definitive theory of capitalism. Volume i of *Capital* was published in 1867, but two more volumes were left uncompleted at his death. Engels edited and published them in 1884 and 1893 respectively. Marx was instrumental in founding the International Working Men's Association in 1864, and guided it through six congresses in nine years. The demise of the First International in 1876 was brought about by a combination of factors, notably the organization's support for the Paris Commune (see Marx's *The Civil War in France*) and internal intrigues by Mikhail Bakunin (expelled in 1872). Marx died of long-standing respiratory ailments on 13 March 1883, and is buried next to his wife in Highgate Cemetery, London.

Marx's interest in philosophical materialism is evident as early as his doctoral dissertation on the philosophy of nature in Democritus and Epicurus. But the dissertation's focus on Epicurus' philosophy of self-consciousness and its historical significance equally displays Marx's education in German idealist philosophy and his preoccupation with its themes. As a philosopher Marx self-consciously sought to marry the tradition of German idealism, especially the philosophy of Hegel, with the scientific materialism of the radical French Enlightenment. This was to some extent the tendency of the Young Hegelian movement generally, but Marx's emphatic admiration for English and French materialism in contrast to the Young Hegelians' depreciation of it is displayed in a well-known passage from *The Holy Family* (1844).

Of greater significance for Marx's later thought is the way in which his famous Paris manuscripts of 1844 address to the 'materialistic' science of political economy a set of issues which Hegel and his followers had treated as questions of religious subjectivity. German idealism was concerned with problems of human selfhood, the nature of a fulfilling human life, and people's sense of meaning, self-worth, and relatedness to their natural and social environment. They saw modern culture as both a scene of 'alienation' for human beings from themselves, their lives, and others, and also as holding out the promise of the conquest or overcoming of alienation. Hegel, however, saw the task of self-fulfilment and reconciliation as a philosophical–religious one. It was Marx in the Paris manuscripts who first attempted to see it as fundamentally a matter of the social and economic conditions in which people live, of the kind of labouring activities they perform and the practical relationships in which they stand to one another. Marx's concern for the plight of the working class was from the beginning a concern not merely with the satisfaction of 'material needs' in the usual sense, but fundamentally with the conditions under which human beings can develop their 'essential human powers' and attain 'free self-activity'.

The Paris manuscripts view human beings in modern society, human beings as they are understood by the science of political economy, as alienated from themselves because their life-activity takes an alien, inhuman form. Truly human and fulfilling life activity is an activity of free social self-expression. It is free because it is self-determined by human beings themselves; it develops and expresses their humanity because, as Hegel had realized, it is the nature of a spiritual being to create itself by objectifying itself in a world and then comprehending that world as its adequate expression, as the 'affirmation', 'objectification', and 'confirmation' of its nature; and it is social because it is the nature of human beings to produce both with others and for others, and to understand themselves in the light of their mutual recognition of one another and their common work. The social relationships depicted by political economy, however, are relationships in which the life-activity of the majority, the working class, is increasingly stunted, reduced to meaningless physical activity which, far from developing and exercising their humanity, reduces them to abstract organs of a lifeless mechanism. They do not experience the products of their labour as their expression, or indeed as theirs in any sense. For these products belong to a non-worker, the capitalist, to whom they must sell their activity for a wage which suffices only to keep them alive so that they may sustain the whole absurd cycle of their lives. Political economy, moreover, depicts human beings whose social life and relationships are at the mercy not of their collective choice but of an alien, inhuman mechanism, the market-place, which purports to be a sphere of individual freedom, but is in fact a sphere of collective slavery to inhuman and destructive forces.

Hegel had earlier conceived of alienation in the form of the 'unhappy consciousness' (a misunderstood Christian religiosity which experiences the human self as empty and worthless, and places everything valuable in a supernatural 'beyond'). The cure for alienation in Hegel's view is the recognition that finite nature is not the absence of infinite spirit but its expression. Feuerbach brought to light the latent humanism in Hegel's view and attacked all forms of religion (and even Hegel's speculative metaphysics) as forms of alienation. The true being of human individuals, he maintained, is in the enjoyment of sensuous nature and of loving harmony with other human beings. What both Hegel and Feuerbach had in common is the perception of alienation as fundamentally a form of false consciousness, whose cure was a correct perception or interpretation of the world. Alienated consciousness contains both a lament that our natural human life is unsatisfying and worthless, and also the hope of consolation in the beyond. Hegel and Feuerbach agree that the illusion of alienated consciousness consists in its negative attitude toward earthly life; the comforting assurances of religion, according to both philosophers, contain the truth, if only we know how to put the right philosophical interpretation on them. To Marx, however, alienation becomes intelligible as soon as we adopt just the reverse supposition: that the alienated consciousness tells the truth in its laments, not in its consolations. Religion, according to Marx, gives expression to a mode of life which is really empty, unfulfilled, degraded, devoid of dignity. Religious illusions have hold on us because they provide a false semblance of meaning and fulfilment for a mode of life which without this illusion would be seen for the unredeemed meaninglessness that it is. For Marx religious misery is both an expression of actual misery and an attempt to flee from it into a world of imagination: it is the 'opium of the people'. The way out of alienation is not, as Hegel and Feuerbach thought, a new philosophical interpretation of life, but a new form of earthly existence, a new society in which the material conditions for a fulfilling human life would no longer be lacking. 'The philosophers have only *interpreted* the world in different ways; the point is to *change* it.'

For Marx the ultimate tendency of history is the Promethean drive of the human species to develop its 'essential human powers', its powers of production. Under capitalism these powers, and the complex network of human co-operation through which they are exercised, have for the first time grown far enough to put within the reach of human beings themselves the collective, rational control of the social form of their own production. This self-conscious self-determination is the true meaning of human freedom. But human beings under capitalism are alienated because capitalist social relations, by dispossessing the vast majority of producers and subjecting the form of social production to the market mechanism, frustrate this collective self-determination. The historic mission of the proletariat is to actualize the capacities for human freedom which the capitalist mode of production has put within our reach, by abolishing class society. In this way, historical materialism gives the working class a full conscious understanding of its historic mission, so that unlike previous ruling classes it may fulfil this mission consciously, and thus truly enable the human species to master itself and its destiny. The materialist conception of history thus serves as the link between Marx's concern with the conditions for human fulfilment, his theoretical enterprise as economist and historian, and his practical activity as a working-class organizer and revolutionary.

According to Marx's materialist conception of history, the goals of a class movement are determined by the set of production relations the class is in a position to establish and defend. This implies that historically conscious revolutionaries should not proceed by setting utopian goals for themselves and then looking around for means to achieve them. Revolutionary practice is rather a matter of participating in an already developing class movement, helping to define its own goals and to actualize them through the use of the weapons inherent in the class's historical situation. The definition of these goals, moreover, is an ongoing process; thus it is pointless to speculate about the precise system of distribution which a revolutionary movement will institute after its victory when the movement itself is still in its infancy.

Marx believed that future society would see the abolition of classes, of private ownership of means of production, and even of commodity production (production of goods and services for exchange or sale). He believed communist society would eventually eliminate all systematic social causes of alienation and human unfulfilment. Yet he never thought of future society as an unchanging state of perfection. On the contrary, he thought of the end of class society as the true beginning of *human* history, of the historical development of human society directed consciously by human beings. Above all, Marx never attempted to 'write recipes for the cookshops of the future' or to say in any detail what distribution relations in future socialist or communist society would be like. He equally scorned those who concerned themselves with formulating principles of distributive justice and condemning capitalism in their name. Marx conceives the justice of economic transactions as their correspondence to or functionality for the prevailing mode of production. Given this conception of justice, Marx very consistently (if rather surprisingly) concluded that the inhuman exploitation practised by capitalism against the workers is not unjust, and does not violate the workers' rights; this conclusion constitutes no defence of capitalism, only an attack on the use of moral conceptions within the proletarian movement. Marx saw the task of the proletarian movement in his time as one of self-definition and growth through organization, discipline, and self-criticism based on scientific self-understanding. He left for later stages of the movement the task of planning the future society which it is the historic mission of the movement to bring to birth.

FRIEDRICH WILHELM NIETZSCHE (1844–1900)

RICHARD SCHACHT

GERMAN philosopher and critic *par excellence*. A classical philologist by training and academic profession, Nietzsche's philosophical efforts—deriving chiefly from the last dozen years of his short productive life—were little heeded until long after his physical and mental collapse in 1889 (at the age of only 44). He subsequently emerged as one of the most controversial, unconventional, and important figures in the history of modern philosophy. His influence upon European philosophy in the twentieth century has been profound; and he has belatedly come to receive considerable attention in the English-speaking world as well, as the shadow cast by the travesty of his appropriation by the Nazis and Fascists has receded, along with the sway of philosophical fashions inhospitable to his kind of thinking and writing. He gave his *Beyond Good and Evil* the subtitle *Prelude to a Philosophy of the Future*; and in this he may well have been prophetic.

Nietzsche's philosophical enterprise grew out of his background as a philologist schooled in the study of classical languages and literatures, his deep concern with issues relating to the quality of life in the culture and society of his time, his conviction that the interpretative and evaluative underpinnings of Western civilization are fundamentally flawed, and his determination to come to grips with the profound crisis he believed to be impending as this comes to be recognized. He sought both to comprehend this situation and to help provide humanity with a new lease on life, beyond what he called 'the death of God' and 'the advent of nihilism' following in its wake. He deemed traditional forms of religious and philosophical thought to be inadequate to the task, and indeed to be part of the problem; and so he attempted to develop a radical alternative to them that might point the way to a solution.

Nietzsche had no formal philosophical training. His introduction to philosophy came through his discovery of Schopenhauer's *The World as Will and Representation* while studying philology at the university at Leipzig. This encounter with Schopenhauer's thought profoundly influenced him, as can be seen in his first book *The Birth of Tragedy* (1872), which he published soon after being appointed to a professorship of philology at Basle University (at the astonishingly early age of 24, before he had even been awarded his doctorate). He was convinced of the soundness of Schopenhauer's basic conception of the world as a godless and irrational affair of ceaseless striving and suffering; but he was repelled by Schopenhauer's starkly pessimistic verdict with respect to the worth of existence in such a world, and sought some way of arriving at a different conclusion. In *The Birth of Tragedy* he made his first attempt to do so, looking to the Greeks and their art for guidance, and to Wagner (with whom he had become acquainted and enthralled) for contemporary inspiration. His attachment to Wagner subsequently gave way to disenchantment and then to scathing criticism (culminating in his late polemic *The Case of Wagner*), and he gradually emancipated himself from Schopenhauer as well; but the fundamental problem of how nihilism might be overcome and life affirmed without illusions remained at the centre of his concern throughout his life.

Nietzsche's brief academic career ended in 1879, owing to the drastic deterioration of his health. His only significant publications after *The Birth of Tragedy* prior to its final year were the four essays he subsequently gathered together under the title *Untimely Meditations*, of which 'The Uses and Disadvantages of History for Life' and 'Schopenhauer as Educator' (both 1874) are of the greatest interest. Then in 1878 he published the first of a series of volumes of aphorisms and reflections under the title *Human, all too Human*. It was followed during the next few years by two supplements which became a second volume under the same title, by *Daybreak* in 1881, and then by the initial four-part version of *The Gay Science* in 1882. In these works, which he described as 'a series of writings . . . whose common goal is to erect *a new image and ideal of the free spirit*', Nietzsche found his way to his kind of philosophy.

It was only in 1886, however, with the publication of *Beyond Good and Evil*, that he pursued it further in something like the same manner. In the interval (1883–5) he published only the four parts of his great literary-philosophical experiment *Thus Spoke Zarathustra*. A mere three more years remained to him prior to his collapse in January of 1889, from which he never recovered. During this brief but phenomenally productive period he wrote prefaces to new editions of most of his pre-*Zarathustra* writings, added a fifth part to a new edition of *The Gay Science* (1887), published *On the Genealogy of Morals* in the same year, and then in the final year of his active life (1888) wrote *Twilight of the Idols*, *The Case of Wagner*, *The Antichrist*, and his autobiographical *Ecce Homo*—all the while filling many notebooks with reflections and thought experiments. (The significance of this 'Nachlass' material is much debated. After his collapse and death, selections from it were gathered into a volume published under the title *The Will to Power*.)

From his early essays to these last works, Nietzsche showed himself to be an astute, severe, and provocative critic on many fronts. Cultural, social, political, artistic, religious, moral, scientific, and philosophical developments and phenomena of many kinds drew his polemical attention. Everywhere he looked he saw much that was lamentably 'human, all too human', even among those things and thinkers generally held in the highest regard. This has given rise to the common impression that the basic thrust and upshot of his thought is radically negative, contributing greatly to the advent of nihilism that he announced (and of worse things as well).

This impression, however, is deeply mistaken. Nietzsche actually was a profoundly positive thinker, concerned above all to discover a way beyond the nihilistic reaction he believed to be the inevitable consequence of the impending collapse of traditional values and modes of interpretation, to a new 'affirmation' and 'enhancement' of life. His critical fire was only a means to this end, preliminary to the twin philosophical tasks of *reinterpretation* and *revaluation* he advocated and pursued with growing explicitness and determination from *The Gay Science* onward.

As a further means to this end, and likewise preliminary to these tasks, Nietzsche developed and undertook a variety of forms of analysis, of which the kind of 'genealogical' inquiry exemplified by his investigations in *On the Genealogy of Morals* is one notable and important example. His analytical acumen was as extraordinary as his critical astuteness; and his writings both before and after *Zarathustra* contain a wealth of cultural, social, psychological, linguistic, and conceptual analyses from many different perspectives, upon which he drew not only in his critiques but also in his reinterpretative and revaluative efforts. His recognition of the importance of engaging in and drawing upon a multiplicity of such analyses in philosophical inquiry is reflected in his insistence that such inquiry is inescapably perspectival—and that this circumstance is by no means fatal to it, if one can learn to capitalize upon the possibility of bringing a variety of perspectives to bear upon many of the matters with which it may concern itself. This is his practice as well as his prescription, in his explorations of issues ranging from moral and religious phenomena to aspects of our human nature and to knowing and reasoning themselves.

The form of Nietzsche's philosophical writings both before and after *Zarathustra*, which for the most part consist of collections of relatively brief aphorisms and reflections on such issues rather than sustained systematic lines of argument, is well suited to this multiply perspectival tactic. It greatly complicates the task of understanding him; but it also makes his thinking far more subtle and complex than is commonly supposed. He returned to problems repeatedly, in one work after another, approaching them from many different angles; and it is only if account is taken of his many diverse reflections on them that anything approaching justice to his thinking about any of them can be done. Even then he can be—and has been, and no doubt will continue to be—interpreted in quite different ways. Precisely for this reason, however, and because he has so much of interest to say (on almost any such interpretation) about so many things, he is certain to continue to attract, deserve, and reward philosophical attention.

Nietzsche was greatly concerned with basic problems he discerned in contemporary Western culture and society, which he believed were becoming increasingly acute, and for which he considered it imperative to try to find new solutions. He prophesied the advent of a period of nihilism, with the death of God and the demise of metaphysics, and the discovery of the inability of science to yield anything like absolute knowledge; but this prospect deeply worried him. He was firmly convinced of the untenability of the 'God-hypothesis' and associated religious interpretations of the world and our existence, and likewise of their metaphysical variants. Having also become persuaded of the fundamentally non-rational character of the world, life, and history, Nietzsche took the basic challenge of philosophy to be that of overcoming both these ways of thinking and the nihilism resulting from their abandonment. This led him to undertake to reinterpret ourselves and the world along lines which would be more tenable, and would also be more conducive to the flourishing and enhancement of life. The 'de-deification of nature', the tracing of the 'genealogy of morals' and their critique, and the elaboration of 'naturalistic' accounts of knowledge, value, morality, and our entire 'spiritual' nature thus came to be among the main tasks with which he took himself and the 'new philosophers' he called for be confronted.

Unlike most philosophers of importance before him, Nietzsche was openly and profoundly hostile to most forms of morality and religious thought. He declared 'war' upon them, on the grounds that they not only are indefensible and untenable, but moreover feed upon and foster weakness, life-weariness, and *ressentiment*, poisoning the wellsprings of human vitality in the process by 'devaluing' all 'naturalistic' values. He further rejected not only the God-hypothesis (as a notion utterly without warrant, owing its acceptance only to naïvety, error, need, or ulterior motivation), but also any metaphysical postulation of a 'true world of "being"' transcending the world of life and experience, and with them the related 'soul-' and 'thing-hypotheses', taking these notions to be ontological fictions reflecting our artificial (though convenient) conceptual shorthand for products and processes. In place of this cluster of traditional ontological categories and interpretations, he conceived of the world in terms of an interplay of forces without any inherent structure or final end, ceaselessly organizing and reorganizing themselves as the fundamental disposition he called 'will to power' gives rise to successive arrays of power relationships among them.

Nietzsche construed our human nature and existence naturalistically, insisting upon the necessity of 'translating man back into nature', in origin and fundamental character, as one form of animal life among others. 'The soul is only a word for something about the body,' he has Zarathustra say; and the body is fundamentally an arrangement of natural forces and processes. At the same time, however, he insisted upon the importance of social arrangements and interactions in the development of human forms of awareness and activity, and moreover upon the possibility of the emergence of exceptional human beings capable of an independence and creativity elevating them beyond the level of the general human rule. So he stressed the difference between 'higher types' and 'the herd', and through Zarathustra proclaimed the 'overman' (*Übermensch*) to be 'the meaning of the earth', representing the overcoming of the 'all-too-human' and the attainment of the fullest possible 'enhancement of life'. Far from seeking to diminish our humanity by stressing our animality, he sought to direct our attention and efforts to the emergence of a 'higher humanity' capable of endowing existence with a human redemption and justification.

Nietzsche proposed that life and the world be interpreted in terms of his conception of 'will to power'; and he framed his 'Dionysian value-standard', and the 'revaluation of values' that he called for, in terms of this interpretation as well. The only positive and tenable value-scheme possible, he maintained, must be based upon a recognition and affirmation of the world's fundamental character, and so must posit as a general standard the attainment of a kind of life in which the assertive–transformative will to power is present in its highest intensity and quality. This in turn led him to take the 'enhancement of life' and creativity to be the guiding ideas of his revaluation of values and development of a naturalistic value-theory.

This way of thinking carried over into Nietzsche's thinking with respect to morality as well. Insisting that moralities as well as other traditional modes of valuation ought to be understood and assessed 'in the perspective of life', he argued that most of them are contrary rather than conducive to the enhancement of life, reflecting the all-too-human needs and weaknesses and fears of less-favoured human groups and types. Distinguishing between 'master' and 'slave' moralities, he found the latter increasingly to have eclipsed the former in human history, and to have become the dominant type of morality at the present time, in the form of a 'herd-animal' morality well suited to the requirements and vulnerabilities of the mediocre who are the human rule, but stultifying and detrimental to the development of potential exceptions to that rule. He further suggested the possibility and desirability of a 'higher' type of morality for the exceptions, in which the content and contrast of the basic 'slave–herd-morality' categories of 'good and evil' would be replaced by categories more akin to the 'good and bad' contrast characteristic of master morality, with a revised (and variable) content.

The strongly creative flavour of Nietzsche's notions of such a higher humanity and associated higher morality reflects his linkage of both to his conception of art, to which he attached great importance. Art, as the creative transformation of the world as we find it (and of ourselves thereby) on a small scale and in particular media, affords us a glimpse of the possibility of a kind of life that would be lived more fully in this manner, and constitutes a step in the direction of its emergence. In this way, Nietzsche's mature thought expanded upon the idea of the basic connection between art and the justification of life which was his general theme in his first major work, *The Birth of Tragedy*.

Nietzsche was highly critical of traditional and commonplace ways of thinking about truth and knowledge, maintaining that as they are usually construed there is and can be nothing of the kind (except in highly artificial contexts), that all thinking is 'perspectival', and that 'there are no facts, only interpretations'. This has led some to suppose that he rejected the idea of truth and knowledge altogether, and so was a radical epistemological nihilist. Yet he manifested a passionate commitment to 'truthfulness', and pursued philosophical tasks which he quite clearly supposed to have something like knowledge as their aim. (So, for example, this is the avowed objective of his 'genealogical' investigations in *On the Genealogy of Morals*, as well as in many of the lines of inquiry he pursues in *The Gay Science*.)

Both in principle and in practice Nietzsche's thinking was avowedly interpretative, multiply perspectival, experimental, and tentative, and made free use of language that is highly metaphorical and figurative. He preferred to offer suggestions, hazard guesses, and propose hypotheses rather than attempt to construct rigorous lines of reasoning. He further acknowledged that the upshot of what he (or anyone else) has to say on any substantive issue neither is nor can ever be beyond all dispute. Yet he repeatedly insisted upon the distinction between the plausibility and soundness of various ideas on the one hand, and their 'value for life' on the other (between their 'truth-value' and their 'life-value', as it were). Although some of his unguarded remarks may seem to suggest otherwise, he inveighed explicitly against the conflation of the two—even while also arguing that the *value* of all knowledge and truthfulness ultimately must be referred to their 'value for life' for human beings with differing constitutions and conditions of preservation, flourishing, and growth, and judged before that tribunal.

Philosophy for Nietzsche involves the *making of cases* for and against various proposed interpretations and evaluations. For the most part he did not present arguments of the sort that one usually finds in the writings of philosophers and expects of them. He attempted to make his criticisms stick and his own ideas stand in other ways. On the attack, he typically sought to make cases against ways of thinking he found wanting by presenting an array of considerations intended collectively first to make us suspicious of them and aware of just how problematical they are, and then to deprive them of their credibility. He generally did not claim that the considerations he marshals actually *refute* the targets of his criticism. Rather he typically aimed to *dispose* of them by undermining them sufficiently to lay them to rest, exposed as unworthy of being taken seriously any longer—at least by those possessed of any degree of intellectual integrity and honesty.

When advancing alternatives to them Nietzsche proceeded in a somewhat similar manner, presenting various supporting considerations—both general and specific—none of which by themselves may be decisive, but which taken together are intended to be compelling. They are purported to establish his 'right' to the ideas he puts forward, notwithstanding the novelty they may have, and the reluctance many may feel to entertain and embrace them. Here, too, he was generally prepared to acknowledge that the cases he makes do not actually *prove* his points, and couched his hypotheses and conclusions in tentative and provisional language. He also not only admitted but insisted that they leave open the possibility of other interpretations as well as of subsequent modifications, as further considerations are hit upon and introduced. But it is clear that he supposed it to be possible to make cases for his interpretations and evaluations, the positive upshot of which is strong and clear enough to warrant confidence that he is at least on the right track, and has got hold of something important. He often did say things to the effect that these are '*his* truths', to which others may not easily be entitled. But this way of speaking may be understood as a challenge to others to *earn their right* to lay like claim to understand what he has grasped, rather than as an admission that they are nothing more than figments of his own creative imagination.

A consequence of the perspectival approach Nietzsche favoured is that one must employ models and metaphors drawn from whatever resources are available to one in conceptualizing and articulating what may be discerned from the perspectives adopted—and, indeed, that these perspectives themselves are to no little extent framed by means of such resources. He himself took his models and metaphors from literature and the various arts, from the natural sciences, and also from the social and behavioural sciences, from economics to psychology. He further availed himself of conceptual resources and images drawn from a multitude of other domains of discourse, including law, medicine, linguistics, and even theology. In this way he was able to take advantage of the different ways of thinking associated with and suggested by them, and to play them off against each other, thereby avoiding becoming locked into any one or particular cluster of them. They afforded him the means of discovering and devising an expanding repertoire of perspectives upon the matters with which he was concerned, and so of developing and sharpening what he called the many and different 'eyes' needed to contribute to a growing and deepening comprehension of them. This has an important bearing upon the question of how his perspectivism is to be understood, and how it works in practice.

Nietzsche clearly held that neither this sort of inquiry nor any other that is humanly possible will suffice to enable one to attain the sort of knowledge to which metaphysicians have traditionally aspired. It by no means follows, however, that for him there is nothing of any significance to be comprehended. He considered the forms of morality that have arisen in the course of human events to admit of better-than-ordinary comprehension if approached in this manner and spirit, for example; and he clearly supposed that the same applies to a broad range of other such phenomena that are to be encountered within the compass of human life, history, and experience—and indeed to our attained and varying human reality itself, down to its basic character and general conditions. Rather like a latter-day Vico, he seized upon the idea that it is humanly possible to comprehend at least something of whatever has been humanly constituted. He came to take this idea quite seriously, concluding that it has important implications for the possibility of knowledge, and that its scope is very wide indeed. For what he called 'the world that concerns us'—which includes ourselves—consists in phenomena that are in various and very real respects 'our doing'.

Nietzsche thus in effect proposed to replace the Holy Grail of an ultimate reality conceived along the lines of a transcendent deity or 'true world' of 'being', and the quest for it conceived as the proper mission and picture of true knowledge, with a different paradigm of reality and associated conception of comprehension. Suppose we take as our paradigm the sort of reality in which human life and the world of our activities and experience consist, and conceive of knowledge in terms of the kind of comprehension of them of which they admit and we are capable. Making them our point of departure, we then can consider how far it is possible to go by expanding the scope of their application into the world with which we find ourselves confronted—while devoting our main efforts to the exploration of those things that are to be encountered *within* the realm of the human, and to the devising and the strategies of inquiry that will be most appropriate to their comprehension. If in this way we manage to achieve some measure of understanding of the kind of world in which our human reality has emerged and taken the various forms and associated expressions it has, so much the better. But even if we cannot do much more than comprehend ourselves and things human, this will at least be something—and something quite significant and well worth achieving at that.

CHARLES SANDERS PEIRCE (1839–1914)

C. J. HOOKWAY

A MERICAN philosopher who is perhaps best known as the origin-
ator of pragmatism. He was educated at Harvard, where his father
was a mathematics professor. His greatest philosophical influence was
Kant, and he saw himself as constructing the philosophical system that
Kant might have developed had he not been so ignorant of logic. But
the influence of Thomas Reid and other common-sense philosophers
became increasingly important: in late writings, the two influences were
combined in his 'critical common-sensism'. Describing himself as a logician, Peirce made major contributions to formal logic (independently of
Frege he and his students developed a logic of quantifiers and relations
after 1880) and to the study of the logic of science. Indeed, he lectured on
these topics at Harvard in the late 1860s and held a lectureship in logic at
Johns Hopkins University from 1879 until 1884. But he also served as an
experimental scientist, working at the Harvard laboratory after he had
graduated in chemistry, and being employed for over twenty years by the
United States Coastal Survey.

Peirce was a difficult man, widely perceived as an immoral libertine,
prone to paranoia and wild mood swings, and possessing an assessment
of his own intellectual powers which may have been accurate but which
was sometimes accompanied by contempt for the capacities of those of
lesser talents. In 1884, when confident of obtaining tenure at Johns
Hopkins, information about his irregular life-style, together with suspi-
cion of his unorthodox religious beliefs, led to his being removed from his
post. From then until his death, it was understood that he could expect no
orthodox academic employment: he lived precariously with his second
wife in north-eastern Pennsylvania, writing extensively and giving a few
important series of lectures arranged by his friend William James. He
never completed the canonical statement of his philosophical position

that he sought, but he published extensively and left hundreds of thousands of manuscripts; his work is gradually becoming more readily available.

Theory of Inquiry and Pragmatism

In a late paper, Peirce described himself as a 'laboratory philosopher', claiming that years of laboratory experience encouraged him, like any experimentalist, to approach all issues in the distinctive manner which comprises his pragmatism. This is clearest in the approach to epistemological matters which emerges in his earliest published work, from the 1860s and 1870s—most clearly in a series of papers in the *Popular Science Monthly* (1877–8).

His epistemological work begins from a rejection of Cartesian strategies in philosophy. They do not, he pointed out, accord with our ordinary practice of carrying out investigations: the latter is a co-operative venture, while Descartes suggests that a responsible investigator should carry out a solitary investigation of his or her cognitive standing. Ordinary inquiry takes for granted all the propositions we find certain as we begin the inquiry, while Descartes's sceptical arguments prompt philosophical doubt about what occasions no real doubt. And ordinary inquiry is impressed by the number and variety of the arguments supporting a conclusion, while the Cartesian requires a single indubitable train of reasoning to ground any belief. Peirce proposes to begin from our everyday and scientific experience of inquiry, and to investigate the norms which govern cognition on that basis.

The first paper of the series suggests that inquiry begins only when one of our previously settled beliefs is disturbed, and it is ended as soon as we have a new answer to the question that concerns us: the aim of inquiry is to replace doubt by settled belief. What methods should we use if we are to carry out our inquiries well? He considers four, the first three being devised to bring to light the key features of the fourth. (1) The method of tenacity requires us to choose any answer, and to take all means necessary to maintain it; (2) the method of authority requires us to defer to an authority and accept whatever the authority requires (it may be no accident that Peirce wrote soon after the bull of papal infallibility had been promulgated); and (3) the a priori method requires us to go by what seems agreeable to reason. It will be no surprise that these methods fail: the second has the advantage over the first that our beliefs will escape the constant buffeting of disputes from those who have decided differently, but we are still likely to meet those who accept a different authority, and our own authority will not be able to settle matters about everything. So fixation of belief must be independent of will or human choice. The third method secures that, but it is likely to make belief a matter of fashion: selection of belief still has a subjective basis. Hence we should adopt (4) the 'method of science', which holds that 'there are Real things, whose characters are entirely independent of our opinions about them; those realities affect our senses according to regular laws, and, though our sensations are as different as our relations to the objects, yet, by taking advantage of the laws of perception, we can ascertain by reasoning how things really are'.

Peirce probably believed that this claim was a presupposition of inquiry and that we should adopt only such methods as were in accord with it. The remainder of the series of papers offers a more detailed account of what this method involves: Peirce was one of the first philosophers to arrive at a satisfactory understanding of statistical reasoning, and this is central to his account of science. He is a 'contrite fallibilist': any of our current certainties might turn out to be mistaken, but relying upon them will not prevent our making cognitive progress; any errors will emerge with time.

The 'pragmatist principle' forms part of this theory of inquiry, and was elaborated in the second paper of the series, 'How to Make Our Ideas Clear'. When William James won notoriety for pragmatism, crediting it to Peirce, the latter renamed his principle 'pragmaticism'. It is a rule for clarifying the content of concepts and hypotheses, and is supposed to reveal all features of the meaning of concepts and hypotheses that are relevant to scientific investigations. Suppose I wish to test whether a sample before me is sodium. In the light of my knowledge of sodium, I can predict that if it is sodium then, if I were to drop it into hot water, it would ignite: I make predictions about the consequences of actions if the hypothesis is true. Peirce expresses his principle: 'Consider what effects, which might conceivably have practical bearings, we conceive the object of our conception to have. Then our conception of those effects is the whole of our conception of the object.' When I have listed *all* the predictions I would make about the consequences of my actions if the substance were sodium, I have a complete clarification of my understanding of the hypothesis: nothing which could be relevant to testing it scientifically has been omitted.

As well as showing its value in clarifying hypotheses, and arguing that it can be used to dismiss some metaphysical 'hypotheses' as empty, Peirce illustrates the value of his pragmatism by clarifying our conception of truth and reality. If a proposition is true, then anyone who investigated the matter long enough and well enough would eventually acknowledge its truth: truth is a matter of long-term convergence of opinion. 'The opinion which is fated to be ultimately agreed upon by all who investigate, is what we mean by the truth, and the object represented in this opinion is the real.' Although the principle bears a superficial resemblance to the verification principle of the later Logical Positivists, there are important differences. First, there is no suggestion that, in clarifying our conception, we list only those conditional expectations that are analytic or true by definition: Peirce expects the content of a conception or hypothesis to develop as our scientific knowledge advances. And, second, as he developed his philosophical position, he insisted that the principle could only be taken seriously by someone who shared his realism about natural necessity: the conceptual clarifications are expressed as subjunctive conditionals ('would-bes'); and such conditionals report real facts about the world.

System

Peirce's logic is a theory of cognitive norms: methods of inquiry, standards of inference, rules for identifying plausible hypotheses, principles for clarifying meanings, and so on. He was unsatisfied with the kind of grounding he provided for cognitive norms in the papers just discussed, and his attempts to correct the Kantian framework were directed at remedying this. His sophisticated architectonic approach to philosophy rested upon a classification of the sciences. Logic was the least fundamental of three normative sciences, being a special application of a system of norms initially developed in ethics and aesthetics. All of these investigations made use of a system of categories, a correction of Kant's system, which was defended through a kind of phenomenological investigation. And these philosophical and phenomenological inquiries used mathematical methods to study experience and reality, mathematics being the only discipline which had, and needed, no foundations. So Peirce's later work developed a highly sophisticated account of how we can have knowledge of cognitive or logical norms.

His system of categories is most easily understood from the perspective of his logic of relations. Properties and relations can be classified according to the number of relata they have: '. . . is blue' is a *one*-place predicate, '. . . respects . . .' is a dyadic, *two*-place relation, and '. . . gives . . . to . . .' is a triadic, *three*-place relation. Peirce argued that a language adequate for scientific or descriptive purposes must contain terms of all these three kinds, but that there are no phenomena which can only be described in a language which contains expressions for four-place relations. Thus he classified phenomena and elements of reality numerically: according to whether they are forms of *firstness*, *secondness*, or (like giving) *thirdness*. The irreducibility of thirdness is, he thinks, a distinctive part of his philosophical outlook, something which allies him with realist philosophers in opposition to nominalism. In early work, his defence of his categories was largely found in his work on formal logic, but later he turned to phenomenology: reflection on experience of all kinds was to convince us that triadicity was ineliminable but that no more complex phenomena were involved in experience.

Thus we are aware that our experiences have raw qualitative characters which do not directly involve relations with other things: they exhibit firstness. They also stand in relations to each other, interacting against one another and so on: this involves secondness, as when fire immediately follows our dropping the sodium in hot water. But we are aware that this interaction is intelligible, it is 'mediated': we can bring it down into a continuous spread of small changes which go together to make up the big one; and we are aware that it conforms to a law. Finding it intelligible introduces thirdness: we understand the two elements of the interaction by reference to a third mediating fact. The aim of inquiry, for Peirce, is to find the thirdness (law and pattern) in the manifold of sensory experiences that we undergo. The norms employed by the scientific method are to be vindicated by showing how they provide means for finding more and more pattern and mediation (more and more thirdness) in the world of our experience.

Signs

According to Peirce, the most important forms of thirdness involve meaning and representation, and all of his work is underpinned by a sophisticated theory of meaning: his semiotics. He probably believed that everything was a sign, but the signs of most interest to him were thoughts and 'the assertions of a scientific intelligence'. This theory of meaning ('speculative grammar') was to provide foundations for his writings in logic.

The key to the thirdness involved in signs was Peirce's notion of *interpretation*. A sign denotes an object only by being understood or interpreted as standing for an object: and this interpretation will always be another sign with the same object. Semiotics is thus primarily a theory of understanding, an account of how we are guided and constrained in arriving at interpretations of signs. Interpretation often involves inference, developing our understanding of the object in question. Thus my understanding of your assertion that you are tired may be manifested in my thinking that you want me to believe you are tired, in my believing you are tired, in my expecting you to fall asleep, in my offering you a cup of coffee, and so on. The interpreting thought mediates between the sign and its object.

Peirce was famous for his classifications of signs, and some of his terminology has acquired wide currency. For example, signs can be distinguished according to the features of them exploited in arriving at an interpretation. A symbol denotes a particular object because there exists a practice of interpreting it as denoting that object: an index denotes an object to which it stands in a direct existential relation: the conventions governing the use of ordinary indexical expressions such as 'this' do not fix the reference unaided but rather guide us in interpreting it as an index. And iconic signs share some feature with their object which each could possess if the other did not exist: maps are straightforward examples, the conventions governing their use fixing how we are to interpret them as icons. Mathematical and logical symbolisms are iconic representations, and it was important for Peirce that sentences of natural languages have iconic elements too: formal inference exploits the fact that sentences exhibit a form which is shared with their subject-matter. Much of Peirce's later work attempted to use this systematic theory of meaning to provide a proof of the pragmatist principle.

Science itself is a process of sign interpretation. And Peirce's account of scientific reasoning has some important elements. As mentioned above, Peirce models all inductive reasoning on statistical sampling: quantitative induction involves attempting to estimate the chance of a member of a population having a particular property; and qualitative induction tests hypotheses by sampling their consequences. He denies that induction ever establishes that a conclusion is true or even probable. Rather, the practice of inductive testing is justified because continued use of it will eventually lead us to converge on the correct value for the chance of a member of the population having the property in question. The pragmatist principle teaches that probability is a propensity: if the chance of a coin coming up heads is 0.43, then, if we were to continue to toss it fairly, the proportion of times on which it comes up heads *would* converge on 0.43.

The logic of abduction is a logic of discovery: it studies how we are guided in constructing new hypotheses from the ruins of defeated ones; and it examines the norms guiding us in deciding which hypotheses are worth testing. All scientific activity is grounded in the hope that the universe is intelligible, and intelligible to us. And we are to take seriously no hypothesis that 'blocks the road of inquiry', forcing us to accept regularities as brute or inexplicable. It is connected to this that Peirce espouses 'synechism', the doctrine that we are to expect the universe to display continuities rather than discontinuities. Peirce contributed to the mathematical analysis of continuity, exploiting his ideas about the logic of relations and trying to use it as the basis of his realism about natural necessity: continuity is 'ultimate mediation'. The logic of abduction advises us to favour theories that posit continuities over those that allow for brute unmediated discontinuities.

Metaphysics

Although Peirce envisaged that pragmatism would eliminate 'ontological metaphysics', he claimed that scientific progress demanded that we construct a 'scientific metaphysics'. Supposedly this was an empirical discipline, differing from the special sciences in using no sophisticated techniques of experiment and observation: it was 'coenoscopic', relying only on familiar everyday observations which are surprising only because their familiarity prevents our noticing them. In part, it was an attempt to describe how the world must be if science was to be possible—if there were to be no inexplicable phenomena, if 'realism' was to be true, if the three categories were to be as Peirce suggested. And in part it was an exercise in 'descriptive metaphysics': drawing out features of our everyday conception of mind or matter (for example) can be a valuable corrective to unthinking theoretical prejudices, especially in psychology.

Two elements of this metaphysics are especially interesting. Peirce defended an evolutionary cosmology, explaining how the world of existing things and law-governed behaviour evolved from pure possibility. Offering an evolutionary explanation of law, he argued, was the only alternative to asserting that fundamental laws are simply true, with no explanation of why they obtain being available. If every regularity must have an explanation, we avoid a regress of ever more general and abstract laws by invoking a historical explanation. And Peirce's account of how this evolutionary process works leads to a form of objective idealism according to which matter is 'effete mind', and physical phenomena are modelled on thought and sign interpretation rather than the mental being reduced to the physical. This is because a 'realist' account of law involves finding 'mediation' in the natural world, and sign interpretation is our best model of mediation.

Secondly, it may accord with the importance he attached to statistical reasoning in science that he accepted *tychism*, the thesis that there is absolute chance, that the universe is not wholly governed by determinist laws. This partly reflects his understanding of the importance of statistical laws in science, and his understanding that observation could never establish that laws were so exact as never to permit slight deviations. He also supposed it was required to explain the evolutionary process discussed in his cosmology: without appeal to such 'chance spontaneity', he doubted that we could make sense of growth and increasing complexity.

WILLIAM JAMES (1842–1910)

T. L. S. SPRIGGE

AMERICAN philosopher and psychologist, son of Henry James, Swedenborgian religious thinker, brother of Henry James, the novelist, and Professor of Psychology and Philosophy at Harvard. Only some of his many concerns are considered here.

1. *The Principles of Psychology* (1890) is officially committed to the scientific study of mind, conceived as the ascertainment of 'the empirical correlation of the various sorts of thought or feeling with definite conditions of the brain'. Although ostensibly avoiding metaphysics, much of it is as philosophical as psychological. Avoiding metaphysics means mainly assuming the existence of a physical world independent of mind, ignoring any philosophical case against this scientifically necessary presupposition. Four themes call for notice here.

(i) For James mind is identified with consciousness, known primarily through introspection; scientific psychology explores its physical basis and biological function. This is evidently to assist the organism to cope with its environment more flexibly than can inherited behavioural patterns. The criterion for the presence of mind is, therefore, the occurrence of behaviour which reaches the same goal, as circumstances alter, through differing means.

James thinks it unlikely that such behaviour could ever be explained mechanistically. While consciousness is too obviously a distinct reality in his eyes for anything like the brain–mind identity theories of today even to be considered, James carefully examines the automaton theory but dismisses it (with debatable logic) as failing to explain why consciousness has been picked out for development by natural selection. (James was strongly influenced by Darwinian ideas.) The old-fashioned idea of a distinct soul is better, but James's own view is rather that 'the stream of consciousness' is generated afresh each moment by the current state of the whole brain and reacts back on it, and hence on behaviour, with a modicum of free spontaneity (a view anticipative of the positions of both Whitehead and Roger Sperry).

(ii) This notion of the stream of consciousness (or thought) is the most famous theme in *The Principles of Psychology*. Among its varied heirs are stream-of-consciousness literature (e.g. Gertrude Stein), aspects of Husserlian phenomenology, and Whiteheadian process thought. Consciousness comes in a continuous flow without sharp breaks or clearly distinguishable components. Thus experience is always of a specious present, a stretch of sensible duration in which the just-past still figures along with the dawning of the future. As against traditional empiricism, for which a state of consciousness is a complex of individually repeatable impressions and ideas, James contends that no item of consciousness is ever exactly repeated. I may perceive or think of the same thing twice but never by way of numerically or qualitatively identical representations.

(iii) James distinguishes between the I and the Me. The I is the ultimate thinker, the Me is the object of all those concerns we call selfish and which the I and its organism primarily seek to preserve. The Me divides into the material me, my body and my possessions; the social Me (or Mes), the image (or images) I present to the various communities to which I belong; and the spiritual Me, which covers both my mental capacities and achievements, and some supposed inner source thereof. As for the ultimate I, which does the thinking, James, having dismissed a permanent ego, decides that (if there is such a thing at all and not simply each total conscious state in turn) it is the momentary thinker of the total present thought. Personal identity through time consists in the fact that the I of one moment adopts the Mes and Is of earlier times by the peculiarly warm and intimate way in which it recollects them. (James pays particular attention to cases of multiple personality in developing his account.)

(iv) The subject of free will was of immense emotional significance to James. He was rescued from a phase of serious psychological depression in 1879 partly by discovering Charles Renouvier's defence of free will as 'the sustaining of a thought because I choose to when I might have other thoughts'. This is James's own view. Consciousness cannot determine what ideas are presented to it but, by effortful selective direction of attention, can decide which will affect behaviour. This power can neither be proved nor disproved scientifically, but belief in it is a legitimate exercise of 'the will to believe'.

James's naturalistic approach (and his role at Harvard) contributed significantly to the development of experimental psychology in America (though he had no love of experiment himself); his treatment of the various types of self has had an influence on social psychology; and his introspectionist investigations enormously influenced Husserlian phenomenology and its offshoots. It should be noted that though James rejects materialism, in any ordinary sense, he does take what might be called a phenomenological materialist view of many mental processes, seeing them as the consciousness of physical states, as in the James–Lange theory of the emotions or his replacement of the Kantian 'I think' as the constant in experience by the 'I breathe'.

2. The best known of James's purely philosophical works is *Pragmatism* (1908). James takes over from C. S. Peirce the idea that the meaning of a concept lies in its practical bearings but puts it to different (not necessarily worse) uses. Truth, for James's pragmatism, consists in useful ideas. Their utility may lie in either the power to predict experience they confer or their encouragement of valuable emotion and behaviour. Obvious objections to this appear less strong when it is realized that James's account incorporates what is currently called an externalist critique of inherent intentionality (sometimes expressed as the rejection of the very idea of consciousness as opposed to experience). Thus an idea (*qua* piece of 'flat' experience) is only about something to the extent that it produces behaviour fitted to deal with it if it exists, and is true only if it does so. (Thus my belief that God exists requires a God it helps me deal with to be true.) This was a response to his colleague Royce, who claimed that only through the mediation of a divine mind can thought be linked to definite external objects and thus enabled James to avoid the absolute idealism to which he had previously felt unwillingly forced. Actually James's pragmatic account of truth is the fulfilment of a variety of strands in his prior thought and takes somewhat different forms according to which is uppermost. Among these are Peirce's operationalism, Royce's account of intentionality, and his own doctrine of the will to believe.

3. James's other chief philosophical doctrine is radical empiricism, the view that the ultimate stuff of reality (or at least all knowable reality) is pure experience. When the natures or qualia which compose this occur in one kind of arrangement they constitute minds, when in another, physical things. (The clash with the earlier denial of repeatable components of consciousness is modified in his final pluralistic metaphysics.) This relates to pragmatism because knowledge is conceived as the way in

which the experience composing a mind leads it to successful negotiation with experience beyond itself (whether in a physical or a mental arrangement). In *Essays in Radical Empiricism* (a posthumous collection of 1904–5 articles) James oscillates between various radical empiricist accounts of the physical world, a phenomenalist view for which the physical consists in possible experience, a 'new realist' position for which it consists in sensory vistas only some of them in minds, and the panpsychist view that the physical consists in its own inner experience of itself. Upon the whole he seems to have thought the last the final metaphysical truth and the second the best analysis of our ordinary conception of things.

4. An inherited concern with religious issues was central to James's thought throughout his life. *The Varieties of Religious Experience* (1902) studies the phenomena of mysticism and religious experience with a view to an eventual empirical assessment of their validity, a concern which also led to James's substantial involvement in psychical research, while later works, such as *A Pluralist Universe* (1909), after sharply attacking the metaphysical monism of absolute idealists like Royce and Bradley, develop a mystical pluralistic metaphysics in which a 'finite God', or more interestingly a 'mother sea of consciousness', plays some of the roles of an infinite God or Absolute, while leaving us an independence we are refused by monism, and avoiding the apology for evil which it, along with orthodox theism, imposes. Death prevented the completion of a final working-out of his metaphysics, but *Some Problems of Philosophy* (1911), which particularly focuses on the nature of relations and continuity, taken with other works, sufficiently exhibits its main outlines.

5. In these later works James allied himself with Henri Bergson in arguing that conceptual thought cannot do proper justice to reality. This arises largely from the fact that concepts can only provide a static picture of a world which is essentially dynamic. (It was partly by exploiting this, he argued, that absolute idealists promoted their specious claim that the familiar world of contingency and change is somehow unreal, and that Reality proper consists in a static Absolute.) This is all right so long as that static picture is used to guide our dynamic dealings with things, but it leads to trouble when we expect it to provide a real grasp of the nature of its object. James's treatment of the limitations of conceptual thought is related to his pragmatic conception of truth in a somewhat curious manner. Truth, he argued, as a pragmatist, is no mere copy of reality in another conceptual or verbal medium. There would be little point in it if it

were, and we should regard the conceptual symbols in which it consists rather as tools for dealing with (and perhaps sometimes as a worthwhile addition to) reality than as revelations of its essence. None the less, James did hanker for something which could provide a sense of the real essence of things and, since concepts and truth were precluded from this role, it had to be sought in a metaphysics which turns us towards reality in some more intimate way than they do. And here the standard logic by which we organize our concepts is more an obstacle than an aid. We should not look for a revelation of reality from what are merely tools for dealing with it but must do so by sinking ourselves perceptually in the flux and be prepared to give an account of a world in process which will capture something of its essence even if conceptually it contains some apparent contradictions. The specific upshot of these reflections is, in effect, a process philosophy, incorporating an 'epochal' view of time, not unlike that later developed by Whitehead and Hartshorne (who, however, aimed to put into satisfactory concepts what James thought could not be adequately conceptualized).

GOTTLOB FREGE (1848–1925)

ANTHONY KENNY

THE founder of modern mathematical logic. As a logician and philosopher of logic he ranks with Aristotle; as a philosopher of mathematics he has had no peer throughout the history of the subject. After taking his doctorate in philosophy at Göttingen, he taught at the University of Jena from 1874 until his retirement in 1918; apart from his intellectual activity his life was uneventful and secluded. His work was little read in his lifetime, and for a long time his influence in philosophy was exercised mainly through the writings of others.

Frege had an influence on analytic philosophy through Russell and on continental philosophy through Husserl. He is often thought of as a philosophers' philosopher, but it was his genius that made possible the work of writers who have caught the attention of the general public, such as Wittgenstein and Chomsky; and his invention of mathematical logic was one of the major contributions to the developments in many disciplines which resulted in the invention of computers.

Frege's productive career began in 1879 with the publication of a pamphlet with the title *Begriffsschrift*, which we can render into English as 'Concept Script'. The pamphlet marked an epoch in the history of logic, for within some hundred pages it set forth a new calculus which has a permanent place at the heart of modern logic. The concept script which gave the book its title was a new symbolism designed to bring out with clarity logical relationships which were concealed in ordinary language.

For generations now the curriculum in formal logic has begun with the study of the propositional calculus. This is the branch of logic that deals with those inferences which depend on the force of negation, conjunction, disjunction, etc. when applied to sentences as wholes. Its fundamental principle is to treat the truth-value (i.e. the truth or falsehood) of sentences which contain connectives such as 'and', 'if', 'or' as being determined solely by the truth-values of the component sentences which are linked by the connectives. Frege's *Begriffsschrift* contains the first systematic formulation of the propositional calculus; it is presented in an axiomatic manner in which all laws of logic are derived, by specified rules of inference, from a number of primitive principles. Frege's symbolism, though elegant, is difficult to print, and is no longer used; but the operations which it expresses continue to be fundamental in mathematical logic.

Frege's greatest contribution to logic was his invention of quantification theory: a method of symbolizing and rigorously displaying those inferences that depend for their validity on expressions such as 'all' or 'some', 'any' or 'every', 'no' or 'none'. Using a novel notation for quantification, he presented a first-order predicate calculus which laid the basis for all recent developments in logic and formalized the theory of inference in a way more rigorous and more general than the traditional Aristotelian syllogistic which up to the time of Kant was looked on as the be-all and end-all of logic. After Frege, for the first time, formal logic could handle arguments which involved sentences with multiple quantification, such as 'Nobody knows everybody' and 'Any schoolchild can master any language'.

In the course of his work Frege developed other branches of logic, including second-order predicate calculus and a version of naïve set theory. He did not explore the areas of logic known as modal logic (that part of logic that deals with necessity, possibility, and kindred notions) or tense logic (the logic of temporal or significantly tensed statements). These branches of logic had been studied in the Middle Ages, and have been studied again in the present century in the light of his innovations.

In the *Begriffsschrift* and its sequels Frege was not interested in logic for its own sake. His motive in constructing the new concept script was to assist him in the philosophy of mathematics. (It was his predominantly mathematical agenda which made him comparatively uninterested in the branches of logic which concern inferences about the transient and the changing.) The question which above all he wanted to answer was this: Do proofs in arithmetic rest on pure logic, being based solely upon general laws operative in every sphere of knowledge, or do they need support from empirical facts? To answer this question, Frege set himself the task of seeing 'how far one could get in arithmetic by means of logical deductions alone, supported only by the laws of thought'.

Not only did Frege show how to conduct logic in a mathematical manner: he believed that arithmetic itself could be shown to be a branch of logic in the sense that it could be formalized without the use of any nonlogical notions or axioms. It was in the *Grundlagen der Arithmetik* (1884) that Frege first set out to establish this thesis, which is known by the name of 'logicism'.

The *Grundlagen* begins with an attack on the ideas of Frege's predecessors and contemporaries (including Kant and J. S. Mill) on the nature of numbers and of mathematical truth. Kant had maintained that the truths of mathematics were synthetic a priori, and that our knowledge of them depended on intuition. Mill, on the contrary, saw mathematical truths as a posteriori, empirical generalizations widely applicable and widely confirmed. Frege maintained that the truths of arithmetic were not synthetic at all, neither a priori nor a posteriori. Unlike geometry—which, he agreed with Kant, rested on a priori intuition—arithmetic was analytic, that is to say, it could be defined in purely logical terms and proved from purely logical principles.

The arithmetical notion of number in Frege's system is replaced by the logical notion of 'class': the cardinal numbers can be defined as classes of classes with the same number of members; thus the number two is the class of pairs, and the number three the class of trios. Despite appearances, this definition is not circular, because we can say what is meant by two classes having the same number of members without making use of the notion of number: thus, for instance, a waiter may know that there are as many knives as there are plates on a table without knowing how many of each there are, if he observes that there is just one knife to the right of each plate. Two classes have the same number of members if they can be mapped one-to-one on to each other. We can define the number zero in purely logical terms as the class of all classes with the same number of members as the class of objects which are not identical with themselves.

In order to pass from a definition of zero to the definition of the other natural numbers, Frege has to define the notion of 'successor' in the sense in which the natural numbers succeed each other in the number series. He defines '*n* immediately succeeds *m*' as 'There exists a concept *F*, and an object falling under it *x*, such that the number of *F*s is *n*, and the number of *F*s not identical with *x* is *m*'. With the aid of this definition the other numbers (one, which is the successor of zero, two, which is the successor of one, and so on) can, like zero, be defined without using any notions other than logical ones such as identity, class, and class-equivalence.

In the *Grundlagen* there are two theses to which Frege attaches great importance. One is that each individual number is a self-subsistent object; the other is that the content of a statement assigning a number is an assertion about a concept. At first sight these theses may seem to conflict, but if we understand what Frege meant by 'concept' and 'object' we see that they are complementary. In saying that a number is an object, Frege is not suggesting that a number is something tangible like a tree or a table; rather, he is denying that number is a property belonging to anything, whether an individual or a collection; he is also denying that it is anything subjective, any mental item or any property of a mental item. Concepts are, for Frege, mind-independent, and so there is no contradiction between the thesis that numbers are objective, and the thesis that number-statements are statements about concepts.

Frege illustrates this latter thesis with two examples. 'If I say "Venus has 0 moons", there simply does not exist any moon or agglomeration of moons for anything to be asserted of; but what happens is that a property is assigned to the *concept* "moon of Venus", namely that of including nothing under it. If I say "the King's carriage is drawn by four horses", then I assign the number four to the concept "horse that draws the King's carriage".'

But if number-statements of this kind are statements about concepts, what kind of object is a number itself? Frege's answer is that a number is the extension of a concept. The number which belongs to the concept *F*, he says, is the extension of the concept 'like-numbered to the concept *F*'. This is equivalent to saying that it is the class of all classes which have the same number of members as the class of *F*s, as was explained above. So Frege's theory that numbers are objects depends on the possibility of taking classes as objects.

It will be seen that Frege's philosophy of mathematics is closely linked to his understanding of several key terms of logic and of philosophy; and indeed in the *Begriffsschrift* and the *Grundlagen* Frege not only founded modern logic, but also founded the modern philosophical discipline of philosophy of logic. He did so by making a sharp distinction between the philosophical treatment of logic and, on the one hand, psychology (with which it had often been confused by philosophers in the empiricist tradition) and, on the other hand, epistemology (with which it was sometimes conflated by philosophers in the Cartesian tradition). In this he was in line with a yet older tradition originating with Aristotle's *De interpretatione*: but in the *Begriffsschrift* and the *Grundlagen* he investigates such notions as *name*, *sentence*, *predicate* with a scope and subtlety greater than Aristotle's.

One of Frege's most fertile devices was the application of the mathematical notions of *function* and *argument* to replace the analysis of sentences in ordinary language in terms of subject and predicate. Consider a sentence such as 'William defeated Harold'—a laconic description, perhaps, of the battle of Hastings. Traditional grammar will say that 'William' is the subject, and 'defeated Harold' the predicate. To say—as Frege did—that we should look on 'William' as an argument, and 'defeated Harold' as a function, may at first look as if it is simply an alternative terminology—and indeed, for much of his life, Frege was willing to call an expression such as 'defeated Harold' a predicate. But to treat a predicate as a function involves a profound change in the understanding of the construction of sentences.

To see this, suppose that we take the sentence 'William defeated Harold' and put into it, in place of the word 'Harold', the word 'Canute'. Clearly this alters the sense of the sentence, and indeed it turns it from a true one into a false one. We can think of the sentence as in this way consisting of a constant component 'William defeated' and a symbol 'Harold' replaceable by other similar symbols— names naming other people, in the way that 'Harold' names Harold. If we think of a sentence in this way, Frege will call the first component a function, and the second its argument: he is making an extension of the mathematical terminology in accordance with which 6 is the value of the function $x \times 3$ for the argument 2, and 9 is the value of the same function for the argument 3. The sentence 'William defeated Harold' is the result of completing the expression 'William defeated' with the name 'Harold', and the sentence 'William defeated Canute' is the result of completing the same expression with the name 'Canute'. That is to say, in the terminology of *Begriffsschrift*, 'William defeated Harold' is the value of the function 'William defeated' for the argument 'Harold', and 'William defeated Canute' is the value of the same function for the argument 'Canute'.

The sentence 'William defeated Harold' is, of course, also the value of the function 'defeated Harold' for the argument 'William'. In the same way, 6 is not only the value of the function $x \times 3$ for the argument 2, but also the value of the function $2 \times x$ for the argument 3. Every sentence, for Frege, can be analysed into argument and function in at least one way, but many can be analysed in more than one way.

Corresponding to the distinction in language between functions of this kind and their arguments, Frege maintained, a systematic distinction must be made between concepts and objects, which are their ontological counterparts. Objects are what proper names stand for: they are of many kinds, ranging from human beings to numbers. Concepts are items which have a fundamental incompleteness, corresponding to the gappiness of a predicate as understood by Frege (i.e. a sentence with a proper name removed from it). Where other philosophers talk ambiguously of the *meaning* of an expression, Frege introduced a distinction between the *reference* of an expression (the object to which it refers, as the planet Venus is the reference of 'the Morning Star') and the *sense* of an expression. ('The Evening Star' differs in sense from 'the Morning Star' though it too, as astronomers discovered, refers to Venus.)

These theories of philosophical logic were worked out by Frege in a series of articles in the early 1890s: 'Funktion und Begriff' (Function and Concept, 1891), 'Begriff und Gegenstand' (Concept and Object, 1892), 'Sinn und Bedeutung' (Sense and Reference, 1892). The most controversial application of Frege's distinction between sense and reference was his theory that the reference of a sentence was its truth-value (i.e. the True, or the False), and the connected theses that in a scientifically respectable language every term must have a reference and every sentence must be either true or false. These theses lead to many difficulties.

In the last years of his life, between 1918 and his death, Frege attempted to write a full treatise of philosophical logic. All that was completed was a series of articles (*Logische Untersuchungen*, 1919–23) in which he returns to the relationship between logic and philosophical psychology or philosophy of mind, and discusses the nature of thought and inference. His work in this area has been largely superseded by the later writings of Wittgenstein, a philosopher much influenced throughout his life, as he himself avowed, by Frege's agenda and Frege's structures of thought.

The climax of Frege's career as a philosopher should have been the publication of the two volumes of *Die Grundgesetze der Arithmetik* (1893–1903), in which he set out to present in formal manner the logicist construction of arithmetic on the basis of pure logic and set theory. This work was to execute the task which had been sketched in the earlier books on the philosophy of mathematics: it was to enunciate a set of axioms which would be recognizably truths of logic, to propound a set of undoubtedly sound rules of inference, and then to present, one by one, derivations by these rules from these axioms of the standard truths of arithmetic.

The magnificent project aborted before it was ever completed. The first volume was published in 1893; the second volume did not appear until 1903 and while it was in the press Frege received a letter from

Russell pointing out that the fifth of the initial axioms made the whole system inconsistent. This was the axiom which, in Frege's words, allowed 'the transition from a concept to its extension', the transition which was essential if it was to be established that numbers were logical objects. Frege's system, with this axiom, permitted the formation of the class of all classes that are not members of themselves. But the formation of such a class, Russell pointed out, leads to paradox: if it is a member of itself then it is not a member of itself; if it is not a member of itself, then it is a member of itself. A system which leads to such paradox cannot be logically sound.

With good reason, Frege was utterly downcast by this discovery, though he strove to patch his system by weakening the guilty axiom. We now know that his logicist programme cannot ever be successfully carried out. The path from the axioms of logic to the theorems of arithmetic is barred at two points. First, as Russell's paradox showed, the naïve set theory which was part of Frege's logical basis was inconsistent in itself, and the remedies which Frege proposed for this proved ineffective. Thus, the axioms of arithmetic cannot be derived from purely logical axioms in the way he hoped. Secondly, the notion of 'axioms of arithmetic' was itself later called in question when Gödel showed that it was impossible to give arithmetic a complete and consistent axiomatization. None the less, the concepts and insights developed by Frege in the course of expounding his logicist thesis have a permanent interest which is unimpaired by the defeat of that programme at the hands of Russell and Gödel.

Wittgenstein once described to Geach his final meeting with Frege. 'The last time I saw Frege, as we were waiting at the station for my train, I said to him "Don't you ever find *any* difficulty in your theory that numbers are objects?" He replied "Sometimes I *seem* to see a difficulty—but then again I *don't* see it." '

EDMUND
HUSSERL (1859–1938)

M. J. INWOOD

GERMAN philosopher who was the founder, and a skilful practitioner, of phenomenology. His early works, *On the Concept of Number* (1887) and *Philosophy of Arithmetic* (1891), were marked by psychologism, the attempt to base logic and arithmetic on psychology. The concept of plurality, for example, was explained in terms of our mental act of combining different contents of consciousness into one representation, of, for example, seeing distinct people as a single group. Influenced in part by Frege's criticism, Husserl abandoned this view, and in his *Logical Investigations* (1900–1; tr. London, 1970) argued that logic is not reducible to psychology. For example, the statement:

(1) If all men are mortal and all Greeks are men, then all Greeks are mortal

neither entails nor is entailed by:

(2) Anyone who believes that all men are mortal and that all Greeks are men also believes that all Greeks are mortal

or:

(3) No one who believes that all men are mortal and that all Greeks are men believes that not all Greeks are mortal.

(Nor is (1) equivalent to a rule of correct thinking:

(4) Anyone who believes that all men are mortal and that all Greeks are men ought to believe that all Greeks are mortal.

We could argue, with equal justification, that an empirical statement, e.g. 'The earth is not flat', amounts to a rule, 'No one ought to believe that the earth is flat'.) If (1) were equivalent to (2) or (3), (1) would be at most probable and would presuppose the existence of mental phenomena. The claim is also viciously circular in that any attempt to derive (1) from (2) or (3), or, more generally, to derive logic from psychology, must presuppose some rule of logic. (Parallel objections can be raised to the claim that the truth of (1) depends on the meanings of the words used to express it or on 'rules of language', if these are interpreted as empirical generalizations about natural languages.)

We need to distinguish between, on the one hand, what is meant or intended, the objects *of* consciousness, and, on the other, our psychical acts or experiences, our consciousness of such objects. (The idea of an 'intended' object stems from medieval philosophy by way of Brentano.) Logic deals with what is meant, not with our acts of meaning it. The objects of consciousness appear to us, are 'phenomena', while our psychical acts are merely experienced. (We may in turn reflect on psychical acts and thus convert them into phenomena. They are then no longer real, experienced acts, but the objects of further acts.) Psychical acts, like any other real entity, must be individual entities; but what is meant is an ideal entity and may be universal. If, for example, I am thinking about love, my thinking is a particular act distinct from other acts of thinking; but the love that I think about may be no particular love, simply love in general. Intended objects are thus 'essences', and it is essences and their interrelations that logic describes. Heidegger (like Adorno) was puzzled by the apparent revival of psychologism in the second volume of the *Logical Investigations*: 'But if such a gross error cannot be attributed to Husserl's work, then what is the phenomenological description of the acts of consciousness? Wherein does what is peculiar to phenomenology consist if it is neither logic nor psychology?'

Husserl published little for some years after the *Logical Investigations*, but continued to develop his ideas in lectures. For example, in his 1905 *Lectures on the Phenomenology of Internal Time-Consciousness* (edited for publication by Heidegger in 1928; tr. The Hague, 1964), he wrestled with a problem that had exercised St Augustine and William James: How can I experience a temporally extended object *as such*? Suppose that I am listening to a tune consisting of a succession of notes, 1, 2, 3, 4, . . ., each of which occurs at a certain time, $t_1, t_2, t_3, t_4, \ldots$. If at any given time, t_n, I hear only the note that occurs at that time, n, and have no awareness of the notes that occur before and after t_n, then at no time am I conscious of a temporally extended tune, but only of the note that is occurring *now*. (I am not strictly aware even of the occurrence of the note *now*, since the awareness of the present *as such* implies some awareness of before and after.) If, on the other hand, at t_n I hear with equal force all the earlier notes, then again I hear not an enduring tune, but a deafening cacophony. The basis of Husserl's solution is this: At any given time, say t_9, I have a 'primal impression' of the note that is occurring now, note 9. I do not now have a primal impression of note 8, but I 'retain' it, that is I am aware of it as just past. When note 10 occurs, I am aware of 9 as just past and of 8 as further past. As the tune proceeds, note 8 recedes further into the past and 'appears' in ever-changing 'retentional modifications'. Thus I retain not only the individual notes of the tune, but the order in which they occurred. Similarly, at any given point in the tune I 'protain' its future course. If I have not heard the tune before, my protention is less determinate than my retention, but following a tune involves an expectation that its future course will lie within certain limits. (If I were to end this article with the words 'And that concludes my account of the Pyramids', the reader's surprise would indicate *both* that on reading this sentence, he retained (his reading of) earlier sentences *and* that while reading earlier sentences he protained, more or less roughly, the future course of the article.) Ordinary, or 'secondary', memory presupposes, but is distinct from, retention, or 'primary' memory. If I am trying to remember an earlier phase of a tune, this impairs my appreciation of its present phase; retention of earlier phases is, by contrast, essential to my appreciation of the present phase. Expectation similarly presupposes, but is distinct from, protention. Husserl does not (as the example of a tune consisting of notes may suggest) regard time as atomized into a series of discrete instants, or periods: our time-consciousness is a 'continuous flux'.

In his next major work, *Ideas: General Introduction to Pure Phenomenology* (1913; tr. London, 1931), Husserl introduces a range of technical vocabulary. The act of consciousness, for example, is *noēsis*, while its intended object is the *noēma*. Logic and pure mathematics rests on the intuition of essences (*Wesensschau*) or *eidē*, and 'phenomenology' is the descriptive analysis of essences in general. Not only objects, such as an object of sense-perception, can be analysed in this way, but also acts of consciousness. But the acts must then be 'reduced' to an essence or *eidos* (the 'eidetic reduction'). The phenomenologist is not concerned, for example, with particular acts of sense-perception, but with the essential features common to all such acts. Moral and aesthetic values, and desires and emotions, are also open to phenomenological investigation.

The phenomenologist must, on Husserl's view, perform an *epochē*, that is, suspend judgement, with regard to the existence of objects of consciousness. In analysing, for example, the essence of perceived objects, we must not assume that such objects as trees and tables exist and causally engage with our sense-organs, but focus exclusively on the essential structure of perceptual consciousness. We must suspend, or 'bracket', the 'natural attitude' to the world. The reason for this is that Husserl, like Descartes, advocated 'philosophy as rigorous science' (the title of an article of 1911), philosophy as the indubitable basis of our dubitable, if for the most part correct, beliefs about the empirical world.

But Husserl disagreed with Descartes in one crucial respect. Descartes moved swiftly from the proposition that 'I think' to the conclusion that I am a 'thinking thing'. The belief that I am a thinking thing is itself, Husserl claims, to be bracketed. I, who am conscious of objects, am neither a thinking substance, nor an embodied person, nor even the stream of my experiences—for I am conscious of, and in that sense distinct from, my experiences; I am the pure or transcendental ego, what Kant called the 'I think' which 'must be able to accompany all my representations'. The transcendental ego or 'transcendental subjectivity' cannot itself be bracketed, any more than Cartesian doubt can extend to the existence of the doubter. Thus only transcendental subjectivity is 'non-relative . . . while the real world indeed exists, but in respect of essence is relative to transcendental subjectivity, in such a way that it can have its meaning as existing reality only as the intentional meaning-product of transcendental subjectivity'. Husserl here infers an idealist conclusion, namely that objects are constituted by consciousness and could not exist without it, from the the true premiss that nothing can be conceived without being an object of consciousness. The error depends on either or both of two confusions: (1) between an intentional and a real object—in conceiving an object, I make it an object of my consciousness, but I do not thereby make it a real object, e.g. a tree; (2) between making something my intentional object by conceiving it and conceiving it *as* my intentional object— I cannot think of a possible lifeless universe without making it the object of my thought, but I do not thereby think of it *as* an object of my thought and thus suppose myself to be one of its inhabitants. (It is a mistake to suppose that Husserl's idealism can only be avoided if we reject the methodological use of *epochē*.) In his *Cartesian Meditations* (1931; tr. The Hague, 1960) Husserl tried to relieve phenomenology of the charge that it entails solipsism by explaining how one transcendental ego can experience another transcendental ego on a par with itself.

From the *Ideas* to the *Cartesian Meditations*, Husserl's enterprise is avowedly akin to Descartes's *Meditations* and, unavowedly, to Fichte's

Wisenschaftslehre. But his last great (unfinished) work, *The Crisis of European Sciences and Transcendental Phenomenology* (1936; tr. 1954) is closer to Hegel's *Phenomenology of Spirit*. For it purports to show, 'by way of a teleological–historical reflection on the origins of our critical scientific and philosophical situation, the inescapable necessity of a transcendental–phenomenological reorientation of philosophy'. This is at odds with his earlier approach in at least two respects: (1) a historical or causal account of the genesis of our consciousness was excluded or 'bracketed' in his earlier works; (2) in so far as Husserl is now concerned not so much with particular past events, as with the *eidos* of history, with the essential historicity of consciousness, its burden of preconceptions derived from the traditions of its social milieu, this casts doubt on his own attempt to found a rigorous science, free of all preconceptions, that goes directly 'to the things themselves'. In part 3 of the *Crisis*, and in other papers intended for incorporation in it (such as 'The Origin of Geometry') he develops the concept of the 'life-world' (*Lebenswelt*), the intersubjective world of our natural, pre-theoretical experience and activity, which, he believes, was neglected by philosophers such as Kant in favour of the world of theoretical science. But the 'theoretical attitude' (exemplified, for Husserl, by Galileo) arose historically, in ancient Greece, against the background of the life-world, and the life-world *essentially* persists even after the development of the theoretical 'spirit'. Even the physicist thinks of the sun as rising and setting, and as marking the phases of his practical life. Husserl's account of the life-world, of its essential priority to theory, and of the emergence of theory from it, owes something to the eidetic method and to *epochē*: to describe the *essential* structures of the life-world involves suspending our scientific presuppositions and our practical engagement with the life-world. Nevertheless, some philosophers, notably Merleau-Ponty, see the *Crisis* as a distinct departure from Husserl's earlier work.

Husserl has had an immense influence in continental Europe. Phenomenological analysis has been applied to psychology (Pfander), law (Reinach), values, aesthetics, and religion (Scheler). Even philosophers who reject Husserl's theoretical doctrines have benefited from his meticulous analyses of particular phenomena. But thinkers such as Heidegger, Sartre, and Merleau-Ponty have used phenomenology in the service of philosophical positions quite different from Husserl's own, and his hope that his rigorous science would put an end to radical philosophical disagreements has remained unfulfilled.

BERTRAND RUSSELL (1872–1970)

MARK SAINSBURY

T HIRD Earl Russell, British philosopher, mathematician, Nobel
Prize-winner (Literature, 1950), civil-rights activist, and public
figure. His most important philosophical works date from the first two
decades of the century, and include the magisterial *Principia Mathematica*
(1910–13), written jointly with Alfred North Whitehead. In the period
between the world wars, he came to public notice through some influential books about morals and mores, which he claimed were written for
money. After the Second World War, he was a prominent member of the
Campaign for Nuclear Disarmament (and was arrested for participating
in one of their protest demonstrations), and helped initiate the Pugwash
conferences, international gatherings of distinguished intellectuals,
mainly scientists, devoted to discussing ways to achieve and maintain
world peace. His *Autobiography* caused a stir by its selective frankness,
and by the rather unattractive picture it conveyed of the great man's
tardy yet intense emotional development.

Russell was a marvellously wide-ranging philosopher, and it is hard to
think of an area of philosophy to which he did not contribute. His best-
known philosophical work, the *History of Western Philosophy*, exemplifies
this breadth of interest and understanding, and shows that no two areas
of philosophy can be guaranteed to be mutually irrelevant.

His own work can be presented under three headings: first, philosophical logic, not so much an area of philosophy as a method which influenced most of his work; second, the foundations of mathematics; third,
epistemology and metaphysics. His interest in mathematics is one of his
earliest, and his main idea, which came to him towards the end of the last
century and was first presented in *Principles of Mathematics* (1903), was
that mathematics is simply logic. Developing this line of thought led
him to fundamental questions in logic, and to the approach he was to

call 'philosophical logic', which came to colour most of his work in philosophy.

Philosophical Logic

A good route to philosophical fame is to found a method, for then even philosophers who disagree entirely with one's results may honour one's name by working within the method. Around 1914 Russell invented the phrase 'philosophical logic' to describe the approach to philosophy which he had already been employing for some years: recasting problematic propositions in their 'logical form', using a language with the formal structure of *Principia Mathematica*. His motivations were various, and not very clearly articulated. He felt that ordinary language enshrines the 'savage superstitions of cannibals' ('Mind and Matter', 143) and other errors, confusions, and vagueness, and makes it impossible to give correct expression to some fundamental philosophical truths. For example, it confuses, in the word 'is', existential quantification (as in 'Serendipity *is*', to be formalized using '∃'), identity (as in 'Hesperus *is* Phosphorus', to be formalized using '='), and predication (as in 'Socrates *is* human', whose 'is' vanishes into the concatenation of the predicate for humanity and the name of Socrates in the formalization 'Fa'); and ordinary language wrongly encourages the view, which Russell urged was nonsensical, that existence is a property of individuals. An example of the way ordinary language embodies cannibalistic superstitions is that expressions like 'Socrates' incline us to think of people and other things as simple metaphysical substances, when they are really complexes.

The best-known application of Russell's philosophical logic is to the problem of denoting phrases. The result is a general account of quantification, including the 'theory of descriptions' presented, in a rather clumsy form, in the famous article 'On Denoting' (1905). The problem is how to understand such phrases as 'a man', 'every man', 'no man', and 'the man'. In his *Principles of Mathematics* (1903), Russell assumed that they should be viewed in the same way as he then thought names like 'Socrates' and predicates like 'red' should be: as standing for some entity in the world. However, it is impossible to discover an appropriate entity, and the 1903 work clearly does not succeed in doing so. The 1905 theory is that these phrases should not be regarded as having any theoretical unity. They contain a quantifier, 'some', 'every', 'no', and, on Russell's view, a quantifier attaches to a 'propositional function', like '. . . is happy' to make a sentence (e.g. 'Someone is happy'). A quantifier attached to a predicate like 'man' (as opposed to a propositional function) in the phrase 'some man' is not an intelligible unit of language: it is essentially 'incomplete' and 'has no meaning in isolation'. A sentence like 'I met a man' is analysed as follows: 'There is some x such that x is human and I met x'. The analysis shows that what corresponds to 'a' has become 'there is some x such that' and it attaches to the propositional function 'x is human and I met x'. In the analysis there is no unit corresponding to 'a man'.

To feel the full impact of Russell's work on quantification, one must recall his background assumption that the fundamental way in which a word has meaning is by standing for something. Russell held to this model for many words, simple singular and general terms, like 'this' and 'red', and it led him to a corresponding view of the world: the basic constituents, the logical atoms, are the things corresponding to such words. Quantifiers, and, if Russell is right, phrases like 'the King of France', function very differently, not standing for anything in the way that the basic words do.

The logic Russell brought to bear in his philosophical logic included the apparatus of classes, originally developed in his philosophy of mathematics, and he used this to provide logical forms within which to analyse various empirical things, like material bodies. (See the section below, 'Epistemology and Metaphysics'.)

The method of philosophical logic, though it has been of great significance in the twentieth century, is now, I suspect, on the wane. Russell himself took an impish and aristocratic delight in claiming that logical forms are very different from surface forms, and that the untrained cannot be expected to appreciate the real complexity of their thoughts. More recently, concern with providing explanations of how the mind actually works has made many philosophers think that one should focus closely on the detailed workings of natural language, rather than treating it as the confused manifestation of some more orderly underlying language of logical forms.

Mathematics

Russell's logicism in the philosophy of mathematics involves two theses: (1) Mathematical truths can be *translated* into truths of pure logic; thus mathematics has no distinctive subject-matter (e.g. numbers). (2) Mathematical truths, once presented in their proper logical form, can be *proved* by logic alone. The first claim concerns the sort of meaning mathematical statements have; the second concerns how they can be established.

The key idea behind the translation is that a number can be treated as a class of classes, and operations on numbers can be regarded as class-theoretic ones, definable in terms of intersection, union, difference, and so on. Thus the number one can be thought of as the class of all one-membered classes, the number two as the class of all two-membered classes, and so on. In these stipulations, number-words like 'one' and 'two' figure as adjectives, and such occurrences can be treated within pure logic by means of quantification and identity. (Thus 'There are two dogs' means 'Something, x, is a dog, and something, y, is a dog, and x is distinct from y, and nothing distinct from either x or y is a dog'.) The addition of one and two (to take an example) is thought of as the class of classes each of which is the union of a member of one with a member of two (cases in which the member of one has a member in common with the member of two to be ignored): in other words, the class of three-membered classes.

The translation assumes that logic includes the theory of classes. In general, this can be disputed; and the dispute gained special prominence from the fact, to which Russell drew attention close to the turn of the century, that the theory of classes, at least as it was understood at that time, is inconsistent. This made it unsuitable for any serious purpose, and, *a fortiori*, unsuitable for serving as a foundation in logic or mathematics.

The inconsistency arises upon the intuitively correct supposition (called, in formal dress, the comprehension axiom) that every coherent condition determines a class. Thus it seems right to say that the condition *being a man* determines the class of men, *not being a man* determines the class of non-men, *being round and square* determines the class of things which are round and square, that is, the class with no members (the empty class). On this supposition, there should be a class, R, satisfying the condition *not being a member of itself*, a class, that is, consisting of just those things, including classes, which are not members of themselves. Is R a member of itself? If it is, then it meets the condition *not being a member of itself*, and so it is not a member of itself; if it is not, then, because it meets this condition, it is a member of itself. So there is no such thing as R; the problem is how to reconcile this with the intuition underlying the comprehension axiom, an intuition apparently forcing us to accept that there is such a class as R.

After exploring many other roads in the early years of the century, Russell finally (1908) arrived at the view that classes are entirely dispensable: the 'no-class' theory of classes, as he called it. The idea is that although his theory has expressions which seem to stand for classes, they do not really. This is not, in itself, enough to ensure that the kind of para-dox illustrated by the Russell class will not arise, for a similar paradox can be formulated without mentioning classes (e.g. on the basis of the prop-erty of not being self-applicable). However, the no-class theory of classes enabled Russell to bypass the intuition underlying the comprehension axiom. In his theory of types, things like 'x is a man', which he called 'propositional functions', cannot be applied to themselves. The ground-ing intuition was that self-application involves a kind of 'vicious circle', and so can justifiably be banned, with the result that the old paradoxes could not be formulated.

In 1931 Gödel published a proof that no consistent theory like Russell's in *Principia Mathematica* (one whose axioms are recursively enumerable) has every mathematical truth as a theorem. This seems to have made Russell think that his logicism had failed. In reality, however, only one component fails, the claim that every mathematical truth can be proved by logical means. It remains open whether every mathematical truth can be expressed in purely logical terms, and whether, thus expressed, it con-stitutes a truth of logic; for perhaps not every logical truth is provable.

Epistemology and Metaphysics

Russell's most important position in this area is his logical atomism, best elaborated in his lectures of that title (1918). The basic idea is that the world is composed of things like little patches of colour, their properties, and the (atomic) facts they compose. His approach is guided by the following considerations: (1) We can non-inferentially know only what is proof against Descartes's demon. (2) A view about the nature of things which vindicates our intuition that we know the things is to be preferred to one which does not. (3) Logical constructions are to be substituted for inferred entities.

The problem of 'knowledge of the external world' presented itself to him in an entirely traditional way: 'I think on the whole the sort of method adopted by Descartes is right: that you should set to work to doubt things and retain only what you cannot doubt because of its clear-ness and distinctness' ('Lectures', 182). This led him to the view that enduring material objects like mountains, thought of in the ordinary way as 'substances', could not be 'retained': no adequate account of how we know about such things, thus regarded, could be provided. The first two guiding considerations thus led him to favour an alternative view of the nature of mountains, one upon which we can account for our apparent knowledge of them, and this is supplied by applying the third consideration: they are to be thought of as logical constructions out of non-inferentially known entities; more specifically, as classes whose only individuals are 'sensibilia', things which, like sense-data, can be known in an immediate and demon-proof way.

It is open to dispute whether this view of mountains gives a better explanation of how we have knowledge about them than the ordinary view. A mountain is construed as a very large class of sensibilia, and no one subject's experience contains them all. Thus no subject can know any proposition of the form 'This mountain is thus-and-so' merely by knowing what sense-data he has. New principles of knowledge are involved, and these principles are no more plausible when they involve extrapolation to the existence of sensibilia with which one will never be acquainted than when they involve extrapolation to material continuants which will never themselves be directly accessible to experience.

Logical atomism involves not only an account of all individuals in terms of the atomic ones, but also an account of all facts in terms of atomic ones. An atomic fact consists of a universal combined with an appropriate number of individuals. The contrast is with a molecular fact, which is expressed by means of such logical expressions as 'and' and 'not'. Russell wanted to believe that at bottom there are only atomic facts: once these are fixed, everything is fixed. Hence there is no *sui generis* fact that '*p* or *q*', since this obtains in virtue of the existence of the fact that *p* or the existence of the fact that *q*. However, Russell argued that general facts, though not atomic, have to be added. Suppose that there are just three cats, c_1, c_2, c_3, and that each is hungry. This does not guarantee that there is such a fact as that all cats are hungry. To guarantee this general fact we have to add to the fact that c_1 is hungry and the fact that c_2 is hungry and the fact that c_3 is hungry the fact that c_1, c_2, and c_3 are all the cats there are, and this is itself a general fact. Russell was also worried that one might have to add negative facts. The fact that Socrates is not alive is guaranteed by the fact that he is dead, and perhaps this is atomic. To generalize this we would have to say something like: the existence of any negative fact is guaranteed by the existence of some incompatible fact, but 'this makes incompatibility fundamental and an objective fact, which is not so very much simpler than allowing negative facts'. However, Russell's reasoning at this point is confused. Russell is happy to use disjunction when explaining what makes disjunctions true, so he should find it legitimate to use negation, or incompatibility, when explaining what makes negations true. The original aim was not to provide an explanation of the meaning of the logical constants, but to expose certain metaphysical relations.

Russell's logical atomism, in particular the technique of logical construction, is in some ways similar to phenomenalism, except that he did not take the atoms (sensibilia) to be mental. At other points in his development, he adopted different views. Thus in *The Problems of Philosophy*, and again in *The Analysis of Matter*, he tries to identify a kind of knowledge (merely structural) of physical continuants which could be acquired even if they are metaphysically very different from the things of which we can have non-inferential knowledge. He laid down the basic postulate that experiences are caused by something other than experiences—call the causes material events. Implicitly assuming some principle of like cause, like effect, he says that one can infer that properties of or relations among experiences mirror properties of or relations among material events. Material continuants are constructed out of material events. The upshot is that we know the structure of matter, but not its intrinsic nature. The strategy leaves room for scepticism about the real nature of material continuants, but is supposed to capture enough for an interpretation of science upon which most scientific beliefs are true.

Yet another approach is provided in *Human Knowledge: Its Scope and Limits* (1948). Here he argues that the alternative approaches do not do justice to all our cognitive capacities. Unless we have a priori knowledge of certain substantive contingent facts, which he called 'postulates of scientific inference', then 'science is moonshine' (p. 524). One postulate is: 'Given any event *A*, it happens very frequently that, at any neighbouring time, there is at some neighbouring place an event very similar to *A*' (p. 506). Russell implies that we do indeed have a priori knowledge of such facts, of a kind which he explains in terms of 'animal expectation'. This kind of knowledge is available to non-language-users and is arguably non-propositional. This is a cognitive faculty often ignored in attempts to show how scepticism can be avoided. In this late work, Russell shows signs of breaking out of the Cartesian problematic in favour of naturalizing epistemology.

The most influential themes in Russell's work have proved those relating to meaning and quantification. It is hard to imagine any new work in this area not confronting Russell's idea that basic words have meaning by standing for a corresponding entity, and that quantifiers and quantifier phrases function quite differently.

Mark Sainsbury 223

LUDWIG
WITTGENSTEIN (1889–1951)

PETER HACKER

THE leading analytical philosopher of the twentieth century, whose two major works altered the course of the subject. Whether by agreement or by disagreement, whether through understanding or misunderstanding, his influence has moulded the evolution of philosophy from the 1920s.

Born in Vienna, Ludwig Josef Johann Wittgenstein studied engineering, first in Berlin, then in Manchester. Gravitating towards philosophy, he went to Cambridge in 1912 to work with Russell. He served in the Austrian army in the First World War, and while on active duty completed his first masterpiece (and only book published in his lifetime) the *Tractatus Logico-Philosophicus* (1921). From 1920 to 1926 he worked as a schoolteacher. The next two years were occupied with designing and building a mansion in Vienna for his sister. During this period he came into contact with the Vienna Circle, a group of philosophers much influenced by his early ideas, which, sometimes through misunderstanding, were the mainspring of their Logical Positivism. In 1929 he returned to philosophical work at Cambridge, where he spent the rest of his teaching life. Between 1929 and 1932 his ideas underwent dramatic change, which he consolidated over the next fifteen years. Reacting against his own early philosophy, he developed a quite different viewpoint. Initially communicated only through pupils, these ideas revolutionized philosophy in mid-century. They were given definitive expression in his second masterpiece, the *Philosophical Investigations* (1953), published two years after his death. Over subsequent decades, a further dozen unfinished books and four volumes of lecture notes taken by pupils were published.

Wittgenstein's greatest contributions to philosophy can be classified under five headings: philosophy of language, philosophy of logic, philosophical psychology, philosophy of mathematics, and the clarification of the nature and limits of philosophy itself. In each of these his views are revolutionary and virtually without precedent. On every subject he tackled, he eschewed received positions and rejected traditional alternatives, believing that where philosophy was caught between apparently unavoidable poles, e.g. realism and idealism, Cartesianism and behaviourism, Platonism and formalism, it was the common presuppositions of both that need to be rejected.

The *Tractatus* is a mere seventy-five pages long, written in sybilline, marmoreal sentences. It ranges over metaphysics, logic, and logical truth, the nature of representation in general and of propositional representation in particular, the status of mathematics and of scientific theory, solipsism and the self, ethics and the mystical.

According to the *Tractatus*, the world is the totality of facts, not things. The substance of all possible worlds consists of the totality of sempiternal simple objects (e.g. spatio-temporal points, unanalysable properties, and relations). The form of a simple object consists in its combinatorial possibilities with other objects. The possible concatenation of objects constitutes a state of affairs. The obtaining of a state of affairs is a fact. A representation of a state of affairs is a model or picture. It must possess the same logical multiplicity as, and be isomorphic with, what it represents. Propositions are logical pictures. They are essentially bipolar, i.e. capable of being true and also capable of being false. In this their nature reflects the nature of what they represent, since it is of the essence of a state of affairs that it either obtains or does not obtain. An elementary proposition depicts an (atomic) state of affairs. Its constituent names (unanalysable, logically simple names) go proxy for the objects in reality which are what they mean. The logico-syntactical form of a simple name must mirror the metaphysical form of the object that is its meaning. Hence the combinatorial possibilities of names mirror the combinatorial possibilities of objects. It is the fact that the names in a proposition are arranged as they are, in accord with the rules of logical syntax, that says that things are thus-and-so in reality. The sense of a proposition is a function of the meanings of its constituent names. Sense must be absolutely determinate; so any vagueness betokens analysability, and will disappear on analysis. The essence of the proposition is given by the general propositional form, which is: 'This is how things are', i.e. the general form of a description of how things stand in reality. A proposition is true if things in reality are as it depicts them as being.

The logical analysis of propositions must yield propositions which are logically independent of each other, i.e. elementary propositions whose truth depends only on the existence or non-existence of (atomic) states of affairs. Elementary propositions can be combined to form molecular propositions by means of truth-functional operators—the logical connectives. These, contrary to Frege and Russell, are not names of anything (logical objects, functions). They are merely truth-functional combinatorial devices, which generate truth-dependencies between propositions. All possible forms of truth-functional combination can be generated by the operation of joint-negation on a set of elementary propositions. All logical relations between propositions turn on the inner complexity (the truth-functional combination) of molecular propositions. The only (expressible) form of necessity is logical necessity. Two limiting cases of combination are senseless (not nonsense): tautologies, which are unconditionally true, and contradictions, which are unconditionally false. In an ideal notation their truth-value would be perspicuous from mere inspection of the symbolism. The necessary truths of logic are not, as Russell thought, descriptions of the most general features of the world; nor are they descriptions of relations between logical objects, as Frege thought. They are tautologies, molecular propositions which are so combined that bipolarity, and hence all content, cancels out; they all say the same thing, namely nothing. They are 'degenerate' propositions in the sense in which a point is a degenerate conic section. So the truths of logic are not a domain for pure reason alone to attain knowledge about reality, since to know a tautology is to know nothing.

Metaphysical utterances, by contrast, are nonsense—violations of the bounds of sense. For the apparent categorial concepts that occur in them, e.g. 'proposition', 'fact', 'object', 'colour', are not genuine concepts at all, but unbound variables that cannot occur in a well-formed proposition. But what one tries to say by means of the pseudo-propositions of metaphysics (e.g. that red is a colour) is *shown* by features (forms) of genuine propositions containing substitution-instances of these formal concepts (e.g. '*A* is red'). What is shown by a notation cannot be said. Truths of metaphysics are ineffable; and so too are truths of ethics, aesthetics, and religion.

Hence there are no philosophical propositions, i.e. propositions describing the essential natures of things or the metaphysical structure of the world. So the very propositions of the *Tractatus* itself are finally condemned as nonsense—attempts to say what can only be shown. The task of the *Tractatus* was to lead one to a correct logical point of view. Once that is achieved, one can throw away the ladder up which one has climbed. Philosophy is not a science; nor is it in competition with the sciences. It is not the accumulation of knowledge about a subject-matter. Its sole function is to monitor the bounds of sense, to elucidate philosophically problematic sentences, and to show that attempts to traverse the bounds of sense are futile.

The achievement of the *Tractatus* is manifold. (*a*) It brought to full fruition the atomist and foundationalist traditions, the conception of philosophy as analysis of hidden logical structures, the venerable quest for an ideal language or notation, the logico-metaphysical picture of language and logical form as a mirror of the logical structure of the world. Thenceforth these were ripe for demolition—a task that was carried out in the *Investigations*. (*b*) Its numerous criticisms of Frege and Russell were definitive. (*c*) The radical conception of philosophy it propounded initiated the so-called 'linguistic turn' characteristic of modern analytical philosophy, and paved the way for the similar, but immeasurably richer, conception of philosophy delineated in the *Investigations*. (*d*) Its elucidation of the nature of logical necessity and logical truth, though still to be modified and elaborated in the later *Remarks on the Foundations of Mathematics*, was its crowning achievement.

Although the *Philosophical Investigations* was meant to be seen against the backcloth of the *Tractatus*, it is the whole tradition of which the *Tractatus* was the culmination that is being criticized. The criticisms are often indirect, confronting not doctrines and theses, but the presuppositions that inform them.

In his philosophy of language, Wittgenstein now rejected the assumption that the meaning of a word is the thing it stands for. That involves a misuse of the word 'meaning'. There is no such thing as *the* name-relation, and it is confused to suppose that words are connected with reality by semantic links. That supposition rests on a misconstrual of ostensive definition. Not all words are or need to be sharply defined, analysable by specification of necessary and sufficient conditions of application. The demand for determinacy of sense was incoherent. Vagueness is not always a defect, and there is no absolute standard of exactness. The very ideal of analysis (inherited from the Cartesians and Empiricists, and developed afresh by Moore and Russell) was misconceived. The terms 'simple' and 'complex', which are relative, were misused. Many concepts, in particular philosophically crucial ones such as 'proposition', 'language', 'number', are united by family resemblance rather than by common characteristic marks. The thought that all propositions share a common essence, a general propositional form, was misguided. Not all propositions are descriptions, and, even among those that are, there are many different logical kinds of description. It was an error to suppose that the fundamental role of the proposition is to describe a state of affairs. It was a mistake to think that the meaning of a sentence is composed of the meanings of its constituents, and confused to think that truth consists in correspondence between proposition and fact. The institution of language can only be elucidated by attending to the use of words and sentences in the stream of life.

In opposition to the conception that makes truth pivotal to the elucidation of meaning, letting understanding take care of itself, Wittgenstein argued that meaning is what is given by explanations of meaning, which are rules for the use of words. It is what is understood when one understands what an utterance means. Understanding is an ability, the mastery of the technique of using an expression. It is exhibited in using an expression correctly, in explaining what it means, and in responding appropriately to its use—which are severally criteria of understanding. Forms of explanation are diverse, formal definition being only one among many, e.g. ostension, paraphrase, contrastive paraphrase, exemplification, explanation by examples, etc. Ostensive definition, which looks as if it links word and world, in fact introduces a sample providing a standard for the correct application of the definiendum. The sample belongs to the method of representation, not to what is represented; hence no link with reality, i.e. with what is represented, is thereby forged.

Consequently the central thought of the *Tractatus*, that any form of representation is answerable to reality, that it must, in its formal structure, mirror the metaphysical form of the world, is misconceived. Concepts are not correct or incorrect, only more or less useful. Rules for the use of words are not true or false. They are not answerable to reality, nor to antecedently given meanings. Rather they determine the meanings of words, are constitutive of their meanings. Grammar is autonomous. Hence what appear to be necessary metaphysical truths (e.g. that red is a colour), which the *Tractatus* held to be ineffably shown by any symbolism (e.g. any language for the description of coloured things), are actually no more than rules for the use of words in the guise of descriptions (e.g. that if anything can be said to be red, it can also be said to be coloured). What seemed to be a metaphysical co-ordination between language and reality, e.g. between the proposition that p and the fact that p which makes it true, is merely an intragrammatical articulation, namely that 'the proposition that p' = 'the proposition which is true if it is a fact that p'. The apparent harmony between language and reality is merely the shadow cast upon the world by grammar. Hence too, puzzles about the intentionality of thought and language are not to be resolved by means of relations between word and world, or thought and reality, but by clarifying intragrammatical connections within language.

Running through the mainstream tradition of European philosophy is the thought that what is given is subjective experience, that a person knows how things are with him (that he is in pain, is experiencing this or that), but must problematically infer how things are 'outside' him. So the private is better known than the public, mind is better known than matter. Subjective experience was conceived not only as the foundations of empirical knowledge, but also as the foundations of language, i.e. that the meanings of words are fixed by naming subjective impressions (e.g. 'pain' means *this*, which I now have). Wittgenstein's 'private language arguments' mount a comprehensive assault on the presuppositions of this conception.

Conceiving of one's current experience as an object of subjective knowledge is misleading, since the ability, for example, to avow one's pain does not rest on evidence, and one does not find out or verify that one is in pain. Being ignorant of or doubting one's own pain makes no sense, nor therefore does knowing or being certain that one is in pain. To say 'I know I'm in pain' is either an emphatic avowal of pain or a philosopher's nonsense. The thought that no one else can have what I have when I am in pain, hence that I enjoy an epistemically privileged position, is confused. For it rests on the assumption that the pains of different people are at best qualitatively, but not numerically, identical. But that is a distinction applicable to substances, not to impressions. Two people have the same pain if their pains tally in intensity, phenomenological features, and occur in corresponding locations of their bodies. The whole traditional picture is a distortion of the 'inner', under the pressure of misleading pictures embedded in our language and of misconstruals of grammatical asymmetries between first- and third-person psychological sentences. Hence we misconstrue the 'outer' likewise. We do often know that others are in pain on the basis of their behaviour, but this is not inductive or analogical evidence. It is a logical criterion for their pain.

Although such criteria are defeasible, in the absence of defeating conditions, it is senseless to doubt whether the sufferer is in pain. The behavioural criteria for the application of a psychological predicate are partly constitutive of its meaning. For expressions signifying the 'inner' are not given their meaning by a private ostensive definition in which a subjective impression functions as a sample. There can be no such thing as a logically private sample, and a sensation cannot fulfil the role of a sample. The elaborate argument to establish this negative conclusion undermines the conception of the 'inner' as a private domain to which its subject enjoys privileged access by means of a faculty of introspection construed on the model of perception.

Contrary to the dominant tradition, Wittgenstein argued that language is misrepresented as a vehicle for the communication of language-independent thoughts. Speaking is not a matter of translating wordless thoughts into language, and understanding is not a matter of interpreting—transforming dead signs into living thoughts. The limits of thought are determined by the limits of the expression of thoughts. The possession of a language not only expands the intellect, but also extends the will. A dog can want a bone, but only a language-user can now want something next week. It is not thought that breathes life into the signs of a language, but the use of signs in the stream of human life.

Wittgenstein also worked extensively on the philosophy of mathematics. His *Remarks on the Foundations of Mathematics* is as original and revolutionary as everything else he wrote. He developed further his earlier account of logical truth, cutting it free from the metaphysical apparatus of the *Tractatus*. He rejected logicism, formalism, and intuitionism alike. In their place he delineated a normative conception of mathematics. Arithmetic is a system of rules (in the form of descriptions) for the transformation of empirical propositions about the numbers or quantities of things. The propositions of geometry are not descriptions of the properties of space, but are rather constitutive rules for the description of spatial relations. A mathematical proof is misconceived as a demonstration of *truths* about the nature of numbers or geometrical forms. It determines concepts and so too forms of inference. It is a matter of invention (concept-formation), rather than discovery. To truth in mathematics corresponds sense in inferences among empirical propositions about numbers and magnitudes of things. Wittgenstein's views here, however, have proved to be too radical and difficult for the age, and have met largely with incomprehension and misinterpretation.

The revolutionary conception of philosophy propounded in the *Tractatus* finds its counterpart in Wittgenstein's later philosophy. Philosophy, he continued to argue, is not a cognitive discipline. There are no philosophical propositions and no philosophical knowledge. If there were theses in philosophy, everyone would agree with them, for they would be mere grammatical truisms (e.g. that we know that someone is in pain by his behaviour). The task of philosophy is to clear away the conceptual confusions that stand in the way of accepting these rule-governed articulations in our language. There is no room for theories in philosophy, for in philosophy we are moving around within our own grammar, dissolving philosophical questions by examining the rules for the use of words with which we are familiar. For there are no such things as hidden rules which are followed, or discoveries about the real meanings of expressions in use which are unknown to all users. Philosophical problems stem from entanglement in linguistic rules, e.g. projecting the grammar of one kind of expression upon another (the grammar of 'pin' on to 'pain'), or projecting norms of representation on to reality and thinking that we are confronting metaphysical necessities in the world (e.g. 'Nothing can be red and green all over'), or placing demands upon certain concepts, e.g. that they lend themselves to certain kinds of explanation, which are only appropriate for concepts of a different category. The methods of philosophy are purely descriptive. The task of philosophy is conceptual clarification and the dissolution of philosophical problems. The goal of philosophy is not knowledge but understanding.

MARTIN
HEIDEGGER (1889–1976)

M. J. INWOOD

GERMAN philosopher who is usually seen as a founder of Existentialism. He prepared the ground for his major work, *Sein und Zeit*
(Being and Time (1927)), with a series of lucid and solid, if unremarkable,
writings, which anticipate several of the themes of his notoriously
obscure mature work. In 'The Problem of Reality in Modern Philosophy'
(1912), his first published article, he argues against various versions of
idealism, including Kant's critical idealism, and in favour of critical realism. He criticizes the stress on epistemology characteristic of philosophy
since Descartes. His 'New Investigations of Logic' (1912) assesses recent
work on logic, including that of Frege, Russell, and Whitehead, from the
standpoint of Husserl's critique of psychologism. (In conformity with his
doctrine of truth as 'unconcealment', the mature Heidegger had little
sympathy for the traditional 'logic of assertion'; like the later Wittgenstein, he would be more inclined to found arithmetic on the everyday
activities of counting and measurement than on the principles of logic.)
In his doctoral dissertation, *The Doctrine of the Judgement in Psychologism*
(1914), he opposed the reduction of logic to psychological processes. His
habilitation thesis, *Duns Scotus's Doctrine of Categories and of Meaning*
(1916), shows a respect for metaphysics, history, and subjectivity which
marks his later work; it examines a treatise, *Grammatica Speculativa*,
which has since been attributed to Thomas of Erfurt, but Heidegger's
thought has often been seen as akin to Duns Scotus', even as 'secularized
Scotism'. His habilitation lecture, 'The Concept of Time in the Science of
History' (1916), argued that time as seen by historians differs from the
quantitative time of physics: it is not uniform, but articulated into qualitatively distinct periods, such as the Victorian era, whose significance
depends on more than their temporal duration.

From 1916 to 1927 he published nothing, but studied widely and intensively, especially the phenomenology of Husserl, Scheler's philosophical anthropology, the hermeneutics of Dilthey, and the texts of St Paul, Augustine, and Luther. Christian texts supplied him not only with examples of momentous, historic decisions, important in his later work, but also with an 'ontology' distinct from our own Greek-derived ontology. At the same time he lectured, with enthralling brilliance, on these and many other themes. (Most of his publications were based on lectures.) He taught at Marburg, 1923–8, and Freiburg, 1928–44. He was elected Rector of Freiburg in 1933, and resigned in 1934. In 1945 he was forbidden to teach, owing to his links with Nazism, until 1951. His initial support for Nazism was rooted in his distaste for technology and industrialized mass society (which he associated with the USA and the USSR) rather than in anti-Semitism. But his conduct as Rector, his private beliefs, and the relationship of his thought to Nazi ideology are still matters of controversy.

Being and Time crystallized his study of virtually the whole range of past and contemporary philosophy. Its central concern is the 'question of being'. Since the beginnings of philosophy in Greece, being (*Sein*) has been ill at ease with time. It has been insulated from change by being seen as *presence*, to the exclusion of past and future—not necessarily temporal presence, but also the atemporal, eternal presence of, for example, Plato's Forms. This affects our conception of the world, including man himself. Heidegger proposes to revive the long-forgotten question of the 'sense of being', and thus to engage in 'fundamental ontology', an ontology which underpins the 'regional' ontologies dealing with the being of particular realms of entity, such as nature and history. But to examine being as such, we need to consider a particular type of entity, namely, the entity that asks the question 'What is being?' and whose understanding of being is an essential feature of its being, i.e. man or *Dasein*. *Dasein*'s being is *Existenz*: it has no fixed nature, but 'its essence lies in its always having its being to be, and having it as its own'. (Despite Heidegger's later denial, this resembles Sartre's view that 'existence precedes essence' and 'man is only what he makes of himself'.) It is not clear why this implies that being is to be approached by way of *Dasein*. In conducting such a large, amorphous inquiry as the question of being, we no doubt need to take our bearings from our ordinary implicit understanding of being, and this will involve a preliminary examination of *Dasein*. But Heidegger also says that 'there is being, only as long as *Dasein* is', suggesting that being, if not entities, depends on our understanding of it, and this would give a stronger reason for approaching being by way of *Dasein*. If this account is correct, Heidegger agrees with Kant and Husserl that how things are depends in large measure on what we contribute to them, with the difference that 'we' are concrete, existing human beings, rather than pure consciousness.

Although *Dasein* is essentially 'ontological', that is, has an understanding of being, the philosopher cannot simply adopt *Dasein*'s own understanding of itself and other entities. For *Dasein* tends systematically to misinterpret itself and its world, regarding itself, for example, as a thing on a par with other things. Much of the vocabulary of traditional philosophy—'consciousness', 'subject', 'object', etc.—is infected with such misinterpretation. Thus Heidegger (like 'analytical' philosophers such as Wittgenstein, J. L. Austin, and Ryle) avoids such terminology, preferring non-committal terms such as '*Dasein*' or down-to-earth words (such as *Sorge*, 'care') which carry no burden of philosophical assumptions. (In accordance with Heidegger's view that silence is an 'essential possibility of discourse', his readers need to bear in mind the words that he purposely avoids, as well as those he uses.) Like Husserl, he attempts to describe 'the things themselves', without the help of theories and preconceptions; but, unlike Husserl, he holds that this requires a determined rethinking of philosophical language. He uses old words in unusual ways, often appealing (like Austin) to etymology, and sometimes coins new words; but his coinages are invariably in the spirit of the German language. It is essential to Heidegger's procedure that in giving the correct or 'authentic' term for, or account of, a phenomenon (such as man, time, or truth) he does not simply counterpose this to the degenerate term or account, but attempts to explain why the degeneration occurred. It is not enough to show, for example, that Descartes was mistaken to regard man as a *res cogitans*. One must also show, in terms of the correct account of man, how the mistake arose. For misinterpretation is not sheer, unaccountable error, but a 'possibility' to which *Dasein* is essentially prone.

For Heidegger, unlike Descartes, *Dasein* is essentially 'in the world' and is inseparable from the world: 'In understanding the world, Being-in is always understood along with it, while understanding of existence as such is always an understanding of the world.' The world is not primarily the world of the sciences, but the everyday world, the 'life-world' (Husserl). It is disclosed to us not by scientific knowledge, but by prescientific experiences, by care and by moods. Entities in the world are not primarily objects of theoretical cognition, but tools that are 'ready to hand' (*zuhanden*), such as a hammer, to be used rather than studied and observed. Theoretical cognition, as when I observe a hammer (or a beetle) disinterestedly, is a secondary phenomenon, which occurs especially when a tool fails to give satisfaction, when, for example, the hammer breaks. Tools are not independent of each other, but belong to a 'context of significance', in which items such as hammers, nails, and work-bench 'refer' to each other and ultimately to *Dasein* and its purposes. Just as *Dasein* is in the world, so it is essentially 'with' others of the same type as itself. It does not first exist as an isolated subject and then subsequently acquire knowledge of and relations to others; it is with others from the start. But others threaten its integrity: 'as being together with others, *Dasein* stands in thrall to others. It itself is not; the others have usurped its being'. 'The self of everyday *Dasein* is the they-self, which we distinguish from the authentic self, the self that has itself in its own grip.' 'They' is the German *man*, 'one': the they-self does and believes what *one* does and believes, rather than what it has independently and authentically decided on. Heidegger's theory of the they or one (*das Man*), like his account of death, is influenced by Tolstoy's *The Death of Ivan Ilyich*: Ivan's carefully redecorated house seems quite exceptional to him, but in fact contains 'all the things people of a certain class have in order to resemble other people of that class'; and when his family discuss Sarah Bernhardt's acting, it is 'the sort of conversation that is always repeated and always the same'. The account of everyday life, which Heidegger first presented as a neutral account of man's bedrock condition, becomes an account of man's 'fallenness' and inauthenticity.

The primary form of discourse, for Heidegger, is not explicit assertion, such as 'This hammer is heavy', but such utterances as 'Too heavy! Give me a lighter one' made in a work situation. Truth too is not primarily the correspondence between an assertion or proposition and a state of the world, but the disclosure of the world to and by *Dasein*, unmediated by concepts, propositions, or inner mental states; at bottom, truth is '*Dasein*'s disclosedness'. (He supported this by appeal to the Greek word for truth, *alētheia*, which, he claimed, means 'unconcealment'.) Meaning, like truth, is extruded from the mind:

Mill's allegedly verbal propositions cannot be completely severed from the beings they intend. Names, words in the broadest sense, have no a priori fixed measure of their significative content. Names, or again their meanings, change with transformations in our knowledge of things, and the meanings of names and words always change according to the predominance of a specific line of vision toward the thing somehow named by the name. All significations, including those that are apparently mere verbal meanings, arise from reference to things. (*The Basic Problems of Phenomenology*, 1927 (1975; 1981 Eng. trans), 197)

The representative theory of perception is rejected along with the correspondence theory of truth: 'What we "first" hear is never noises or complexes of sounds, but the creaking wagon, the motor-cycle . . . It requires a very artificial and complicated state of mind to "hear" a "pure noise".' The problem of the reality of the external world, like that of the existence of other minds, is a pseudo-problem: for Kant, the 'scandal of philosophy' is that no proof has yet been given of the 'existence of things outside of us', but for Heidegger the scandal is 'not that this proof has yet to be given, but that *such proofs are expected and attempted again and again*'.

Dasein must be considered as a whole, and this requires an account of death. *Dasein* can be genuinely authentic only in its 'being towards death', since here it accepts its finitude. *Dasein* is individualized by death: it dies alone, and no one else can die in its place. Thus death is a criterion of authenticity: I must recognize that I will die, not simply that 'one' dies. There is, Heidegger believes, a pervasive tendency to conceal the inevitability of one's own death. (Like Kierkegaard and Tolstoy, he refers to the old syllogism 'All men are mortal, Caius is a man, so Caius is mortal': 'That Caius, man in the abstract, was mortal', mused Tolstoy's Ivan, 'was perfectly correct, but he was not Caius, not an abstract man, but a creature quite, quite separate from all the others.') Authentic being towards death is related to 'resoluteness' (*Entschlossenheit*): it is only if I am aware of my finitude that I have reason to act now, rather than to procrastinate, and it is the crucial decision made with a view to the whole course of my future life that gives my life its unity and shape.

The future is thus the primary aspect or 'ecstasis' of time. But a decision is also constrained by a situation inherited from the past and the more important it is, the more it will be taken in view of the past. The third ecstasis, the present, is now the 'moment' of decision:

To the anticipation which goes with resoluteness, there belongs a present in accordance with which a resolution discloses the situation. In resoluteness, the present is not only brought back from distraction with the objects of one's closest concern, but it gets held in the future and in having been. That *present* which is held in authentic temporality and which thus is *authentic* itself, we call the 'moment of vision' (*der Augenblick*).

(Russell's claim that it would make little difference if our present position were reversed, that is, if we barely remembered the past, but foresaw much of the future, applies to the time of physics, but not to the time of action and decision: in deciding whether to do this or that, I characteristically do not yet know which I shall do.)

Several central features of time have been ignored by the traditional account deriving from Aristotle. Time is significant: it is time *to do* such-and-such. Time is datable by events: it is the time *when*, for example, Napoleon became emperor. Time is spanned: now is not a durationless instant, but now, *during*, for example, the lecture. Time is public: we can all indicate the same time by 'now' or 'then', even if we date it by different events. Time is finite: (my) time does not run on for ever, but is running out. History is to be understood in terms of this account of time and of the 'historicality' of *Dasein*. *Dasein*'s understanding of itself and the world depends on an interpretation inherited from the past. This interpretation regulates and discloses the possibilities open to it. Inauthentic *Dasein* accepts tradition unthinkingly and fulfils the possibilities shaped by it; authentic *Dasein* probes tradition and thereby opens up new and weightier possibilities. Heidegger, for example, does not simply contribute to contemporary philosophical controversy, but by 'repeating' and 'de(con)structing' crucial episodes in the development of our philosophical tradition hopes to change the whole course of philosophical inquiry. It is only because *Dasein* is historical that history in the usual sense is possible: 'Our going back to "the past" does not first get its start from the acquisition, sifting and securing of such material [namely, remains, monuments, and records]; these activities presuppose *historical Being towards* the *Dasein* that has-been-there—that is to say, they presuppose the historicality of the historian's existence.'

Being and Time remained unfinished: the third section of part 1, which was to explicate being in terms of time, and the whole of part 2, which was to examine Kant, Descartes, and Aristotle, never appeared. But shorter works of the same period fill some of the gaps. His Freiburg inaugural lecture, 'What is Metaphysics?' (1929), expands on the nothing, which made a brief appearance in *Being and Time*, and which is disclosed in the *Angst* that reveals to *Dasein*, in its freedom and finitude, the ultimate groundlessness of itself, its world, and its projects. *Kant and the Problem of Metaphysics* (1929) argues that the first *Critique* is not a theory of knowledge or of the sciences (as such neo-Kantians as Hermann Cohen, Paul Natorp, and Ernst Cassirer held), but lays the foundation for metaphysics. Kant saw that reason, knowledge, and man in general are finite, and thus made the transcendental imagination the basis of the possibility of synthetic a priori knowledge. But since this threatens the primacy of reason and the foundations of 'Western metaphysics', Kant recoiled from the 'abyss' in the second edition of the *Critique* and made the imagination a 'function of the understanding'. Heidegger's interpretation was attacked by most Kant scholars, including Cassirer; he implicitly retracts some of his views in later essays on Kant.

Heidegger published little in the 1930s, but lectures delivered around 1930 but published later suggest that at that time he abandoned many of his earlier views, especially on the centrality of *Dasein*. In 'On the Essence of Truth' (1943), truth, and by implication being, is no longer located primarily in *Dasein*, but is the 'open region' to which man is exposed. In 'Plato's Doctrine of Truth' (1942) he argued that in Plato's allegory of the cave truth ceased to be 'unhiddenness' and became, 'under the yoke of the *idea*', mere 'correctness'. This set in train the degeneration of thought about being into metaphysics: man moves into the centre of things. The history of Western philosophy is a history of decline. This view reached its more or less final form in his 1935 lectures, *An Introduction to Metaphysics* (1953).

Heidegger's late philosophy emerges for the most part in discussions of past thinkers, especially the 'most unbridled Platonist in the history of Western metaphysics', Nietzsche (*Nietzsche* (1961)); poets such as Hölderlin who offer a way out of 'forgetfulness of being'; and the Pre-Socratic thinkers who precede it. (Nietzsche is seen as metaphysical, since his claim that 'truth is the sort of error without which a definite type of living entity could not live. Ultimately, the value for life decides' presupposes that truth lies in man's thought and that there is a realm of values distinct from the world.) Being becomes ever more elusive in his writings, barely describable except in such tautological terms as 'It is itself'. The 'ontological difference', the crucial distinction between being and beings, is differently described at different times. Despite Heidegger's denials, being resembles God. It is not at man's disposal, but rather disposes of man. Whatever happens comes from being. Man, the 'shepherd of being', must respond to its directions. It is above history, but since the time of Plato it has been hidden, and the 'history of being' can be reconstructed from the texts of philosophers and poets. Forgetfulness of being, or 'nihilism', has culminated in the domination of the world by technology, which is primarily an event in the history of being, 'the completion of metaphysics'. Whether or not man can return to genuine thinking of being will determine the future of the planet. On this he was not wholly pessimistic: 'But where there is danger, the remedy grows too' (Hölderlin).

The appropriate response to being is thinking. Thinking is our obedient answer to the call of being: the early Greeks did it, but we have forgotten it. Thinking contrasts with assertion, logic, science ('science does not think'), metaphysics, philosophy itself, and especially technology, which is merely an instrument for the calculation and domination of entities. Language, which, like thinking, played a subordinate part in *Being and Time*, now becomes central, not language as an instrument of manipulation—into which it has degenerated under the auspices of metaphysics—but language as the 'abode of being': 'Language speaks, not man. Man only speaks, when he fatefully responds to language.' Art, especially poetry, are of crucial importance for thinking and language. Poetry is not a secondary phenomenon: it has a special relation to being and truth. Poetry is 'founding of truth': it discloses the (or 'a') world and creates a language for its adequate expression. When a painting, such as Van Gogh's peasant shoes, 'sets up' a world, the world of the peasant, it is essentially poetry. Unpoetic thought and language are parasitic on poetry and its vision. Poetry is close to the sacred: 'The thinker says being. The poet names the holy.'

The change from *Being and Time* to Heidegger's later thought is often called 'the turn' (*die Kehre*). Heidegger used this expression in his *Letter on Humanism* (1947) for the change of direction involved in his intended, but unfulfilled, continuation of *Being and Time*. (He also used it for the hoped-for change, in the history of being, from forgetfulness of being to thinking.) But he regularly denied that his early thought differed significantly from his later thought and that it bore any similarity to Sartre's existentialism. Heidegger's interpretation of his own work, as of much else, is of continuing interest, but open to question.

The ultimate worth of Heidegger's thought is still *sub judice*. Like his great rival Hegel (who also made life difficult for his non-German readers by trying to 'teach philosophy to speak German'), he is alternately worshipped, reviled, or sympathetically assimilated to other, more accessible philosophers, especially Wittgenstein. (Heidegger's relation to Husserl is not dissimilar to the relation of the late to the early Wittgenstein.) But his immense learning, his profound and innovative intelligence, his commitment to philosophical inquiry, and, above all, his intense influence on modern thought, are not open to doubt. Philosophers such as Sartre,

Gadamer, and Derrida derive many of their basic concepts from him, and his philosophical influence extends to Japan and China. Theologians, Catholic (Karl Rahner) as well as Protestant (Rudolf Bultmann), are in his debt, as are psychologists (Ludwig Binswanger) and literary critics (Emil Staiger). Whether or not Heidegger's thought is 'true' in the traditional sense, it has disclosed something of the world, and of the possibilities for our 'comportment' to it, that was previously concealed.

JEAN-PAUL SARTRE (1905–1980)

THOMAS BALDWIN

S ARTRE's œuvre is a unique phenomenon. No other major philoso-pher has also been a major playwright, novelist, political theorist, and literary critic. It is still too early to judge which facet of Sartre's extraordinary genius posterity will regard as the most important, but since his philosophy permeates his other works, its enduring interest is assured.

After a provincial childhood spent, if we can trust Sartre's captivating autobiographical essay *Words*, in his grandfather's library, Sartre studied philosophy at the École Normale in Paris. In 1931 he became a teacher of philosophy in Le Havre, which he hated (Le Havre is 'Bouville' in *Nausea*). In 1937 he moved to Paris, and the next year his brilliant philosoph-ical novel *Nausea* was published. Many of the themes of this book recur in his first major philosophical book *L'Imaginaire* (1940) (whose botched English translation bears the title *The Psychology of Imagination*). But then the war intervened: Sartre was mobilized in 1939, and served as a meteor-ologist in the French Army. He later described the war as the turning-point in his life, one which changed him from an academic philosopher and avant-garde writer into an intellectual deeply committed to the fate of the 'Wretched of the Earth' (the title of the famous work by Fanon for which Sartre wrote an eloquent preface). Military service did not, how-ever, stem the flow of words: he wrote voluminous diaries (excellently translated as his *War Diaries*), which contain early drafts of his philosoph-ical work, mixed in with marvellous descriptions of his experiences and colleagues. In 1940 Sartre was captured and imprisoned: in prison he con-tinued his study of Heidegger's philosophy and wrote his first play. Released a year later, he returned to occupied Paris and to his post as a teacher of philosophy. His desire to work with the Resistance was complicated by his unwillingness to commit himself to either the

Communists or the Gaullists, and in the end he devoted most of this time to writing his most important philosophical work, *Being and Nothingness* (1943).

With the liberation came instant fame, as dramatist (thanks to *Flies* and *No Exit*) and philosopher: his optimistic 1945 lecture *Existentialism and Humanism* seized the imagination of a generation. Sartre could have continued his academic career, but he chose to refuse all academic positions and to make his living as a writer, an occupation which he combined with an active concern for the political and social affairs of the day. The nature of Sartre's engagements was at first largely shaped by his complex relationships with the Communist Party, which he joined at the time of the Korean War and then left, never to return, after the Russian suppression of the Hungarian Revolution in 1956. Not surprisingly, his reflections on Marxism date from this period, and over the next decade he developed the 'existentialist Marxism' first expounded in his 1957 essay *Search for a Method*, and then further developed in his second large-scale philosophical treatise, *Critique of Dialectical Reason* (1960). Towards the end of this period he committed himself whole-heartedly to the struggle for liberation in Algeria (a cause which nearly cost him his life in 1961). A few years later the same passions stirred him to lead the French opposition to the American involvement in Vietnam, and these commitments are reflected in several long essays on behalf of the Third World. In 1964 he was offered the Nobel Prize for Literature, but chose to decline the offer. The student uprising of May 1968 seemed to show that Sartre's writings were still as influential as ever, as he addressed thousands in the Sorbonne; but in truth, his intellectual reputation was now eclipsed by structuralists (such as Lévi-Strauss and Althusser), and post-structuralists (such as Derrida and Deleuze). Sensing this loss of intellectual sympathy, and combating increasing blindness and other illnesses, Sartre largely withdrew from public affairs and turned his attention to the completion of his final *magnum opus*, his vast study of Flaubert, *L'Idiot de la famille*; sadly, his eyesight gave out in 1973, when only three out of five projected volumes had been completed. Yet his funeral showed that he retained an extraordinary hold on the public imagination: over 50,000 people turned up in a spontaneous demonstration of respect.

In his early philosophical writings from the 1930s Sartre was primarily concerned to develop Husserl's phenomenological methods and apply them to the study of the imagination. He argues that the traditional conception of mental imagery derived from the theory of ideas is incoherent, and needs to be replaced by a recognition that imagination, like perception, is a distinctive mode of intentional consciousness whose contents should not be treated as if they were inner objects. Sartre's special interest in the imagination derives partly from its connections with aesthetics and the use of the imagination in creating ideal worlds which contrast with the perceived actual world (this is a prominent theme of *Nausea*); but also from the fact that he regards the exercise of the imagination as the paradigmatic exercise of freedom. He argues that, because the content of the imagination, 'the imaginary', characteristically goes beyond the actual world, there simply cannot be an adequate causal theory of the imagination, since the effects of actual causes cannot be anything but actual. This argument is unsatisfactory, for Sartre confuses the fact that what is imagined is characteristically not actual with the claim that the act of imagination itself is not actual; but we can agree with him that the imagination is a primary manifestation of human freedom without accepting his argument.

Freedom is not just a phenomenon of the imagination, however: according to Sartre, all consciousness is in some way free (so that the imagination is a privileged manifestation of consciousness in general). In order to understand Sartre's conception of the essential freedom of consciousness we need now to turn to *Being and Nothingness*. Sartre begins this work by arguing that consciousness belongs to a different ontological category from that of the physical world. The key premiss for this ontological distinction is an obscure thesis that consciousness is always constituted by a tacit self-consciousness. Sartre argues that the conception of a conscious mental state which does not include this self-conscious dimension is incoherent, since it would be an unconscious conscious state; but this argument is plainly fallacious, although there may be other reasons for thinking that consciousness implies the possibility of self-consciousness. What is distinctive about the Sartrean conception, however, is not just the association between consciousness and self-consciousness, but the claim that the self-conscious dimension is constitutive. It is not easy to see why Sartre holds this, but it seems to rest on a presumption, similar to that employed in his discussion of the imagination, that the intentional content of consciousness is in principle inexplicable in causal terms. If that presumption is granted, then it follows that consciousness cannot get its essential intentional content from the physical world; in which case, if there is to be an explanation of any kind for it, it is tempting to have recourse to a constitutive self-consciousness, though this requires the dubious assumption that the content of this self-consciousness is itself unproblematic.

This constitutive role for self-consciousness, however exactly it is understood, explains why Sartre now proceeds to call those aspects of human life which involve consciousness the 'for-itself' *(pour-soi)*. This contrasts with all physical facts, which are independent of consciousness and comprise the 'in-itself' *(en-soi)*. This distinction is not, however, one between substances of two different kinds; for Sartre denies that consciousness is a substance at all. Instead, the distinction is one between types of fact. Physical facts satisfy ordinary classical logic: 'they are what they are'. But, according to Sartre, the same logic does not hold of consciousness: here things 'are what they are not and are not what they are'. This thesis connects with the feature of Sartre's philosophy which is most difficult to come to terms with—his treatment of negation. Like other opponents of negative facts, Sartre argues that negation does not reside 'in things themselves'; instead, he holds, it is introduced into our conception of the world as a quasi-Kantian category whose transcendental justification lies in the fact that the self-conscious structure of consciousness involves negation—'the being by which Nothingness comes to the world must be its own Nothingness' *(Being and Nothingness,* 23). This baffling doctrine implies that the constitutive role of self-consciousness is at the same time self-nihilating. One would like to set this doctrine aside as a rhetorical extravagance; but this is impossible, since, according to Sartre, this capacity for reflexive self-negation is the core of human freedom and, indeed, human life. The best one can do to grasp Sartre's intention is to point to the phenomena he uses to illustrate our self-directed 'nothingness'—such facts as that we can always detach ourselves from the roles we find ourselves occupying (as in Sartre's famous example of the waiter in a café), and that in cases of self-deception we convince ourselves of something precisely because we already believe the opposite.

This theory of consciousness so far lacks any reference to the self, or subject of consciousness. This omission is deliberate, for in one of his first essays (*The Transcendence of the Ego*) Sartre took issue with Husserl's doctrine of the transcendental subject and argued that consciousness is fundamentally impersonal. In *Being and Nothingness* this thesis is significantly modified in the light of that of the constitutive role of self-consciousness: Sartre argues here that this self-consciousness characteristically includes a set of commitments and aspirations that gives a projective unity to the acts of consciousness that they inform, and, in doing so, strings them

together as the acts of a single person—'consciousness by the pure nihil-
ating movement of reflection makes itself *personal*' (*Being and Nothingness*, 103). In the last part of the book Sartre develops this theme in a rich
and detailed elucidation of the purposive structures of psychological
explanations. Two aspects of this account are specially worthy of notice.
The first concerns Sartre's attitude to Freud. In an early section of the
book Sartre launches a well-known critique of Freud's theory of the
unconscious which is motivated by Sartre's claim that consciousness is
essentially self-conscious. Sartre also argues here that Freud's theory of
repression is internally flawed, but this argument is based on a misunderstanding of Freud. What is of more interest, however, is Sartre's attempt,
towards the end of the book, to adapt some of Freud's ideas to his own
account of human life, and thereby to develop an 'existential psycho-
analysis' in which Freud's causal categories are replaced by Sartre's own
teleological ones. The theme of consciousness is not so dominant here,
and the method of psychological inquiry Sartre began here is one that he
was to employ fruitfully in several biographical works (including *Baude-
laire* (1946), *Saint Genet—Actor and Martyr* (1952), and *The Idiot of the
Family* (1971–2)).

One feature of these studies is the emphasis Sartre comes to place
upon the formation during childhood of a 'fundamental project' which
gives unity to the person's subsequent life, and this brings me to the second notable aspect of Sartre's psychological theory. In *Being and Nothingness* Sartre writes of the formation of this fundamental project as a
'choice', and it is easy to see why he says this in the light of his emphasis
on freedom—he calls this choice 'the fundamental act of freedom' (*Being
and Nothingness*, 461). Sartre is here reviving a doctrine central to Kant's
conception of freedom, but, like Kant, Sartre faces insoluble problems in
explaining how such an act can be a choice at all, since all the subject's reasons for choice are referred back to their fundamental project. Hence it is
not surprising that when Sartre attempted to apply this conception in his
biographical studies, a causal mode of explanation concerning the formation in childhood of one's fundamental project appears to replace the
abstract schemata of *Being and Nothingness*.

We have seen how subjectivity is achieved through the reference of
acts of consciousness, through their tacit self-conscious structure, to a
single project. Sartre makes it clear in *Nausea* that Roquentin's abandonment of his project brings with it the end of his subjectivity—'suddenly
the I pales, pales and goes out' (*Nausea*, 241). One can ask whether

subjectivity does not also involve reference to other persons, perhaps, as Hegel supposed, to their recognition of one's status as a subject. In *Being and Nothingness*, however, Sartre argues that although, for each of us, there is an aspect of ourselves that is dependent on recognition by others (our 'being-for-others'), this is an alienated conception of ourselves that we cannot integrate into our own self-consciousness; in relation to ourselves as we are for ourselves we are not dependent upon others. Sartre's discussion of this thesis includes a sustained analysis of a variety of situations in which we become aware of each other (most famously, that of the peeping Tom who hears someone behind him), and in my judgement these analyses provide the finest example of the application of phenomenological methods of analysis, not only by Sartre, but by any philosopher. Yet their conclusion is paradoxical—that we are always '*de trop* in relation to others' (*Being and Nothingness*, 410).

The ethical implication of this is that 'respect for the Other's freedom is an empty word' (*Being and Nothingness*, 409). Yet how can this be combined with the thesis which he proclaims in his 1945 lecture *Existentialism and Humanism*, that 'I am obliged to will the liberty of others at the same time as mine' (p. 52)? One part of the explanation is that *Being and Nothingness* is incomplete, and was always intended primarily as an exploration of human life as guided by illusions such as a belief in determinism and in the independent reality of ethical values. It was supposed to be balanced by a further book in which a life freed from these illusions was explored. This book was never completed, though *Existentialism and Humanism* and Sartre's 1947 notebooks *Cahiers pour une morale* (now published) reveal his broad intentions. The crucial point that emerges from them is that Sartre maintains that although our metaphysical freedom does not depend upon others, there is another kind of freedom, moral freedom, which does depend upon others; as he puts it in the 1947 notebooks, 'morality is only possible if everyone is moral'.

Sartre's acceptance of this thesis coincides with his growing awareness of the need to fill out the rather abstract account of consciousness he had offered with an account of the relationships between an individual and their society. His approach to these relationships is, of course, deeply influenced by his study of Marx, and he likes to portray himself as a historical materialist ('I have said—and I repeat—that the only valid interpretation of human History is historical materialism' (*Critique of Dialectical Reason*, 39–40)). But in *Search for a Method* he is a brilliant critic of the reductive historical materialism familiar from orthodox Marxist theory; he offers instead a version which incorporates parts of the account of human life presented in *Being and Nothingness*. But the theme of human freedom is now given little direct emphasis: in a striking passage in the *Critique of Dialectical Reason* (pp. 233–4) he describes how workers who have some monotonous task are prone to engage in sexual fantasies—thereby contradicting his youthful insistence that the imagination is a citadel of absolute freedom. Indeed in a 1972 essay ('The Itinerary of a Thought') Sartre describes his earlier views about freedom as 'scandalous' and 'incredible'. Yet he remains as strongly committed as ever to the distinctiveness of human affairs: 'dialectical reason' is the mode of rationality characteristic of social and psychological explanations, and contrasts with 'analytical reason', which is the rationality appropriate to the physical sciences.

A central mark of 'dialectical reason' is the involvement of holistic explanations. This was already a feature of the account of psychological explanation given in *Being and Nothingness*, and to some extent the account of social explanation in Sartre's later works is an extrapolation into a broader historical and interpersonal field of the earlier account. In this case, however, the holistic theme is underpinned by an assumption basic to all Sartre's later work, that all human affairs are conducted under conditions of relative scarcity. For this implies that humans always confront each other as potential competitors, and, according to Sartre, it is this threat which both motivates all social and economic structures, and, in the end, unifies human history. This assumption of scarcity also provides one basis for the alienation which Sartre, like Marx, regards as an endemic feature of human history up to the present. But Sartre differs significantly from Marx in holding that alienation also arises from the fact that the realization of human purposes creates material structures (houses, machines, etc.—the 'practico-inert') that are inherently liable themselves to place further demands on people and, in some cases, to subvert the very purposes they were intended to promote. A central theme of Sartre's *Critique of Dialectical Reason* is, indeed, one of the attempt to overcome the constraints of the practico-inert through social institutions, and then of the failure of this attempt as social institutions themselves ossify and join the practico-inert. In the *Critique of Dialectical Reason* as published, this theme is developed with particular reference to the French Revolution; in the projected second volume of the *Critique* (which was published posthumously) the same theme is discussed with reference to the Russian Revolution.

Thomas Baldwin 251

The *Critique* bears witness to Sartre's disillusionment with the fate of communist states (though not with Marxism), and in it he returns to the pessimism of *Being and Nothingness*. The kind of moral freedom that he had envisaged in *Existentialism and Humanism* is now presented as entirely utopian. Yet it was the themes of that lecture which once captivated the post-war generation, and, I suspect, it will be as protagonist of the value of existential freedom that he will be remembered.

A CHRONOLOGICAL TABLE
OF PHILOSOPHY *A. R. Lacey*

Any table of this nature must reflect a certain arbitrariness. The left column represents philosophers or events of philosophical importance. Some attempt has been made to list philosophers in the order in which they produced their main work or had their main influence; normally each philosopher is listed once only, at the time when he was most active or most influential. Titles are given in the language in which they are most familiar. Similar considerations in general apply to the right column, which lists, with considerably greater arbitrariness, public events or people, partly to give a general temporal framework and partly to pick out items that might be thought to have some relevance to the development of philosophy. The correlation between the columns, however, cannot be anything but very rough and approximate.

600 BC	First flourishing of Greek philosophy (Thales, Anaximander, Anaximenes) through the sixth century in the town of Miletus in Asia Minor	Zoroaster c.630–c.553
		Solar eclipse, allegedly predicted by Thales, 585
		Beginnings of Greek mathematics, attributed to Thales
	Pythagoras and his followers found religious movement in southern Italy	Buddha c.563–?
	Xenophanes criticizes anthropomorphic religion	First systematic edition of *Iliad* and *Odyssey* (probably composed two or three centuries earlier)
	Heraclitus propounds a bold metaphysics in Ephesus	Cleisthenes expels tyrants from Athens 510, and introduces democracy 508
500 BC		Ionian revolt against Persia 499–494
	Parmenides discusses philosophical method in verse	Persian wars unite Greece, temporarily; Persia effectively defeated in 479
		Persian-war veteran Aeschylus becomes first great European dramatist
	Confucius c.557–479	Athens founds Delian League as bulwark against Persia, but uses it for imperialist purposes (and to finance building of Parthenon, completed 438)
	Lao Tsǔ founds Taoism	
	Zeno of Elea develops Parmenides' ideas	
	Empedocles in Sicily; Anaxagoras in Athens; Melissus in Samos	Periclean age c.460–429, ending with plague which killed Pericles
	Protagoras, the leading Sophist, visits Athens	Sophocles writes prize-winning tragedies from 468 until his death in 406
		Abortive attempt to found Panhellenic colony at Thurii in Italy 444, with Protagoras invited to write its laws
		Herodotus presents a panorama of the world known to the Greeks in his *Histories*
		Peloponnesian War between Sparta and Athens, 431–404, ends in defeat of Athens,
	Democritus develops early atomism	which quickly revives

THE ARCHAIC PERIOD IN GREECE

EASTERN CHOU ERA IN CHINA

THE CLASSICAL PERIOD IN GREECE

BC		
		Earliest of many medical treatises attributed to Hippocrates (c.450–c.370)
	Socrates (469–399)	Euripides' tragedies show Sophists' influence
		Aristophanes mocks Socrates in his comedy *Clouds*
		Thucydides examines political behaviour and motivation in his history
400 BC	Death of Socrates, 399, has profound effect on Plato and others	Pentateuch of Old Testament receives definitive form
	'Socratic schools' (Megarians, Cynics, Cyrenaics) form	Xenophon (c.428–c.354), historian and one source for our knowledge of Socrates
	Plato (427–347) founds Academy c.380	Greek mathematics flourishes under Theodorus and Theaetetus
	Plato's *Republic* c.380–370	Greek oratory and rhetoric flourish under Isocrates, Demosthenes, Aeschines
	Diogenes the Cynic c.400–c.325	
	Aristotle (384–322) enters Academy 367, tutors Alexander c.343–339, founds Lyceum c.336, writes main works c.350–323	Aristoxenus, theorist of Greek music
	Headship of Academy falls to Speusippus 347, and then Xenocrates	Second battle of Chaeronea 338 ends independence of Greek city states, thereafter under Macedonian rule
	Theophrastus (Aristotle's successor in Lyceum) 370–c.288	Greek comedy turns, especially with Menander, from political and social to domestic satire
	Pyrrho the Sceptic c.365–c.275	Alexander succeeds Philip of Macedon 336
	Epicurus (341–270) founds Epicurean school	Death of Alexander 323
	Zeno of Citium (335–263) founds Stoic school	Euclid the geometer active
300 BC	Mencius (c.372–289) and Chuang Tzŭ active	Aristarchus presents heliocentric hypothesis
	Arcesilaus (c.316–c.242) founds 'Middle Academy', representing Sceptical rival to Stoics	Septuagint (Greek version of Old Testament) written
	Cleanthes and Chrysippus (c.280–207) second and third heads of Stoic school	Scientist-engineer Archimedes c.287–212 (killed at fall of Syracuse)
		Asoka emperor and law-giver in India
		Eratosthenes (c.276–194) makes good estimate of earth's circumference
		Hannibal in Italy; finally defeated at Zama (near Carthage) 202
200 BC		Plautus and Terence develop Roman comic theatre
	Carneades (c.214–c.129) founds 'New Academy', continuing Sceptical tradition	Sack of Corinth by Rome finally ends Greek independence of Rome 146
	Panaetius the Stoic c.185–109	Political reforms attempted by the Gracchi in Rome

Posidonius the Stoic c.135–c.51	Aristotle's works brought to Rome by Sulla 84, and subsequently edited by Andronicus
	Rebellion of slaves under Spartacus defeated 71
Cicero 106–43	Caesar crosses Rubicon and starts civil war 49
	Julian calendar adopted 46
Lucretius (98–c.51) publishes poetic version of Epicureanism c.60	Library of Alexandria wholly or partially destroyed 47
	Battle of Actium ends Roman republic and independence of Egypt (where defeated parties, Antony and Cleopatra, were based), thereby closing the Hellenistic or Alexandrian period, 31
	Augustan or Golden Age of Roman literature: Virgil, Livy, Horace, Ovid, et al.

	Jesus Christ 4 BC–AD c.29
	Augustus dies 14; succeeded by Tiberius
Seneca c.1 BC–AD 65	Nero (emperor 54–68) orders suicide of Seneca and persecutes Christians
Beginning of Nyāya philosophy (Hindu logical school) in India	Naturalist Pliny the Elder dies while investigating eruption of Vesuvius which destroyed Pompeii 79
	Silver Age of Roman literature begins: Tacitus, Suetonius, Pliny the Younger, Martial, Juvenal, Quintilian, et al.
	Greek historian Plutarch of Chaeronea

	Trajan (emperor 98–117) extends Roman Empire to its greatest size
Epictetus c.55–135	
	Encyclopaedic medical writer Galen 129–99
Marcus Aurelius 121–80	
	Origen (c.185–254) tries to reconcile Christianity with Platonic philosophy by interpreting the Bible

Mahāyāna Buddhism inaugurated by Nāgārjuna	Diogenes Laertius, important source for history of philosophy, writing
Alexander of Aphrodisias lecturing in Athens	Diophantus the mathematician active c.250
Sextus Empiricus active	Manichean religion founded by Mani
Plotinus (205–c.269) introduces Neoplatonism	Roman Empire begins to be invaded from the north-east
Porphyry c.232–c.305	Roman Empire first divided into east and west by Diocletian 285

	Constantinople founded 324, becoming seat of Roman Empire 331; start of Byzantine era
	First Council of Nicaea condemns Arians (who stressed God's unity and so gave Christ subordinate status) in favour of Athanasius 325

THE HELLENISTIC PERIOD

HAN DYNASTY IN CHINA

ROMAN EMPIRE

Books start to replace scrolls c.360

Roman Empire finally divided into east and west after death of Theodosius 395

400

Augustine (354–430) composes his major philosophical works

Proclus c.410–85

Western Roman Empire falls to Germans under Odoacer 476

First schism between Eastern and Western Churches 484

500

John Stobaeus' literary anthology, of some importance as source for history of philosophy

Boethius c.480–524

Philoponus (c.490–570) and Simplicius active, Simplicius being the last main Neoplatonist, and Philoponus helping to replace Neoplatonism with Christianity in Alexandria

Closing of Athenian schools by Justinian 529

Simplicius temporarily migrates to Persia

Justinian promulgates legal code

600

Hegira: flight of Muhammad (570–632) from Mecca to Medina, 622; start of Muslim calendar

Islam replaces Zoroastrianism in Persia 641

Nestorians translate ancient Greek philosophers into Syriac

700

Muslim Empire reaches its height, with capital first at Damascus and then at Baghdad

Beginning of Arabic science and philosophy at Baghdad

'Arabic' (in fact Indian) numerals known in Baghdad 760

800

Charlemagne crowned at Aix (Aachen) as first Holy Roman Emperor 800

Al-Kindī c.801–66

John Scotus Eriugena active

Revival of classical learning at Aix

900

Buddhist influence in India starts to decline

Start of Christian reconquest of Spain

Al-Fārābī 870–950

Cordoba becomes centre of Arabic culture in Spain, with university founded 968

1000

Avicenna (Ibn Sīnā) 980–1037

Avecebrol (Ibn Gabirol) 1020–c.1070

Anselm 1033–1109
Al-Ghazālī 1058/9–1111

Arabic philosophers start to be translated into Latin

Norman Conquest of England 1066

Greek medicine brought to West by Constantine the African 1071

First Crusade launched by Pope Urban II 1095

1100

First modern European university founded at Bologna 1113

Philosophers	Events and works	Era
Abelard 1079–1142	Arabs in Spain manufacture paper 1150	
	University of Paris founded 1150	
	University of Oxford founded 1167	
Averroës 1126–98	Thomas à Becket murdered at Canterbury 1170	BYZANTINE ERA
Maimonides 1125–1204		
1200		
	Francis of Assisi 1182–1226	
	Magna Carta 1215	
	Genghis Khan (c.1162–1227) establishes Mongol Empire	
Albert the Great c.1200–80	Fourth Crusade captures Constantinople 1204, giving West access to Greek writings	
Roger Bacon c.1214–c.1292		
Bonaventure 1221–74		
Thomas Aquinas c.1224–74	Cordoba falls to Spain 1236	
Duns Scotus c.1266–1308		
1300		
William of Ockham c.1285–c.1349	Dante (1265–1321), one of the earliest writers in Italian rather than Latin, writes *Divine Comedy*	
	Black Death ravages Europe, killing one-third of English population 1347–51	
	Boccaccio (1313–75) publishes *Decameron* 1348–53	
	Chaucer (1340–1400) writes *The Canterbury Tales*	
1400		
	Constantinople falls to Ottomans 1453, ending Byzantine era	
Nicholas of Cusa c.1400–64	Caxton prints Chaucer's *Canterbury Tales* 1477	
Marsilio Ficino 1433–99	Granada falls to Spanish, ending Moorish power in Spain, 1492	
	Columbus crosses Atlantic 1492	
1500		EUROPEAN RENAISSANCE
	Leonardo da Vinci 1452–1519	
	Raphael 1483–1520	
	Michelangelo 1475–1564	
Erasmus 1465–1536	Physician and alchemist Paracelsus 1493–1541	MOGUL EMPIRE IN ASIA
Machiavelli (1469–1527) writes *Il Principe* 1513	Luther (1483–1536) instigates Reformation at Wittenberg 1517	
	Rabelais (1494–1553) publishes *Pantagruel* 1532	
	St Ignatius Loyola founds Society of Jesus 1534	
	Copernicus (1473–1543) publishes heliocentric theory 1541–3	
	Calvin 1509–64	
Suarez 1548–1607	Montaigne (1533–92)	

Queen Elizabeth I crowned 1558

First microscope invented by Janssen 1590

Thermometer invented by Galileo

Edict of Nantes, tolerating Huguenots, issued by Henri IV 1598

Shakespeare (1564–1616) writes *Hamlet* c.1600

Telescope invented by Dutch 1600

Francis Bacon (1561–1626) publishes *Advancement of Learning* 1605, *Novum Organum* 1620

Philosophy starts to be written in the vernacular rather than in Latin

Gassendi 1592–1655

Descartes (1596–1650) publishes *Meditations* 1641, *Principles of Philosophy* 1644

Bruno (born 1548) accused of heresy and burnt by Inquisition 1600

Kepler (1571–1630) discovers elliptical orbits of planets

Harvey discovers circulation of blood 1628

Galileo sentenced by Inquisition 1633

Harvard University founded 1636

English Civil War 1642–6

Louis XIV (1638–1715) becomes King of France 1643

Hobbes (1588–1679) publishes *Leviathan* 1651

Charles I executed 1649, inaugurating eleven-year Commonwealth period under Puritans in Britain

Fermat (1601–65) and Pascal (1633–62) inaugurate study of probability 1654

French drama flourishes with Corneille (1606–84), Molière (1622–73), Racine (1639–99)

Plague in England 1665

Great Fire of London 1666

Milton (1608–74) publishes *Paradise Lost* 1667

Decline of Latin as a language in which the educated are fluent

Spinoza (1632–77) publishes *Ethics* 1677

Cambridge Platonists (Whichcote (1609–83), More (1614–87), Cudworth (1617–88), *et al.*) active

Locke (1632–1704) publishes *Essay Concerning Human Understanding* 1690, *Two Treatises of Government* 1690

Malebranche (1628–1715) publishes *De la recherche de la vérité* 1674

Bunyan (1628–88) publishes *The Pilgrim's Progress* 1678–84

Newton publishes *Principia* 1687

'Glorious Revolution' rids Britain of Stuart monarchs 1688

Dryden (1631–1700), poet, dramatist, and critic

Leibniz 1646–1716

Vico 1668–1744

Shaftesbury (1671–1713) publishes *Characteristics* 1711

Berkeley (1685–1753) publishes *Principles of Human Knowledge* 1710, *Three Dialogues* 1713

Hutcheson (1694–1746/7) publishes *Inquiry into the Origin of our Ideas of Beauty and Virtue* 1725

Fahrenheit (1686–1736) constructs mercury thermometer 1714

Pope (1688–1744), poet and social critic

MOGUL EMPIRE IN ASIA

ERA OF EUROPEAN COLONIZATION

Butler (1692–1752) publishes *Fifteen Sermons* 1726, *The Analogy of Religion* 1736

Jonathan Edwards 1703–58

Hume (1711–76) publishes *A Treatise of Human Nature* 1739, *An Enquiry Concerning Human Understanding* 1748, *An Enquiry Concerning the Principles of Morals* 1751

Richard Price (1723–91) publishes *A Review of the Principal Questions in Morals* 1758

Adam Smith (1723–90) publishes *The Theory of Moral Sentiments* 1759, *Wealth of Nations* 1776

Rousseau (1712–78) publishes *Le Contrat social* 1762

Bentham (1748–1832) publishes *A Fragment of Government* 1776, *An Introduction to the Principles of Morals and Legislation* 1789

Condillac 1715–80

Kant (1724–1804) publishes *Critique of Pure Reason* 1781, *Fundamental Principles of the Metaphysic of Morals* 1785, *Critique of Practical Reason* 1788, *Critique of Judgement* 1790

Reid (1710–96) publishes *Essays on the Intellectual Powers of Man* 1785, *Essays on the Active Powers of Man* 1788

Condorcet 1743–94

Fichte 1762–1814

Maine de Biran 1766–1824

Schleiermacher 1768–1834

Hegel (1770–1831) publishes *The Phenomenology of Mind* 1807

James Mill 1773–1835

Diderot (1713–84) begins work on the *Encyclopédie* 1745

Mathematician D'Alembert (1717–83)

Montesquieu (1689–1755) publishes *De l'esprit des lois* 1748

Encyclopédie published 1751–80

Lisbon earthquake 1755 (referred to by Voltaire and others when discussing divine justice)

Voltaire (1694–1778) publishes *Candide* 1759

Süssmilch inaugurates study of statistics 1761

Samuel Johnson (1709–84), publishes *Dictionary of the English Language* 1755–73

Cook (1728–79) discovers Australia 1770

Boston Tea Party 1773

Watt (1738–1819) invents steam-engine, which pioneers Industrial Revolution

American Declaration of Independence 1776

Lavoisier (1743–94) analyses air into oxygen and nitrogen, opening the way for overthrow of phlogiston theory of combustion (dominant since early in the century) 1777

Mesmerism practised in Paris 1778

French Revolution 1789

Burke (1729–97) publishes *Reflections on the Revolution in France* 1790

Tom Paine (1737–1809) publishes *The Rights of Man* 1791–2, *The Age of Reason* 1794–5

Benjamin Franklin 1752–1828

French Reign of Terror 1793, followed by Napoleonic wars

Goethe 1749–1832

Schiller 1759–1805

Malthus (1766–1834) publishes *Essay on the Principle of Population* 1798

Dalton (1766–1844) introduces atomic theory *c.*1800

Wordsworth 1770–1850

Coleridge 1772–1834

Thomas Jefferson (1743–1836), third President of USA 1801–9

Battle of Waterloo brings comparative stability to Europe 1815

1800

AGE OF ENLIGHTENMENT IN EUROPE

ERA OF EUROPEAN COLONIZATION

AGE OF REVOLUTION

Schelling 1775–1854

Schopenhauer (1788–1860) publishes *The World as Will and Representation* 1819

John Austin (1790–1859) publishes *The Province of Jurisprudence Determined* 1832

Comte 1798–1857

Feuerbach 1804–72

Hamilton (1805–65), philosopher-mathematician criticized by J. S. Mill

Whewell 1794–1866

John Stuart Mill (1806–73) publishes *A System of Logic* 1843, *On Liberty* 1859, *Utilitarianism* 1863

Kierkegaard 1813–55

Byron 1788–1824

Shelley 1792–1822

Ricardo writing on economics 1809–17

Lamarck (1744–1829) propounds theory of inheritance of acquired characteristics

Non-Euclidean geometries developed by Lobachevsky (1793–1856) and Riemann (1826–66)

Faraday (1791–1867), experimental physicist

Carnot (1796–1832) propounds second law of thermodynamics

Carlyle (1795–1841) publishes *The French Revolution* 1837

British franchise widened to include male middle class 1832, and much of male working class 1867

Dickens 1812–70

Engels (1820–95) publishes *The Condition of the Working Class in England* 1845

Marx (1818–83) publishes *Manifesto of the Communist Party* (with Engels) 1848, *Das Kapital* 1867, 1885, 1893

Emerson 1803–82

Spencer 1820–1903

Pre-Raphaelite Brotherhood founded by Hunt, Millais, Rossetti 1848

Major unrest in Paris. Louis-Philippe abdicates throne and Louis-Napoléon elected President 1848

Louis-Napoléon largely reverses reforms of 1848 in 1851

Great Exhibition in London 1851

Thoreau 1817–62

Dostoevsky 1821–81

Ruskin (1819–1900) publishes *Modern Painters* (1843–60)

Crimean War 1854–5

George Eliot 1819–80

Indian Mutiny repressed 1857

Darwin publishes *The Origin of Species* 1859

American Civil War 1861–5

Cardinal J. H. Newman (1801–90) publishes *Apologia pro vita mea* 1864

Courbet (1819–77) promotes realist movement in painting

Women get the vote in the American state of Wyoming 1869

Dilthey 1833–1911

Sidgwick (1838–1900) publishes *The Methods of Ethics* 1874

Mach (1838–1916) publishes *The Science of Mechanics* 1883, *Popular Scientific Lectures* 1894 (or 1896)

Franco-Prussian War 1870–1

Matthew Arnold 1822–88

Tolstoy 1828–1910

Brentano (1838–1917) publishes *Psychology from an Empirical Standpoint* 1874, *The Origin of our Knowledge of Right and Wrong* 1889

Peirce 1834–1914

Nietzsche (1844–1900) publishes *Thus Spake Zarathustra* 1883–5, *Beyond Good and Evil* 1886

William James (1842–1910) publishes *The Principles of Psychology* 1890, *The Varieties of Religious Experience* 1902, *Pragmatism* 1907

Cantor 1845–1914

Bradley (1846–1924) publishes *Appearance and Reality* 1893

Frege (1848–1925) publishes *The Foundations of Arithmetic* 1884, 'On Sense and Reference' 1892

Poincaré 1854–1912

Husserl (1859–1938) publishes *Philosophy of Arithmetic* 1891, *Logical Investigations* 1900–1, *Cartesian Meditations* 1931

Bergson (1859–1941) publishes *Time and Free Will* 1889, *Matter and Memory* 1896, *Creative Evolution* 1907, *The Two Sources of Morality and Religion* 1932

Dewey 1859–1952

Meinong (1853–1920) publishes *On Assumptions* 1902, 'On the Theory of Objects' 1904

Croce (1866–1952) publishes *Aesthetic* 1902

Scheler 1874–1928

Moore (1873–1958) publishes *Principia Ethica* 1903, 'Refutation of Idealism' 1903

Russell (1872–1970) publishes *The Principles of Mathematics* 1903, *Principia Mathematica* (with Whitehead) 1910–13, *Our Knowledge of the External World* 1914

Duhem (1861–1916) publishes *The Aim and Structure of Physical Theory* 1906

Santayana 1863–1952

Alexander (1859–1938) publishes *Space, Time and Deity* 1920

William Thomson, Lord Kelvin (1824–1907), physicist

Maxwell (1831–74) unites electricity and magnetism 1873

Impressionist exhibitions in Paris 1874–86

Michelson–Morley experiment shows that speed of light is unaffected by direction of travel, 1888 and after

Oscar Wilde 1854–1900

Boer War 1899–1902

Freud (1856–1939) publishes *The Interpretation of Dreams* 1900, *The Psychopathology of Everyday Life* 1905, *Totem and Taboo* 1913

Bloomsbury Group of intellectuals including the Woolfs, the Bells, J. M. Keynes, Lytton Strachey, E. M. Forster, etc., influenced by Moore's *Principia Ethica* 1903, comes into existence *c.*1905

Einstein (1879–1955) devises special relativity theory 1905

Bohr (1885–1962) publishes theory of hydrogen atom 1913

First World War 1914–18

Einstein (1879–1955) introduces general relativity theory 1915, confirmed by solar eclipse 1919

Jung, psychologist, 1875–1961

Lenin (1870–1924) masterminds Bolshevik Revolution in Russia 1917, inaugurating communism there

Treaty of Versailles, imposing crippling war reparations on Germany 1919

J. M. Keynes (1883–1946) publishes *The Economic Consequences of the Peace* 1919; start of Keynesian economics

1900

McTaggart (1866–1925) publishes *The Nature of Existence* 1921

Wittgenstein (1889–1951) publishes *Tractatus Logico-Philosophicus* 1921

Schlick 1882–1936

Ramsey 1903–30

Broad (1887–1971) publishes *The Mind and its Place in Nature* 1925, *Five Types of Ethical Theory* 1930

Heidegger (1889–1976) publishes *Sein und Zeit* 1927

Whitehead (1861–1947) publishes *Process and Reality* 1929

Carnap (1891–1970) publishes *Der Logische Aufbau der Welt* 1928, *The Unity of Science* 1932, *Meaning and Necessity* 1947, *Logical Foundations of Probability* 1950

Gödel (1906–78) publishes his incompleteness theorems 1931

Maritain 1882–1973

Jaspers 1883–1969

Bachelard 1884–1962

Marcel 1889–1973

Reichenbach 1891–1953

H. H. Price (1899–1984) publishes *Perception* 1932

Popper (1902–94) publishes *The Logic of Scientific Discovery* 1935, *The Open Society and its Enemies* 1945

Ayer (1910–89) publishes *Language, Truth and Logic* 1936

Collingwood (1889–1943) publishes *An Essay on Metaphysics* 1940

Merleau-Ponty (1908–61) publishes *La Structure du comportement* 1942, *La Phénoménologie de la perception* 1945

Sartre (1905–80) publishes *L'Être et le néant* 1943

Mussolini (1883–1945) forms Fascist government in Italy 1922

T. S. Eliot (1888–1965) publishes *The Waste Land* 1922

James Joyce (1882–1941) publishes *Ulysses* (burnt by American Post Office) 1922, *Finnegan's Wake* 1939

General strike in Great Britain defeated 1926

Trotsky (1879–1940) expelled from Russian Communist Party 1927

Heisenberg's uncertainty principle 1927

Eddington (1882–1944) publishes *The Nature of the Physical World* 1928

Fleming (1881–1954) discovers penicillin 1928

Economic depression hits Europe and America 1929

Roosevelt elected US President 1932

Karl Barth, theologian, 1886–1968

Hitler (1889–1945) takes power 1933 and annexes Austria 1938, causing exodus of many intellectuals including philosophers

Alan Turing (1912–54) conceives universal digital computing machine

Franco (1892–1975) gains power in Spain after Civil War 1936–9

Munich Agreement offers 'peace in our time' 1938

German–Soviet pact 1939

Second World War, ended by atomic bombs, 1939–45

Orwell (1903–50) publishes *Animal Farm* 1945, *Nineteen Eighty-Four* (written in 1948) 1949

Labour government introduces socialist measures in Great Britain 1945–51

Camus (1913–60) publishes *L'Étranger* 1946

'Iron Curtain' named by Churchill 1946

First meeting of the General Assembly of the United Nations 1946

India given independence 1947

Ryle (1900–76) publishes *The Concept of Mind* 1949

De Beauvoir publishes *Le Deuxième Sexe* 1949

Quine (1908–) publishes *Methods of Logic* 1950, *From a Logical Point of View* 1952, *Word and Object* 1960

Tarski 1902–83

Hare publishes *The Language of Morals* 1952

Wittgenstein's *Philosophical Investigations* published posthumously 1953

'Australian materialism' develops in 1950s

Goodman (born 1906) publishes *Fact, Fiction, and Forecast* 1955

Marcuse (1898–1979) publishes *Eros and Civilization* 1955

Church 1903–

Chisholm (born 1916) publishes *The Philosophy of Perception* 1957

Adorno 1903–69

Ricœur 1913–

P. F. Strawson (born 1919) publishes *Individuals* 1959

Gadamer (born 1900) publishes *Truth and Method* 1960

Foucault (1926–84) publishes *Histoire de la folie* 1961

Kuhn (born 1922) publishes *The Structure of Scientific Revolutions* 1962

Sense and Sensibilia and *How to Do Things with Words*, by J. L. Austin (1911–60), published 1962

Habermas (born 1929) publishes *Theorie und Praxis* 1963

Althusser (born 1918) publishes *Pour Marx* 1965

Derrida (born 1930) publishes *L'Écriture et la différence* 1967

Davidson (born 1917) publishes 'Truth and Meaning' 1967, 'Mental Events' 1970

Berlin (born 1909) publishes *Four Essays on Liberty* 1969

Putnam 1926–

Kripke (born 1940) publishes 'Naming and Necessity' 1972

Rawls (born 1921) publishes *A Theory of Justice* 1972

Mahatma Gandhi (born 1869) assassinated 1948

'Steady state' cosmology proposed 1948

Communists under Mao Tse-tung take over China 1949

Korean War 1950–3

Joseph McCarthy (1908–57) conducts campaign against Communists in USA, 1950–4

Stalin (born 1879) dies 1953

Russia suppresses Hungarian revolt 1956

Russia launches first Sputnik 1957

Chomsky (born 1928) publishes *Syntactic Structures* 1957

European Common Market established 1958

Castro becomes leader of Cuba 1959

Berlin Wall constructed 1961

Cuba crisis threatens nuclear war 1962

US 'military advisers' in Vietnam 1962

J. F. Kennedy assassinated 1963

Campaign for civil rights in USA

Russell active in campaign against British nuclear deterrent

Expansion of British universities during 1960s

Arab–Israeli Six Day War 1967

Soviet forces suppress 'Prague Spring' 1968

Student riots in Paris and elsewhere 1968

Women get the vote in Switzerland 1971

Withdrawal of US troops from Vietnam 1971

Dummett (born 1925) publishes *Frege: Philosophy of Language* 1973

Mackie (1917–81) publishes *The Cement of the Universe* 1974

Nozick (born 1938) publishes *Anarchy, State and Utopia* 1974

Spain returns to democracy 1975

Searle (born 1932) publishes 'Minds, Brains, and Programs' 1980

Rorty (born 1931) publishes *Philosophy and the Mirror of Nature* 1980

'Thatcherism' introduced in UK after Conservative election victory 1979

War in Afghanistan between Soviet troops and Mujaheddin guerillas 1979–89

Shipyard strike in Poland leads to the concession of workers' rights and the formation of the Solidarność union confederation 1980

MacIntyre (born 1929) publishes *After Virtue* 1981

Parfit (born 1942) publishes *Reasons and Persons* 1984

Bernard Williams (born 1929) publishes *Ethics and the Limits of Philosophy* 1985

Thomas Nagel (born 1937) publishes *The View from Nowhere* 1986

Deaths of IRA hunger strikers 1981

German Green party wins first parliamentary seats 1983

John Paul II becomes the first pope to visit a synagogue

Gorbachev campaigns for *glasnost* (openness) in the Soviet Union 1987

Collapse of communism in Soviet Union and Eastern Europe 1989, followed by political fragmentation and intellectual liberation

100-day war against Iraq by UN (mainly US) forces 1991

Nelson Mandela elected president in South Africa's first universally representative elections 1994

Demilitarization of Northern Ireland begins 1994, after 25 years

GUIDE TO
FURTHER READING

SOCRATES

Represented in the dialogues written by Plato. Plato's Socrates is considered to be closest to the historical Socrates in the following works:

Early Socratic Dialogues (*Ion, Laches, Lysis, Charmides, Hippias Major, Hippias Minor, Euthydemus*) translated by Trevor J. Saunders, Iain Lane, Donald Watt, and Robin Waterfield, with introduction by Trevor J. Saunders (Penguin, 1987): 400 pp.

Defence [*Apology*] *of Socrates, Euthyphro, Crito*, translated with introduction by David Gallop (Oxford UP, 1997): 160 pp.

Protagoras, Gorgias, Phaedo: see under PLATO below.

Another source is:

Xenophon: *Memoirs of Socrates* and *Apology*, translated by H. Tredennick, revised by Robin Waterfield (Penguin, 1990): 384 pp.

C. C. W. Taylor: *Socrates* (Past Masters, Oxford UP, 1998): 120 pp.

Gregory Vlastos: *Socrates: Ironist and Moral Philosopher* (Cambridge UP, 1991): 320 pp.

Thomas C. Brickhouse and Nicholas D. Smith: *Plato's Socrates* (Oxford UP, 1994): 254 pp.

PLATO

Collected Dialogues, edited by E. Hamilton and D. Cairns (Princeton, 1961).

Protagoras, translated with introduction and notes by C. C. W. Taylor (Oxford UP, 1996): 122 pp.

Gorgias, translated with commentary by Terence Irwin (Oxford UP, 1979): 280 pp.

Meno, translated by G. M. A. Grube, 2nd edn. (Hackett, 1990): 39 pp.

Phaedo, translated with notes by David Gallop (Oxford UP, 1993): 134 pp.

Phaedrus, with Letters VII and VIII, translated by W. Hamilton (Penguin, 1973): 160 pp.

Symposium, translated with introduction and notes by Robin Waterfield (Oxford UP, 1994): 150 pp.

Republic, translated with introduction and notes by Robin Waterfield (Oxford UP, 1993): 548 pp.

Parmenides, translated by Mary Louise Gill and Paul Ryan, with introduction by Mary Louise Gill (Hackett, 1996): 144 pp.

Theaetetus, translated by M. J. Levett, revised by Myles Burnyeat, with introduction by Bernard Williams (Hackett, 1992): 128 pp.

Timaeus and *Critias*, translated with introduction by Desmond Lee (Penguin, 1971): 176 pp.

Sophist, translated by Nicholas P. White (Hackett, 1993): 144 pp.

Statesman, translated by Robin Waterfield, edited by Julia Annas (Cambridge UP, 1995): 200 pp.

Philebus, translated by Dorothea Frede (Hackett, 1993): 176 pp.

The Laws, translated with introduction by Trevor J. Saunders (Penguin, 1970): 560 pp.

G. M. A. Grube: *Plato's Thought*, 2nd edn. (Hackett/Blackwell, 1980): 218 pp.

Richard Kraut (ed.): *The Cambridge Companion to Plato* (Cambridge UP, 1992): 576 pp.

Julia Annas: *An Introduction to Plato's Republic* (Oxford UP, 1981): 370 pp.

Terence Irwin: *Plato's Ethics* (Oxford UP, 1995): 464 pp.

Gail Fine (ed.): *Plato*, two volumes (Oxford Readings in Philosophy, Oxford UP, 1999).

ARISTOTLE

Nicomachean Ethics, translated with introduction by W. D. Ross (Oxford UP, 1954): 320 pp.

Politics, translated by Ernest Barker, revised with introduction and notes by R. F. Stalley (Oxford UP, 1955): 456 pp.

De Anima, translated with introduction by Hugh Lawson-Tancred (Penguin, 1987): 256 pp.

Physics, translated by Robin Waterfield, with introduction and notes by David Bostock (Oxford UP, 1996): 382 pp.

Poetics, translated by Richard Janko (Hackett, 1987): 261 pp.

The Complete Works of Aristotle: The Revised Oxford Translation, edited by Jonathan Barnes, two volumes (Princeton UP, 1983).

The *Categories, De Interpretatione, Posterior Analytics, Politics*, and selected books from the *Eudemian Ethics, Nicomachean Ethics, Metaphysics, De Anima, Topics*, and the scientific works are available in translation with detailed philosophical commentaries in the Clarendon Aristotle Series (Oxford UP).

Anthologies:

Introductory Readings, translated and edited by Terence Irwin and Gail Fine (Hackett, 1996): 386 pp.

Selections, translated and edited by Terence Irwin and Gail Fine (Hackett, 1995): 650 pp.

A New Aristotle Reader, translations edited by J. L. Ackrill (Oxford UP, 1987): 600 pp.

Jonathan Barnes: *Aristotle* (Past Masters, Oxford UP, 1982): 112 pp.

J. L. Ackrill: *Aristotle the Philosopher* (Oxford UP, 1981): 168 pp.

W. D. Ross: *Aristotle* (6th edn. Routledge, 1995): 336 pp.

Terence Irwin: *Aristotle's First Principles* (Oxford UP, 1988): 720 pp.

R. R. K. Sorabji: *Necessity, Cause, and Blame: Perspectives on Aristotle's Theory* (Duckworth, 1981): 326 pp.

G. E. R. Lloyd: *Aristotle: The Growth and Structure of his Thought* (Cambridge UP, 1968): 324 pp.

AUGUSTINE

The Confessions, translated with introduction by Henry Chadwick (Oxford UP, 1991): 340 pp.

On Christian Teaching, translated by R. P. Green (Oxford UP, 1998).

City of God, translated by H. Bettenson, edited by D. Knowles (Penguin, 1984): 1152 pp.

On Free Choice of the Will, translated with introduction by Thomas Williams (Hackett, 1993): 192 pp.

Against the Academicians and *The Teacher*, translated with introduction and notes by Peter King (Hackett, 1995): 208 pp.

Political Writings, translated by Douglas Kries and Michael W. Tkacz, edited with introduction by E. L. Fortin (Hackett, 1994): 304 pp.

Henry Chadwick: *Augustine* (Past Masters, Oxford UP, 1986): 128 pp.

C. A. Kirwan: *Augustine* (Arguments of the Philosophers, Routledge, 1989): 224 pp.

John M. Rist: *Augustine: Ancient Thought Baptized* (Cambridge UP, 1996): 356 pp.

AQUINAS

Selected Philosophical Writings, translated with introduction by Timothy Mc-Dermott (Oxford UP, 1993): 490 pp.

Basic Writings, translations edited with introduction by Anton C. Pegis (1945; reissue by Hackett, 1997): two volumes, 2362 pp.

On Law, Morality, and Politics, translations edited by W. P. Baumgarth and R. J. Regan (Hackett, 1988): 316 pp.

Anthony Kenny: *Aquinas* (Past Masters, Oxford UP, 1979): 94 pp.

Brian Davies: *The Thought of Thomas Aquinas* (Oxford UP, 1992): 408 pp.

Norman Kretzmann and Eleonore Stump (eds.): *The Cambridge Companion to Aquinas* (Cambridge UP, 1993): 312 pp.

Frederick Copleston: *Aquinas* (Penguin, 1956): 272 pp.

HOBBES

Leviathan, edited by Richard Tuck (Cambridge UP, 1996): 612 pp.
Leviathan, edited by Edwin Curley (Hackett, 1994): 672 pp.
De Homine and *De Cive*, edited by Bernard Gert (Hackett, 1991): 394 pp.
The Elements of Law, edited by J. C. A. Gaskin (Oxford UP, 1994): 340 pp.

Richard Tuck: *Hobbes* (Past Masters, Oxford UP, 1989): 136 pp.
Jean Hampton: *Hobbes and the Social Contract Tradition* (Cambridge UP, 1988): 311 pp.
Tom Sorell (ed.): *The Cambridge Companion to Hobbes* (Cambridge UP, 1996): 416 pp.

DESCARTES

Meditations on First Philosophy, translated with selections from the *Objections and Replies*, edited by John Cottingham with introduction by Bernard Williams (Cambridge UP): 166 pp.
Discourse on Method, translated by Donald A. Cress (Hackett, 1980): 58 pp.
Passions of the Soul, translated by S. H. Voss (Hackett, 1989): 191 pp.
Selected Philosophical Writings, translated and edited by John Cottingham, Dugald Murdoch, and Robert Stoothoff (Cambridge UP, 1993): 272 pp.

John Cottingham: *Descartes* (Blackwell, 1986): 184 pp.
Anthony Kenny: *Descartes: A Study of his Philosophy* (1968; reissue Thoemmes, 1993): 252 pp.
Bernard Williams: *Descartes: The Project of Pure Inquiry* (Penguin, 1978): 320 pp.
Margaret D. Wilson: *Descartes* (Arguments of the Philosophers, Routledge, 1982): 276 pp.
Stephen Gaukroger: *Descartes: An Intellectual Biography* (Oxford UP, 1995): 520 pp.
John Cottingham (ed.): *Descartes* (Oxford Readings in Philosophy, Oxford UP, 1998): 250 pp.
John Cottingham (ed.): *The Cambridge Companion to Descartes* (Cambridge UP, 1992): 455 pp.

SPINOZA

Ethics, translated by Edwin Curley, with introduction by Stuart Hampshire (Penguin, 1996): 208 pp.
Ethics, translated with introduction and notes by G. H. R. Parkinson (Oxford UP, 1999).
Ethics, with *Treatise on the Emendation of the Intellect* and *Selected Letters*, translated by Samuel Shirley (Hackett, 1992): 304 pp.
Theological-Political Treatise, translated by Samuel Shirley, with introduction by Seymour Feldman (Hackett, 1998): 316 pp.

Roger Scruton: *Spinoza* (Past Masters, Oxford UP, 1986): 128 pp.

Jonathan Bennett: *A Study of Spinoza's Ethics* (Hackett, 1984): 406 pp.

Genevieve Lloyd: *Spinoza and the Ethics* (Routledge Philosophy GuideBooks, 1996): 176 pp.

Stuart Hampshire: *Spinoza* (Penguin, 1951): 192 pp.

Don Garrett (ed.): *The Cambridge Companion to Spinoza* (Cambridge UP, 1995): 479 pp.

Alan Donagan: *Spinoza* (University of Chicago Press, 1989): 238 pp.

Edwin Curley: *Behind the Geometrical Method: A Reading of Spinoza's Ethics* (Princeton UP, 1988): 200 pp.

LOCKE

An Essay concerning Human Understanding, edited by Peter H. Nidditch (Oxford UP, 1975): 924 pp.

An Essay concerning Human Understanding, edited by R. S. Woolhouse (Penguin, 1997): 816 pp.

An Essay concerning Human Understanding, abridged and edited with introduction by Kenneth P. Winkler (Hackett, 1996): 416 pp.

Two Treatises of Government, edited by Peter Laslett, 3rd edn. (Cambridge UP, 1988): 480 pp.

A Letter concerning Toleration, edited by James H. Tully (Hackett, 1983): 72 pp.

Some Thoughts concerning Education and *Of the Conduct of the Understanding*, edited by Ruth Grant and Nathan Tarcov (Hackett, 1996): 256 pp.

John Dunn: *Locke* (Past Masters, Oxford UP, 1984): 112 pp.

E. J. Lowe: *Locke on Human Understanding* (Routledge Philosophy GuideBooks, 1995): 216 pp.

R. S. Woolhouse: *Locke* (Harvester, 1983).

Nicholas Jolley: *Locke* (Oxford UP, 1999): 248 pp.

J. L. Mackie: *Problems from Locke* (Oxford UP, 1976): 248 pp.

Michael Ayers: *Locke* (Arguments of the Philosophers, Routledge, 1993): 704 pp.

Vere Chappell (ed.): *Locke* (Oxford Readings in Philosophy, Oxford UP, 1998): 280 pp.

Vere Chappell (ed.): *The Cambridge Companion to Locke* (Cambridge UP, 1994): 343 pp.

LEIBNIZ

Philosophical Texts, translated with introduction and notes by Roger Woolhouse and Richard Francks (Oxford Philosophical Texts, Oxford UP, 1998): 320 pp.

Discourse on Metaphysics and Other Essays, translated by Daniel Garber and Roger Ariew (Hackett, 1991): 96 pp.

New Essays on Human Understanding, translated by Peter Remnant and Jonathan Bennett (Cambridge UP, 1981).

Benson Mates: *The Philosophy of Leibniz* (Oxford UP, 1986): 280 pp.
Nicholas Rescher: *Leibniz: An Introduction to his Philosophy* (Gregg Revivals, 1993): 170 pp.
Robert M. Adams: *Leibniz: Determinist, Theist, Idealist* (Oxford UP, 1994): 444 pp.
Nicholas Jolley (ed.): *The Cambridge Companion to Leibniz* (Cambridge UP, 1994): 512 pp.

BERKELEY

The Principles of Human Knowledge, edited with introduction and notes by Jonathan Dancy (Oxford Philosophical Texts, Oxford UP, 1998): 244 pp.
Three Dialogues between Hylas and Philonous, edited with introduction and notes by Jonathan Dancy (Oxford Philosophical Texts, Oxford UP, 1998): 192 pp.
Philosophical Works, edited by M. R. Ayers (Everyman, 1993).

A. C. Grayling: *Berkeley: The Central Arguments* (Duckworth, 1987): 230 pp.
David Berman: *George Berkeley: Idealism and the Man* (Oxford UP, 1994): 241 pp.
Kenneth Winkler: *Berkeley: An Interpretation* (Oxford UP, 1989): 322 pp.

HUME

A Treatise of Human Nature, edited by L. A. Selby-Bigge, revised by P. H. Nidditch (Oxford UP, 1978): 764 pp.
An Enquiry concerning Human Understanding, edited with introduction and notes by Tom L. Beauchamp (Oxford Philosophical Texts, Oxford UP, 1999): 304 pp.
An Enquiry concerning the Principles of Morals, edited with introduction and notes by Tom L. Beauchamp (Oxford Philosophical Texts, Oxford UP, 1998): 298 pp.
Dialogues concerning Natural Religion and *The Natural History of Religion*, edited with introduction by J. C. A. Gaskin (Oxford UP, 1993): 250 pp.
Political Essays, edited with introduction by Knud Haakonssen (Cambridge UP, 1994): 414 pp.
Selected Essays, edited with introduction by Stephen Copley and Andrew Edgar (Oxford UP, 1993): 438 pp.

Barry Stroud: *Hume* (Arguments of the Philosophers, Routledge, 1981): 292 pp.
David Fate Norton (ed.): *The Cambridge Companion to Hume* (Cambridge UP, 1993): 416 pp.
David Pears: *Hume's System* (Oxford UP, 1990): 216 pp.
David Fate Norton: *David Hume: Common Sense Moralist, Sceptical Metaphysician* (Princeton UP, 1982).

J. C. A. Gaskin: *Hume's Philosophy of Religion*, revised version (Macmillan, 1987): 264 pp.

KANT

Critique of Pure Reason, translated by Norman Kemp Smith (Macmillan): 682 pp.

Prolegomena to Any Future Metaphysics, translated by Lewis White Beck (Prentice-Hall, 1950).

Groundwork of the Metaphysic of Morals, translated by H. J. Paton (*The Moral Law*, Routledge, 1976): 144 pp.

Critique of Practical Reason, translated by Lewis White Beck, new edition (Macmillan, 1992): 198 pp.

Critique of Judgement, translated by James Creed Meredith (Oxford UP, 1952): 436 pp.

The Metaphysics of Morals, English translation (Cambridge UP, 1991): 400 pp.

Lectures on Ethics, translated by Louis Infield (Hackett, 1981): 269 pp.

Perpetual Peace and Other Essays on Politics, History, and Morals, translated by Ted Humphrey (Hackett, 1983): 162 pp.

Roger Scruton: *Kant* (Past Masters, Oxford UP, 1982): 112 pp.

Stephan Körner: *Kant* (Penguin, 1955): 249 pp.

H. E. Allison: *Kant's Transcendental Idealism* (Yale UP, 1986): 400 pp.

Ottfried Höffe: *Immanuel Kant*, translated by M. Farrier (SUNY Press, 1994): 290 pp.

Roger J. Sullivan: *An Introduction to Kant's Ethics* (Cambridge UP, 1994): 191 pp.

Paul Guyer (ed.): *The Cambridge Companion to Kant* (Cambridge UP, 1992): 492 pp.

R. C. S. Walker: *Kant* (Arguments of the Philosophers, Routledge, 1978).

P. F. Strawson: *The Bounds of Sense: An Essay on Kant's Critique of Pure Reason* (Routledge, 1966): 296 pp.

Ernst Cassirer: *Kant's Life and Thought* (Yale UP, 1981): 464 pp.

BENTHAM

Introduction to the Principles of Morals and Legislation, edited by J. H. Burns and H. L. A. Hart (Oxford UP, 1970, revised edition 1996): 456 pp.

A Fragment on Government, edited by J. H. Burns and H. L. A. Hart (Cambridge UP, 1988): 158 pp.

Panopticon and Other Prison Writings (Verso, 1995): 240 pp.

Bentham's Theory of Fictions, edited by C. K. Ogden (1932; reissue AMS Press).

J. R. Dinwiddy: *Bentham* (Past Masters, Oxford UP, 1989): 140 pp.

Ross Harrison: *Bentham* (Arguments of the Philosophers, Routledge, 1985): 224 pp.

H. L. A. Hart: *Essays on Bentham: Jurisprudence and Political Theory* (Oxford UP, 1982): 280 pp.

Gerald J. Postema: *Bentham and the Common Law Tradition* (Oxford UP, 1986): 508 pp.

David Lyons: *In the Interests of the Governed: A Study in Bentham's Philosophy of Utility and Law* (Oxford UP, 1973; revised edition 1991): 175 pp.

Frederick Rosen: *Jeremy Bentham and Representative Democracy: A Study of 'The Constitutional Code'* (Oxford UP, 1983): 138 pp.

Shirley Robin Letwin: *The Pursuit of Certainty: David Hume, Jeremy Bentham, John Stuart Mill* (1965; reissue Liberty Fund, 1998): 379 pp.

HEGEL

Phenomenology of Spirit, translated by A. V. Miller (Oxford UP, 1977): 632 pp.

Philosophy of Right, translated by T. M. Knox (Oxford UP, 1967): 396 pp.

Hegel's Logic (Part One of *The Encyclopaedia of the Philosophical Sciences*), translated by William Wallace (3rd edn., Oxford UP, 1975): 386 pp.

Hegel's Philosophy of Mind (Part Three of *The Encyclopaedia of the Philosophical Sciences*), with the *Zusätze*, translated by A. V. Miller (Oxford UP, 1971): 342 pp.

Introduction to The Philosophy of History with selections from *The Philosophy of Right*, translated by Leo Rauch (Hackett, 1988): 123 pp.

On Art, Religion, and the History of Philosophy: Introductory Lectures, edited by J. Glenn Gray, with introduction by Tom Rockmore (new edn. Hackett, 1997): 342 pp.

Introductory Lectures on Aesthetics, translated by Bernard Bosanquet, with introduction by Michael Inwood (Penguin, 1993): 240 pp.

The Hegel Reader, edited by Stephen Houlgate (Blackwell, 1998): 400 pp.

Peter Singer: *Hegel* (Past Masters, Oxford UP, 1983): 110 pp.

Michael Inwood: *Hegel* (Arguments of the Philosophers, Routledge, 1983): 544 pp.

Charles Taylor: *Hegel* (Cambridge UP, 1977): 580 pp.

H. S. Harris: *Hegel: Phenomenology and System* (Hackett, 1995): 128 pp.

Robert Solomon: *In the Spirit of Hegel* (Oxford UP, 1983) 668 pp.

Michael Inwood: *A Hegel Dictionary* (Blackwell, 1992): 260 pp.

Frederick Beiser (ed.): *The Cambridge Companion to Hegel* (Cambridge UP, 1993): 592 pp.

SCHOPENHAUER

The World as Will and Representation, translated by E. F. J. Payne, two volumes (Dover, 1966): 562 and 694 pp.

On the Basis of Morality, translated by E. F. J. Payne, with introduction by David E. Cartwright (Hackett, 1996): 272 pp.

Essays and Aphorisms, translated by R. J. Hollingdale (Penguin, 1970): 240 pp.

On the Fourfold Root of the Principle of Sufficient Reason, translated by E. F. J. Payne (Open Court, 1977): 288 pp.

Christopher Janaway: *Schopenhauer* (Past Masters, Oxford UP, 1994): 122 pp.
Patrick Gardiner: *Schopenhauer* (Penguin, 1971; Thoemmes, 1997): 315 pp.
Bryan Magee: *The Philosophy of Schopenhauer*, revised edition (Oxford UP, 1997): 464 pp.
John Atwell: *Schopenhauer on the Character of the World* (University of California Press, 1995): 236 pp.

KIERKEGAARD

Either/Or: A Fragment of Life, abridged and translated with introduction by Alastair Hannay (Penguin, 1992): 640 pp.
The Sickness Unto Death, translated with introduction by Alastair Hannay (Penguin, 1989): 192 pp.
Concluding Unscientific Postscript, translated by H. V. and E. H. Hong, two volumes (Princeton UP, 1992).
Papers and Journals: A Selection, translated with introductions by Alastair Hannay (Penguin, 1996): 704 pp.
Fear and Trembling, translated by Alastair Hannay (Penguin, 1985): 160 pp.

Alastair Hannay: *Kierkegaard* (Arguments of the Philosophers, Routledge, 1982): 262 pp.
Patrick Gardiner: *Kierkegaard* (Past Masters, Oxford UP, 1988): 128 pp.
Anthony Rudd: *Kierkegaard and the Limits of the Ethical* (Oxford UP, 1993): 198 pp.
Alastair Hannay and Gordon Marino (eds.): *The Cambridge Companion to Kierkegaard* (Cambridge UP, 1997): 446 pp.
Jonathan Rée and Jane Chamberlain (eds.): *Kierkegaard: A Critical Reader* (Blackwell, 1997): 200 pp.

MILL

On Liberty and Other Essays, edited with an introduction by John Gray (Oxford UP, 1991): 638 pp.
Utilitarianism, edited with introduction and notes by Roger Crisp (Oxford Philosophical Texts, Oxford UP, 1998): 164 pp.
Principles of Political Economy and Chapters on Socialism, edited with an introduction by Jonathan Riley (Oxford UP, 1994).
The Subjection of Women, edited by Susan M. Okin (Hackett, 1988): 127 pp.
Autobiography, edited with an introduction by John Robinson (Penguin, 1989): 240 pp.
A System of Logic (Lincoln-Rembrandt, 1986).

John Skorupski: *John Stuart Mill* (Arguments of the Philosophers, Routledge, 1989): 448 pp.

Jonathan Riley: *Mill on Liberty* (Routledge Philosophy GuideBooks, 1998): 256 pp.

Roger Crisp: *Mill on Utilitarianism* (Routledge Philosophy GuideBooks, 1997): 256 pp.

Alan Ryan: *The Philosophy of John Stuart Mill*, new edition (Macmillan, 1998): 304 pp.

John Skorupski (ed.): *The Cambridge Companion to Mill* (Cambridge UP, 1998): 607 pp.

MARX

Selected Writings, edited by David McLellan (Oxford UP, 1977): 636 pp.

Early Political Writings, edited by Joseph O'Malley (Cambridge UP, 1994): 230 pp.

Writings of the Young Marx on Philosophy and Society, edited and translated by Loyd D. Easton and Kurt M. Guddat (1967; Hackett, 1977): 512 pp.

Capital: A Critique of Political Economy, translated by Ben Fowkes and David Fernbach, with introductions by Ernest Mandel, three volumes (Penguin, 1990–2): 1152 pp., 624 pp., 1152 pp.

Grundrisse: Foundations of the Critique of Political Economy, translated by Martin Nicolaus (Penguin, 1993): 912 pp.

Political Writings, edited with introductions by David Fernbach, three volumes (Penguin, 1993): 368 pp., 384 pp., 432 pp.

With Friedrich Engels: *The Communist Manifesto*, translated by David McLellan (Oxford UP, 1998): 190 pp.

Peter Singer: *Marx* (Past Masters, Oxford UP, 1980): 92 pp.

Allen Wood: *Karl Marx* (Arguments of the Philosophers, Routledge, 1985): 290 pp.

John Elster: *An Introduction to Karl Marx* (Cambridge UP, 1986): 200 pp.

G. A. Cohen: *Karl Marx's Theory of History: A Defence* (Oxford UP, 1980): 386 pp.

Isaiah Berlin: *Karl Marx: His Life and Environment*, revised edition (Fontana, 1995): 335 pp.

David Conway: *A Farewell to Marx: An Outline and Appraisal of his Theories* (Penguin, 1987): 231 pp.

NIETZSCHE

On the Genealogy of Morality, translated with introduction by Maudemarie Clark and Alan Swensen (Hackett, 1998): 192 pp.

Beyond Good and Evil, translated by R. J. Hollingdale, with introduction by Michael Tanner (Penguin, 1990): 240 pp.

Twilight of the Idols and *The Anti-Christ*, translated by R. J. Hollingdale, with introduction by Michael Tanner (Penguin, 1990): 208 pp.

The Birth of Tragedy, translated by Shaun Whiteside, edited with introduction by Michael Tanner (Penguin, 1993): 160 pp.

The Gay Science, English translation (Random House, 1974).

Ecce Homo, translated by R. J. Hollingdale (Penguin, 1992): 144 pp.

Thus Spoke Zarathustra, translated by R. J. Hollingdale (Penguin, 1969): 352 pp.

Untimely Meditations, translated by R. J. Hollingdale, edited with introduction by Daniel Breazeale (Cambridge UP, 1997): 336 pp.

Human, All Too Human, edited by Richard Schacht (Cambridge UP, 1996): 429 pp.

Daybreak: Thoughts on the Prejudices of Morality, translated by R. J. Hollingdale, edited with introduction by Maudemarie Clark and Brian Leiter (Cambridge UP, 1997): 260 pp.

On the Advantage and Disadvantage of History for Life, translated by Peter Preuss (Hackett, 1980): 70 pp.

Michael Tanner: *Nietzsche* (Past Masters, Oxford UP, 1994): 94 pp.

Richard Schacht: *Nietzsche* (Arguments of the Philosophers, Routledge, 1985): 568 pp.

Alexander Nehamas: *Nietzsche: Life as Literature* (Harvard UP, 1985): 272 pp.

John Richardson: *Nietzsche's System* (Oxford UP, 1996): 328 pp.

Maudemarie Clark: *Nietzsche on Truth and Philosophy* (Cambridge UP, 1991): 312 pp.

Bernd Magnus and Kathleen Higgins (eds.): *The Cambridge Companion to Nietzsche* (Cambridge UP, 1996): 415 pp.

Arthur C. Danto: *Nietzsche as Philosopher* (Columbia UP, 1980): 250 pp.

Walter Kaufmann: *Nietzsche: Philosopher, Psychologist, Antichrist* (Princeton UP, 1975).

Ronald Hayman: *Nietzsche: A Critical Life* (Phoenix, 1995): 448 pp.

PEIRCE

The Essential Peirce, edited by N. Hauser and C. Kloesel: vol. 1 (1992): 448 pp.; vol. 2 (1998): 640 pp.

Philosophical Writings, edited by J. Buchler (Dover, 1940): 386 pp.

Reasoning and the Logic of Things, edited by K. L. Ketner (Harvard UP, 1993): 312 pp.

Christopher Hookway: *Peirce* (Arguments of the Philosophers, Routledge, 1985): 328 pp.

Murray G. Murphy: *The Development of Peirce's Philosophy* (Hackett, 1993): 438 pp.

Max Fisch: *Peirce, Semiotic and Pragmatism* (Indiana UP, 1986): 480 pp.

Carl R. Hausman: *Charles S. Peirce's Evolutionary Philosophy* (Cambridge UP, 1993): 288 pp.

J. Brent: *Charles Sanders Peirce: A Life*, revised edition (Indiana UP, 1998): 448 pp.

Israel Scheffler: *Four Pragmatists* (see under JAMES).

JAMES

The Principles of Psychology (Harvard UP, 1983): 1392 pp.

The Varieties of Religious Experience, edited by Martin E. Marty (Penguin, 1982): 576 pp.

Pragmatism: A New Name for Some Old Ways of Thinking, edited by F. H. Burkhardt and F. Bowers (Harvard UP, 1978): 400 pp.

Some Problems of Philosophy (University of Nebraska Press, 1996): 249 pp.

Selected Writings, edited by Graham Bird (Everyman, 1995).

Graham Bird: *William James* (Routledge, 1987): 221 pp.

Marcus Ford: *William James's Philosophy: A New Perspective* (University of Massachusetts Press, 1982): 136 pp.

Ruth Anna Putnam (ed.): *The Cambridge Companion to William James* (Cambridge UP, 1997): 418 pp.

Israel Scheffler: *Four Pragmatists: A Critical Introduction to Peirce, James, Mead and Dewey* (Routledge, 1986): 288 pp.

FREGE

The Frege Reader, edited by Michael Beaney (Blackwell, 1997): 432 pp.

Now out of print are:
The Foundations of Arithmetic, translated by J. L. Austin (Blackwell)
and
Philosophical Writings, edited by Peter Geach and Max Black (Blackwell).

Anthony Kenny: *Frege* (Penguin, 1995): 240 pp.

Hans Sluga: *Gottlob Frege* (Arguments of the Philosophers, Routledge, 1980); 224 pp.

Michael Dummett: *Frege: Philosophy of Language* (Duckworth, 1973): 708 pp.

Michael Dummett: *Frege: Philosophy of Mathematics* (Duckworth, 1991): 331 pp.

Michael Dummett: *The Interpretation of Frege's Philosophy* (Harvard UP, 1987): 752 pp.

Joan Weiner: *Frege in Perspective* (Cornell UP, 1990): 304 pp.

HUSSERL

Cartesian Meditations (Kluwer, 1977): 169 pp.

Logical Investigations, two volumes (Humanities Press, 1970).

Ideas for a Pure Phenomenology, three volumes (Kluwer, 1982–9).

Phenomenology of The Consciousness of Internal Time, translated by J. B. Brough (Kluwer, 1992): 468 pp.

The Crisis of European Sciences and Transcendental Phenomenology (Northwestern UP, 1970): 405 pp.

David Bell: *Husserl* (Arguments of the Philosophers, Routledge, 1991): 288 pp.

Barry Smith and David Woodruff Smith (eds.): *The Cambridge Companion to Husserl* (Cambridge UP, 1995): 528 pp.

RUSSELL

The Basic Writings of Bertrand Russell, edited by Robert E. Egner and Lester E. Denoun (Routledge, 1992): 744 pp.

Logic and Knowledge (Routledge, 1959): 400 pp.

Problems of Philosophy, with introduction by John Skorupski (Oxford UP, 1998): 128 pp.

Introduction to Mathematical Philosophy, with introduction by John G. Slater (Routledge, 1993): 208 pp.

The Principles of Mathematics, with introduction by John G. Slater (Routledge, 1992): 592 pp.

Our Knowledge of the External World, with introduction by John G. Slater (Routledge, 1993): 56 pp.

An Inquiry into Meaning and Truth, with introduction by Thomas Baldwin (Routledge, 1996): 68 pp.

Theory of Knowledge, edited by Elizabeth Ramsden Eames and Kenneth Blackwell (Routledge, 1992): 248 pp.

Philosophical Essays (Routledge, 1994): 160 pp.

The Analysis of Matter, 3rd edition, with introduction by John G. Slater (Routledge, 1992): 424 pp.

Autobiography (Routledge): 752 pp.

R. M. Sainsbury: *Russell* (Arguments of the Philosophers, Routledge, 1979).

A. C. Grayling: *Russell* (Past Masters, Oxford UP, 1996): 124 pp.

Peter Hylton: *Russell, Idealism, and the Emergence of Analytic Philosophy* (Oxford UP, 1990): 438 pp.

WITTGENSTEIN

Tractatus Logico-Philosophicus, translated by D. F. Pears and B. F. McGuiness (Routledge, 1961): 112 pp. (216 pp. with German)

Philosophical Investigations, edited by G. E. M. Anscombe (Blackwell, 1953).

Philosophical Remarks, edited by Rush Rhees (Blackwell, 1978): 357 pp.

Philosophical Grammar, edited by Rush Rhees (Blackwell, 1980): 495 pp.

The Blue and Brown Books (Blackwell, 1974): 180 pp.

On Certainty, edited by G. E. M. Anscombe and G. H. von Wright (Blackwell, 1975): 195 pp.

Remarks on the Foundations of Mathematics, edited by G. H. von Wright, Rush Rhees, and G. E. M. Anscombe, third edition (Blackwell, 1981): 444 pp.

The Wittgenstein Reader, edited by Anthony Kenny (Blackwell, 1994): 320 pp.

Anthony Kenny: *Wittgenstein* (Penguin, 1973).

Marie McGinn: *Wittgenstein and the Philosophical Investigations* (Routledge Philosophy GuideBooks, 1997): 240 pp.

David Pears: *The False Prison: A Study of the Development of Wittgenstein's Philosophy*, two volumes (Oxford UP, 1987 and 1988), 224 and 340 pp.

Robert Fogelin: *Wittgenstein*, second edition (Arguments of the Philosophers, Routledge, 1995): 272 pp.

P. M. S. Hacker: *Insight and Illusion*, second edition (Thoemmes, 1998).

Saul Kripke: *Wittgenstein on Rules and Private Language* (Blackwell, 1984): 256 pp.

Hans Sluga and David G. Stern (eds.): *The Cambridge Companion to Wittgenstein* (Cambridge UP, 1996): 518 pp.

HEIDEGGER

Being and Time, translated by J. Macquarrie and E. S. Robinson (1962; Blackwell, 1978): 590 pp.

The Basic Problems of Phenomenology, translated by A. Hofstadter (Indiana UP, 1981): 430 pp.

An Introduction to Metaphysics, translated by R. Mannheim (Yale UP, 1974): 214 pp.

Kant and the Problem of Metaphysics, translated by R. Taft (Indiana UP, reissued 1997): 256 pp.

Basic Writings, edited by David Farrell Krell (Routledge, 1993): 214 pp.

Stephen Mulhall: *Heidegger and* Being and Time (Routledge Philosophy GuideBooks, 1996): 224 pp.

Charles Guignon (editor): *The Cambridge Companion to Heidegger* (Cambridge UP, 1993): 411 pp.

Hubert Dreyfus: *Being-in-the-World: A Commentary on Heidegger's* Being and Time, *Division I* (MIT Press, 1991): 384 pp.

John Richardson: *Existential Epistemology: A Heideggerian Critique of the Cartesian Project* (Oxford UP, 1986): 222 pp.

SARTRE

Being and Nothingness, translated by Hazel Barnes, new edition with introduction by Mary Warnock (Routledge, 1990): 682 pp.

The Psychology of the Imagination, with introduction by Mary Warnock (Routledge, 1995): 282 pp.

Sketch for a Theory of the Emotions (Routledge, 1971): 100 pp.

The Transcendence of the Ego (Hill & Wang, 1991): 119 pp.

La Nausée (1938), translated as *Nausea* (Penguin, 1990): 256 pp.

Critique of Dialectical Reason (Verso, 1991): 512 pp.

Existentialism and Humanism, translated by Philip Mairet (Eyre Methuen, 1974): 70 pp.

Les Mots (Folio, 1964), translated as *Words* (Penguin, 1969): 160 pp.

War Diaries (Verso, 1984): 366 pp.

Arthur Danto: *Sartre* (Modern Masters, Fontana, 1975): 160 pp.

Gregory McCulloch: *Using Sartre: An Analytical Introduction to Early Sartrean Themes* (Routledge, 1994): 160 pp.

David Cooper: *Existentialism: A Reconstruction* (Blackwell, 1990): 288 pp.

Peter Caws: *Sartre* (Arguments of the Philosophers, Routledge, 1984): 224 pp.

Christina Howells (ed.): *The Cambridge Companion to Sartre* (Cambridge UP, 1992): 407 pp.

Francis Jeanson: *Sartre and the Problem of Morality*, translated by R. V. Stone (Indiana UP, 1980): 320 pp.

Annie Cohen-Solal: *Sartre, 1905–1980* (Folio).

Now out of print are
Mary Warnock: *The Philosophy of Sartre* (1953)
and
Iris Murdoch: *Sartre: Romantic Rationalist* (1963).

Compiled by Peter Momtchiloff

PHOTOGRAPHIC ACKNOWLEDGEMENTS

The editor and publisher wish to thank the following, who have kindly given permission to reproduce illustrations on the pages indicated:

Pages 14, 22, 32, 38 Archivo Alinari; 66, 76, 86, 114, 130, 148, 196, 202, 210, 216, 234 AKG London; 8 Bildarchiv Preussischer Kulturbesitz; 166, 174 Hulton Getty; 156 Mansell/Time Inc./Katz; 48, 94, 122 Courtesy of the National Portrait Gallery; 58 Louvre, Paris: © RMN; 102 Scottish National Portrait Gallery; 186 © Stock Montage; 224 Courtesy of Trinity College, Cambridge; 244 © Lipnitzki, Viollet.

INDEX

Feuerbach 167, 170
Fichte 136
form and matter:
  Aquinas on 44–5
  Aristotle on 30
Forms/Ideas, Plato's theory of 17, 19–20,
  143, 236
freedom:
  in Aristotle's state 28
  Hegel on 132–4
  Marx on 171
  Mill on 163–4
  Plato's disregard for 19, 21
  Sartre on 247, 250–2
  see also free will
free will, freedom of action:
  Aquinas on 42–3
  Augustine on 35
  Hobbes on 51–2
  James on 198–9
  Kant on 118–20
  Leibniz on 91
  Sartre on 246–7
  Schopenhauer on 144–5
  Spinoza on 73
Frege **203–9**
Freud 249

Galileo 91, 214
Geist 135–7
God:
  Berkeley on 97–9
  and causation 41–2, 61–2, 89, 97–8,
    112–13
  divine attributes 42, 70–1
  and evil 91–2
  existence of 41, 61–2, 70–1, 91, 97, 111–12
  and free will 35, 42–3, 51
  Hegel on 136
  Hume on 111–12
  as infinite 70–2
  Kant on 120
  Kierkegaard on 152
  knowledge of 40–2, 78–9
  love of 74
  Nietzsche on 178–9
  as perfect substance 71
  as physical 70–2
  in Platonism 34
  as source of reason 55–6, 62
  Spinoza on 69–74

and time 35, 42–3, 70
and truth 43–4, 61–2
Gödel 209
Goethe 139
good:
  Aristotle on the good for humans 26–7,
    29
  and desire 43, 51–2
  and God, in Augustine 34
  Kant on the highest good 120
government:
  Bentham on 124–5
  Locke on 77

happiness:
  Aristotle on 26–7
  Bentham on 124–6
  in Mill's ethics 162–4
  Plato on 19, 20
  in Schopenhauer's ethics 144–5
  as the ultimate end of action 46
Harvard University 187, 197
hedonism 149
Hegel **131–7**, 215
  criticized by Kierkegaard 149, 152, 154
  and Marx 168–70
  influenced by Spinoza 69
Heidegger 2, 155, 212, 214, **235–43**
history:
  Hegel's philosophy of 132–3, 135, 137
  Heidegger on 240
  Husserl on 215
  Marx's philosophy of 167–71
  Nietzsche on 178
  Sartre on 250–1
Hobbes 3, **49–56**, 68
human nature:
  Hegel on 134
  Hobbes on 51
  Nietzsche on 179–80
  Schopenhauer on 142
Hume 4, 63, **103–12**, 160
Husserl 198, 203, **211–15**, 235, 237, 246,
  248

idealism:
  Berkeley's 87–8
  Hegel's absolute 136–7
  Husserl's 213
  Kant's 117–18
  Schopenhauer's 139

Compiled by Peter Momtchiloff